Cherrill Hicks was born in 1950 in North London where she was brought up, and studied English at Sussex University. She has been working as a specialist health writer and editor for the last ten years, and has written on health, social welfare and related issues for numerous magazines and newspapers including the *Observer*, *Guardian*, *Independent*, *Good Housekeeping*, *Nursing Times*, and *Social Work Today*. In 1981 she undertook a major investigation into racism in nursing, published in the *Nursing Times*, and in the same year won a commendation from the Lilly Research Award for medical journalism. From 1983 to 1985 she was editor of *Amnesty*, the human rights journal published by Amnesty International. She lives in London and now works regularly for the *Independent*.

Cherrill Hicks first became interested in women and men looking after disabled and elderly people at home through the experiences of some of her friends and relatives. She has carried out research into the subject from 1985, during which time she interviewed more than eighty carers from all over Britain. *Who Cares: Looking After People at Home* is a timely and moving account of what it means to be one of the 1.3 million people in Britain looking after someone at home.

'*Who Cares* is a record of great suffering and great love hidden within the family – Cherrill Hicks has given us an important and vivid social document' – Oliver Gillie, the *Independent*

CHERRILL HICKS

Who Cares: Looking after people at home

Published by VIRAGO PRESS Limited
20–23 Mandela Street, Camden Town, London NW1 0HQ

British Library Cataloguing in Publication Data

Hicks, Cherrill
Who cares: looking after people at home.
1. Great Britain. Dependent persons.
Home care
I. Title   649.8

ISBN 0–86068–834–8

Typeset by Goodfellow & Egan, Cambridge

Printed in Great Britain by Cox and Wyman Ltd, Reading, Berkshire

Contents

Author's Note

The first national survey of adults looking after elderly and disabled people at home was published in June 1988,* just after this book was printed, and too late to be included in the main text. Carried out by the Office of Population Censuses and Surveys, the survey indicates that the number of carers has previously been underestimated. It reveals that about one adult in seven in Great Britain is involved in looking after an elderly or disabled person, a figure which represents six million carers overall. About 1.7 million carers are looking after someone in the same household, and one in four carers, or 1.4 million, devote at least twenty hours a week to caring. One in five carers look after more than one person and nearly one in five have looked after the same person for at least ten years. The report also indicates that the number of men involved in caring is higher than previously thought: there are 2.5 million male carers compared to 3.5 women.

* Green, H (1988) *Informal Carers* (General Household Survey 1985–GHS No. 15, Supplement A), HMSO, London

Acknowledgements

First and foremost I would like to thank all the carers who agreed to be interviewed for this book, and who, in spite of their own difficulties, showed me kindness and hospitality. Since the majority wished to remain anonymous, the names of most of those interviewed have been changed; but their experiences have been faithfully recorded.

Many other people have contributed to this book. I am especially grateful to Judith Oliver, former director of the Association of Carers (now the Carers' National Association), who proved an invaluable source of advice and information. I would also like to thank Martin Bould, from the King's Fund Informal Caring Programme; Jackie Hockings, from the Terrence Higgins Trust; Roma Iskander, from the Health Visitors' Association; Margaret Jefferies, from the Association of Carers; Linda Lennard, from the Disability Alliance; Noreen Miller, from Contact-a-Family; Jill Pitkeathley, from the National Council for Carers and their Elderly Dependants (now the Carers' National Association); Ros Rawlins, from Counsel and Care for the Elderly; Philippa Russell, from the Voluntary Council for Handicapped Children; Reg Talbott, from Headway; and Elizabeth Tan, from the Royal Society for Mentally Handicapped Children and Adults.

It would have been impossible to contact so many carers without the help of a number of individuals. I am particularly grateful to Iris Bruce, Julie Burman, Kate Eldridge, Sharon Haffenden, Pam Harris, Jean Johnston, Shabira Moledina, Pat Purcell, Elizabeth Reid, and Dorothy Thompson.

This book would never have been finished but for the

support and encouragement of my friends. I would like to thank Bernard Becker, Simon Farr, Jackie Fosbury, Caroline Howie, Fiona Kay-Kreizman, John Knepler, Hugh Rollo, Sue Lanzon, Anne Lee, Lilian Lees, Corinne Perlman, Lynda Phillimore, Jane Salvage, Rose Shapiro, Katie Simmons (and Rosa), Dave Taylor, Jane Walker, Cynthia Westley, and Sheila Willson. Special thanks to Terry Ilott, who cared for me through long periods of self doubt, and who did an invaluable job in reading the manuscript. Thanks to my editor, Ruthie Petrie and to my agent, Mic Cheetham. Thanks to Madge and Ted, my parents, and to Doreen, my aunt.

1

Who cares: An introduction to the 1.3 million carers at home

There is in Britain a growing group of people, mainly women, who have aptly been described as a forgotten army. They are the carers – over one million women and men – who have given up much of their lives to look after disabled and elderly dependants. This book is about carers. It is based on over eighty interviews with people in all circumstances and from all over the UK. It intends, as far as possible, to give the carers a voice and to let their stories speak for themselves.

What do we know about carers? Very little. We know that at present there are around 1.3 million people looking after an elderly or disabled relative virtually as a full-time job, and five or six million more for whom caring is a major responsibility. We know that most of them – three out of every four – are women, usually the daughters, wives and mothers of their dependants. We know that in most families it is usually one person, and one alone, who takes on the job of carer, with little or no support from other family members, friends, neighbours or statutory services. We know that most carers are in middle or late middle age, that growing numbers are themselves elderly, and that the majority of their dependants are very old – 75 plus. We know that caring is a long term commitment which can be measured in years rather than months, and that many people are 'multiple carers', looking after more than one relative. We also know that something like half of all women, and increasing numbers of men, can at some point in their lives expect to become carers over and above their 'normal' family responsibilities. And we know that by keeping their dependent relatives out of institutions, carers save the British state over £11 billion a year.

Of course, there have always been people, mostly women, who have given up their lives to look after a disabled parent or child. But in the past, this role has been accepted as an extension of women's normal responsibilities, as a natural sacrifice taken on out of love and duty. It is only in the last few years that these people have been given what now amounts to an almost official title – 'carer' – and that their needs have begun to be taken seriously by government.

Why? Because caring is in crisis, and because carers are saying they can no longer cope. For one thing, the number of people with disabilities who need long term care is growing, largely as a result of the major improvements in public health and the advances which have been made in medical technology over the last century. These same improvements have resulted in an explosive rise in the number of old people – the over-75 age group now stands at 3 million, an increase of 500 per cent since the turn of the century – and with it an increase in the non-fatal illnesses and disabilities associated with old age. Medical changes have also made it possible to keep disabled children and adults – whether congenitally handicapped or the victims of accidents – alive for longer than would have been possible in the past.

In addition, the need for care is growing because the nature of illness and disability has itself changed. Having wiped out with antibiotics the lethal epidemics and infections of the past, we have been left to cope with a new scourge: the chronic diseases and disabilities of middle and late age, namely arthritis – the biggest disabling disease of all – stroke, dementia, cancer and heart disease.

Caring is also in crisis because of other changes in the nature of our society. The rise of smaller, more mobile families has reduced the number of people available to care: in modern families, for example, there are fewer adult children among whom to spread the load of looking after an elderly parent; while the fact that the vast majority of women

2

now get married means there are fewer of those traditional carers, the single daughters who sacrified everything to stay at home and help. The last fifty years have also seen radical changes in women's roles and expectations, especially in relation to work. Half of all married women are now part of the labour force, and most women expect to return to work once they have raised their children – precisely the age at which they are most likely to be required to start looking after an elderly relative. In other words, growing numbers of women now find themselves having to perform an intolerable number of roles: as wives, mothers, workers, and carers.

And, despite all the official expressions of concern, and the growing realisation that informal carers, as they are now called, have to be given support if a major crisis is to be averted, the problems carers face have been exacerbated by government moves towards 'community care' – a policy which has come to mean unpaid, 'invisible' care taken on by families, neighbours and volunteers.

As the interviews in this book demonstrate, carers cannot be lumped into one category, any more than can 'the disabled' or 'elderly' they are looking after. Their experiences of caring and their ways of coping are as diverse as their personalities, their relationships with their dependants, their environments, and their incomes: looking after a frail and incontinent old lady while living on supplementary benefit on the fourth floor of an inner city tower block is a quite different experience from doing the same in a spacious and specially adapted bungalow in the Kent commuter belt. Having said that, most carers share a common experience: one of physical drudgery, emotional stress, social isolation, anxiety about money, loss of employment, and the erosion of independence, freedom and their own sense of identity.

The few surveys which have been carried out into caring back up the impressions given by the interviews in this book. They indicate, for example, that two-thirds of carers are themselves in poor health, that one-half may be at risk of psychiatric illness, and that nearly seven out of ten suffer physical injury, especially back injuries, caused by lifting and the other heavy work involved in looking after a disabled person. Research also indicates that carers lose out financially, not only because of loss of earnings but because of all the extra costs associated with disability: of laundry, heating, special aids and trips to hospital. One study published in 1982 put these extra costs, for each carer, at nearly £11,000 a year. Another recent survey revealed that carers are almost totally isolated and that four out of five get no help at all, either from statutory services, friends or neighbours.

Whatever their circumstances, and however well they cope, most carers feel resentment, frustration, despair, and chronic guilt – torn between the desire to look after the person who needs them and the need for a life and identity of their own. Most women seem to find it easier to give in to this guilt than to assert their own needs: trying to break a pattern of behaviour which may have been built up over years – one which is, after all, an extension of the 'normal' roles which women are expected to play – is no easy task. It is easier for a caring wife, for instance, to give up all idea of organising a sitter for the evening than to deal with opposition from her disabled husband; easier for a daughter to be called a 'credit' to her elderly mother by neighbours and friends – and in the process to be swallowed up by her parents' demands – than to strike out for a separate life, and in doing so be labelled 'callous' or 'unnatural'. It takes insight and self-knowledge to care successfully, qualities which few of us would claim to have in abundance, least of all when it comes to our own family relationships. The bond between a carer and dependant often becomes so introverted, and so isolated from the rest of the world, that the carer needs more strength and more detachment than do most of us, simply in order to survive.

The woman who first set me on the path to writing this book would never think of herself as a carer. In her fifties and looking after a husband semi-paralysed by a stroke, she is too proud, too stoical and too loyal to think of herself as doing anything more than would be expected of her. She sees what she is doing, not as 'care', but as part of her natural role and responsibilities, taken on out of love, loyalty and duty. She would hate to identify herself as a 'carer', and her husband as 'dependent', because to do so would be to imply that he is a burden rather than a partner, and would devalue their relationship and the life they have built up together.

Of course, she is right: the role which she has now taken on is an extension of one she has been performing all her life. Despite the official label, 'carers' are not a sociological sub-group whose lives can be neatly divided off from those of the rest of us. The reality is that most women are already caring for someone, either a parent, partner or child, and that this role, which for the most part is regarded as normal and unremarkable, will at one time or another take over their lives completely, bringing with it, in most cases, almost unendurable stress.

I was reluctant to write a book about 'carers' as opposed to one about 'people'. I did not want to divide them off from the rest of the population or label them as different; enough damage has already been caused by doing this to elderly and disabled people themselves. What I did want to do was to show that the pressures and problems faced by carers reflect the common experience of women, and that the caring role is an extension of normal family roles and relationships, and would not exist without them.

This book is not only for the carers who recognise themselves as such, but also for the millions of women who do not identify with that label, but whose role in life amounts to much the same thing.

In spite of the seemingly intolerable burdens many of them face, it would be wrong to think of all carers as victims; most are able to draw on immense resources of strength and willpower in order to survive. It takes courage for the woman described above, for instance, to keep going to the restaurants she and her husband so enjoyed before his stroke, and to cut up her husband's food and wipe his mouth in public; to put

5

up with the television on at full-blast because it is the only thing which gives him comfort; to organise a holiday abroad for the two of them every year despite the problems of just getting from one train to another; to put up with the lack of conversation and companionship; and to carry on as though everything were normal.

The last thing most carers want is to be thought of as heroic or wonderful. But it is hard not to be moved by their courage and their ability to carry on in what often seem unbearable circumstances.

Many of the women in this book are fighting for better lives for themselves and for their dependants, shocked into action by simple desperation, often after years of trying to cope alone. Some of the most organised and active women interviewed – the ones running local self-help groups and sitting on voluntary committees – were those who would previously never have thought of joining a pressure group. Kind, conservative, conventional, polite, often running immaculate homes, many of them said they had never asked for anything from the state in their lives, believing that they would always get help if it was needed. They had been shocked into taking action by the lack of support with which they have been faced.

Ask someone about caring and you are asking them about their whole life: no wonder so many, when interviewed, found it difficult to know where to begin, or to describe in a few hours a relationship and experience which in some cases had gone on for twenty or thirty years. Yet, whatever difficulties they had, most of the carers interviewed for this book were grateful: glad to have someone to talk to, someone who

---

* This book concentrates on carers of physically disabled and elderly people. There are several other groups of carers whose experiences are not specifically included: among them are the thousands of families looking after mentally ill relatives, especially parents caring for young people suffering from schizophrenia; and those looking after people with terminal illnesses such as cancer. The problem of length made it inevitable that some groups would be left out. They will, however, find that their experiences are at least partially reflected in this book.

would listen to feelings which had been suppressed for years and which now poured from them for hours. It is their stories which make this book.

Christina Stanson

Tina Stanson is 40, married with two children, a son, 21, and a daughter, 12. Three years ago her mother, 77, had a severe stroke which paralysed her left side and left her unable to walk or stand without support; she also has diabetes, glaucoma, incontinence and a recurring bladder infection. Her father, 78, is getting confused and frail and suffers from angina. 'It's all to do with Mum. He was in good health until the stroke. She did all the cooking and sewing – it's come as a great shock to him. They want to be together. Mum doesn't want to be in a home and I don't want her to be.'

Her parents' two-up, two-down unmodernised cottage – no bathroom and an outside toilet – is around the corner from Tina's house, in a London suburb. The small front room has been turned into a makeshift bedroom and is full of family photos, with a crucifix on the wall and a television in the corner. Everywhere smells of talcum powder.

Tina, who divides her time between her own house and family and her parents, is waiting for her mother to come home from daycare.

I'm up at six. The children rough it along, get their own breakfast. I give Dad his drugs, look around, make sure everything is all right. Mum can't sit up by herself, I have to pull her up from lying flat. She's 14 stone. The bed is made up from bits of the children's old beds; she's got a ripple mattress but the backrest is no good. We're trying to get her another. She's got a chemical commode; I lift her onto it. I take all her clothes off. They'll be soaking wet, along with the duvet cover and the sheets. The incontinence service is very good: we get paper sheets every day and 100 nappies a week and pads for the chairs. I do three machine washes a day, her dresses and pants and so on.

Then I get her into the chair and wash her all over, she has two blanket baths a day. I put drops in her eyes every two hours for the glaucoma. I dress her – everything, bra, petticoat, vest. It's difficult because she can't move. Then it's back onto the pot because she's on diuretics. This is all before breakfast. Then, while she's on the pot, I'll clear up and see to Dad. I get him a cooked breakfast. Mum

7

sits over here with the pillows and things. She doesn't like going into the other room, or even our garden. This room is like a security to her – she never used to be like that – so we try and fit as much as you can into it.

Then I clear away the breakfast, do Dad's bed, clean the room, do the washing up, do the housework, clean the commode, hoover, dust. Then I'll prepare everything for lunch. At around 10.30 I'll go home for half an hour, take the washing. I'll leave two nappies on her because Dad can't move her onto the commode. I come back, put Mum on the pot, get lunch, clear it up, then it's back on the pot. I put the TV on in the afternoon, around one. Then I say, if you want me I'm going for a bath and to read the newspaper. I'll be back here by 2.45, earlier if Dad phones. Then the routine goes into reverse – Mum goes on the pot, her clothes go off, she's creamed all over, has the eye drops, I make sure her toes are dry in between. Her hand is like a claw; she had some physio in the hospital but never at home, never, so you have to make sure every little crack is clean. Then back into bed; then it's supper time, we have a light supper. I clear it all away, put out the pills for the night, make sure her legs are all right, pop home about six. At seven my husband or I will come down to turn Mum and check her; we check again at nine and give her two sleeping pills.

Dad goes to bed about 7.30 or eight. Sometimes I help wash him. He takes a pot to bed. I try to keep him doing as much as he can, even if he doesn't do it very well. There's so much to do with Mum, I almost neglect him. The first year, I didn't even know he existed. I come down for another check at ten. If she's really ill, I'll stay the night. Hopefully she'll be all right until the morning, until I get here.

The district nurse comes once a week. The two I've had, they've been like friends. If I didn't have them I couldn't have gone on. One of them said, if I tried to do this twenty-four hours a day I'd be dead in a month; said not to bother with things like disinfectant. They've always said, we'll come any time, but they can't come when I want them to, between six and twelve, when if I wasn't here Mum would lay in her pee all hours. They can't help me put Mum to bed – that's when I need them. It's not that they don't want to. (She had not seen a district nurse since the last one left three weeks before.) She goes twice a week to the day hospital, from eleven till three. They've been very good. She loves the nurses there; the consultant says she can go as long as I'm looking after her. It gives me a break.

8

I've had so many home helps, most have been awful. One brought her children here; can you imagine, two teenage children in this place? Another put the washing away wet. One was wonderful, Dad and Mum really loved her, she even used to cut their hair. But then she left. I was supposed to have one five mornings a week, then it went down to three, then two. I ended up having a terrible row with the supervisor. Whose fault? I don't know, I was fed up. I suppose I'm so angry.

When Mum left the hospital – after the stroke – we saw no one. No one said, look, you're going to have to watch your back with the lifting. I put on three stone in weight, I was so depressed. You almost need something like a teacher training course before you bring them home. It's not fair to anyone. We didn't have a commode, we didn't know about the inco service. I didn't know who to turn to; I was given no telephone numbers. She didn't have a telephone for a year. I said, she must have a telephone; but they said there were two people in the house. I said my mother can't move, Dad had to keep coming round in the cold to get me, what if he's ill? It was the same when I asked for Meals on Wheels. Mum had just had the stroke and I was still working. She (someone from social services) came and looked at me and said, can't you do it? She wouldn't let me have it.

Now there's a super girl (at social services), she said if there's anything you need just ask. They've given me £500 backdated to cover her clothing and washing. At first I paid out pounds in electric bills, with the fire always on in Mum's room. Now social services pay the bills, rent, rates, telephone.

I've a sister in Cheshire we haven't seen for three years, since Mum had the stroke. I don't know why, there's been no letter. I can't understand it. She wanted Mum in a home. But I had to look after her. Not because I owe it to her, I've got nothing against people who put them in a home. But I can't do it. My sister's not been anywhere near. They want her in a home. My other sister, in Essex, we used to be very close, we haven't spoken in two years. She said I'd broken the family up by not putting Mum in a home. She's turned to religion. They don't want to come here because I'm here. They say it's me. I'm beginning to think it is me.

My brother comes once a week, Saturdays, to see Mum for an hour, but my sister-in-law won't come. She says she's never going to forgive me. Forgive me for what? For what?

They all think she should be away. It makes me terribly angry and bitter because they could be supporting me psychologically. I feel I should be able to phone up and say, I'm desperate. But you know what they'd say? They'd say I told you so, you should have put her away.

I must be able to have a break, to say I've got a headache. I've worked nine months now day and night; I must have a break or I'll be ill. The social worker says, what do you want, someone to hold your hand? Maybe that's what you do want – when you're coming down here at six every morning and you're terrified of someone being so dependent on you.

Two ambulancemen bring her mother to the door; her father, who has been sitting watching television next door, gets up, half excited, to put the kettle on. He waves hopefully from the other room. 'There she is! Hallo Mum!' Tina lifts her with difficulty onto the edge of the bed; the first thing to do is get out the commode. Her mother jokes and shouts raucously. 'Listen to Mum enjoying herself,' says her father.

The stroke has changed her. She used to be a very private person, very quiet, liked her own company. She enjoyed being by herself. Now she says some terrible things sometimes. It upsets Dad when she shouts at him, I think that's why he goes to bed so early. Get out, she tells him, get out. They had a very active sex life until the stroke, so it's very sad for him. She was the easiest going person you could hope to meet. Now she's so particular about what she eats, how it's presented. She's got a huge appetite; she's very overweight. She used to smoke and they told her to stop and she couldn't cope with a diet, she got so huge, that's when she had the stroke. She always wants sweets, but I'm the one who gets into trouble if she has a sweet. Sometimes you get so desperate, you think, have a bloody sweet.

I'm tired out. Tired and depressed. I get so low that I can't do the things I want to do. Just as the children are moving away from me and I can be independent, I've got Mum. You think, you're 40 – will it be another ten years? I couldn't nurse her for another ten years. The doctor said it could be another twenty. What do you do? I try not to think ahead, I go from day to day. It's as though I'm living by the graveside sometimes. Sometimes Dad'll phone and I'll think hope-fully, she's going to be dead. But you can't think like that.

I used to work in an art gallery. I used to love walking and bird watching and cycling; I used to do aerobics, I like classical music, I used to read a lot. I've got so much I want to do with my life. My daughter loves horses, goes to the three-day events; I'd love to go. I went to Harrods the other day, just to look around, but I was rushing everywhere; I didn't enjoy it.

Her husband is a taxi driver, in the third year of a social sciences course. They had a holiday in Italy last year, when her mother went into respite care.

He's very supportive, he thinks if I want to do it . . . In Italy I was much better. You lose the fun out of life. You become so serious. Also I argue with everybody. That's what Dad and Mum find so difficult; I've changed, changed a lot. I've had to argue to make people understand.

What I need is someone like me who'd come in at 6 a.m., say one day a fortnight. There was a lady from the Manpower Services, she came every Friday afternoon for two hours. What's two hours to me? Where can I go? What can I do in two hours? It's the mornings I need it; I'm not good in the mornings; you've got to come down here and face it seven days a week, and the house looks as though a bomb's hit it. If only someone would do that once a week, once a fortnight.

You can't entertain people here, with Mum on the pot there isn't room. They're always on my mind; sometimes it feels like a nightmare. I say to Dad when I'm low, the only way out is if I die, Dad dies or Mum dies. I used to be really smart, but you come down here and get stuff on your pants. Even my way of dressing has changed. I liked to think about what I was going to wear, meeting interesting people. I used to enjoy all that. It makes me feel maybe I'm selfish. The social worker says to me, well, life just turns out that way. Chrissie, she calls me; Chrissie. I don't think they're trained for it.

I said I'd like a new backrest, that one is hopeless. She says to Mum, I'm sorry, it's not my department. Not, I'll see to it for you. I don't know what she's meant to do, what she comes for. She's a nice enough girl, but I asked her, what is your role? Not my department, she says.

I only hit Mum once, I got really angry. Mum had pooed in bed, it took three hours to clean up. I walk through the door and she's pooed again. Mum said, you're paid to do it, you've chosen to do it, you've got to do it. I really got so angry. She says, why don't you dress like you used to, why don't you behave like you used to? I said I'm too bloody tired and washed out. I had to walk out and leave them that time. Dad phoned, he was crying. I had to wait before I could go back, restrain myself. I can honestly say, with my two children, I've never struck them. With Mum I was nearly there. I went to the GP and told him how I had nearly killed Mum; it was then I got the break and she went into Putney (minimal care hospital) for two weeks.

You can't read here: the moment you sit down, it's I want. I say to her, before I sit down tell me what you want, but it's no use. She used to have me up and down with the commode every day. They get a thing about the pot, it was up and down forty times a day. Dad tried to get her on it once, he had to leave her there till I came back. Whoever comes in, she wants them to lift her on the pot. Now I've got it down to five times a day. I say, if you're desperate, pee in your nappy. If I come down at night and she needs the pot I can't put her back into a wet bed. Some people say put her back, but I can't. I have to take it all off and put clean on.

She says, what do you want to go home and have a bath for? Why do you want to go spending your money? We used to get on really well, never a cross word, but now. She does feel terrible that I have to look after her; when she's OK she says to me, it won't be long. She's awful to Dad – he can't fight back. He lives for his telly and she tells him to turn it off. Sometimes when I come down, he's sitting there without any sound.

In the end you have to be callous and say, this is it. You can understand why these nurses are like that – you just can't do everything they want. If you did, you'd be like a slave. The nurses say she's thoroughly ruined here. It's always, I want a sweet give me a sweet; I say you can't eat sweets. I'm more selfish now, I take every chance I can to get away. I always say, tomorrow's another day, it won't be the same. I hope she dies. For us all. But she doesn't want to die. Dad's quite able to accept death, he's more philosophical, but Mum, even with her religion she hasn't been able to accept it. I don't want to die, she says. I'm too young.

2

_____ • _____

What shall we do with Mother?: Daughters caring for elderly parents

Someone asked me recently, do you hate your mother? I said no, I don't hate her. I resent what she's done to me and what she's doing to me. She goes to bed saying thank God the day is over. I say Mother, that's my life you're talking about. (Delia Holland, 63 and widowed, caring for an 82-year-old mother with Parkinson's disease and partially paralysed by five strokes)

The largest group of carers in this country comprises adult children looking after their elderly parents. Most of these carers are women, either daughters or daughters-in-law; most are in middle or early old age and either married or widowed; and, because women tend to outlive men, they are usually looking after a parent who is female and widowed too. Like Delia Holland, growing numbers of elderly women are looking after mothers in their eighties.

Old age, especially when accompanied by the loneliness of being without a partner, has always been viewed as a time of increasing frailty and vulnerability, and millions of families expect to give some support and care, in the broadest sense, to relatives who are getting old. But the unprecedented growth in the UK's elderly population is beginning to make this kind of support far more difficult to provide. In the last 80-odd years, for instance, the 65-plus age group has jumped from 1.7 to more than 8 million. The numbers of old people, and especially the very old, have grown not only in absolute terms but also in proportion to the rest of the population: whereas in 1901 one person in every twenty was over 65 and one in every 82 over 75, these ratios have now changed to one in seven and one in eighteen respectively.

This rapid growth in the numbers of very old people looks set to continue, both in the immediate and the longer term future: in the next forty years, the numbers of those aged 75 and over will increase by 30 per cent and the over 85 age group, which now stands at half a million, will have almost doubled. The very elderly will make up a growing proportion of the UK's total retired population and will represent nearly one-half of it by the turn of the century.

It would be wrong to portray all old people as a problem population in need of special care: the majority of those past retirement age are leading fit, active and independent lives and are determined to go on doing so. That said, there is no doubt that as the numbers of very old people have grown, so have the numbers of those with disabilities. Recent surveys have shown, for example, that about two-thirds of all those over 75 suffer chronic health problems such as arthritis, stroke, bronchitis and heart disease, and that many suffer from more than one. Up to a fifth of our elderly population is now thought to suffer from some degree of mental infirmity, including senile dementia, while vast numbers have less serious problems such as constipation and poor circulation.

The everyday problems resulting from these disabilities range from being bedridden or housebound to difficulties with walking, washing, using the lavatory or getting upstairs. Again, research indicates that in England and Wales alone, around one million old people are too frail or ill to get their own meals, and that about 1.3 million have problems with shopping and laundry; that over a million need help in taking a bath and going outdoors; and that probably over half a million are housebound.

Despite all the popular assumptions about old age, not all these disabilities are an inevitable part of the ageing process: as some of our new departments of geriatric medicine are now demonstrating, many of them are treatable, even reversible, although they have in the past been neglected, put down to the 'natural' decline of old age. Similarly, handicap, dependence and the need for care are not created by physical disability alone, but by the social and economic vulnerability of many elderly people and by other factors such as class, income, and lifestyle: much depression and confusion in old people is caused by poverty and loneliness, for example, and much dependence on others by the simple fact that two-thirds of all old people have no access to a car.

Poverty is perhaps the greatest handicap which our elderly population faces – about two million old people are dependent on supplementary benefit (or income support, as it is now called) to 'top up' their incomes – and old women are particularly vulnerable as a result of a social security system which has penalised them for stopping work to have children. Housing is another handicap: almost half of all elderly persons' households lack a basic amenity such as warmth or a proper bathroom. And, because of their low incomes and their corresponding lack of power, old people are often denied the goods and services – cars, suitable houses, central heating and washing machines – which other groups take for granted, and which could give them more independence. In other words, the 'dependence' of old people – and their corresponding need for 'care' – is not caused by disability alone, but by their social and financial circumstances.

Who, if anyone, is looking after the growing numbers of handicapped old people? The common assumption – often made by professionals – that families are keen to dump their elderly on the state is a myth: the proportion of old people going into residential care – about 6 per cent – is still only a tiny part of the total and has not risen significantly since the turn of the century. And, despite the belief that families 'don't care as much as they used to', all the evidence indicates that the vast majority of disabled and handicapped old people are still managing to live in the community, supported and cared for by their families. Some researchers have even argued that the three-generation extended family, which many of us look back to with nostalgia as a truly caring social unit, never really existed, and that the familiar modern

15

image of a lonely and neglected old age shut out by the 'selfish' nuclear family is far from accurate: that today's families care more extensively and for more disabled elderly people than ever before.

To talk about family care is misleading, however, since it suggests that whole families are involved in supporting the elderly, when in fact the bulk of this care is provided by women, most of them the daughters and daughters-in-law of dependants.

Delia Holland

Delia Holland lives in a small council flat on the outskirts of Liverpool with her mother, 82, who has suffered five strokes in the last few years and who also has Parkinson's disease: illnesses which have left her brain-damaged, confused and easily agitated. She needs help with walking, even with a frame, and with dressing, washing and cutting her food; at times she loses her memory completely. 'It's like living with a zombie, you try and make conversation and she doesn't want to talk. Actually, she just wants to die.' Her mother, who has always lived nearby, moved in four years ago, only a few months after Delia's husband had died of a stroke. 'My advice to anyone is, don't do it,' says Delia. 'It's just too much.'

Many times I've thought why didn't I put her in a home. She could live long after me. All sorts of stupid things go through my mind. But I feel very sorry for her. She wasn't dominant before, we each lived our own lives. She was a very quiet woman.

It's changed her personality. Even now there are so many times I could really hit her. But there's nobody more upset than me when she's ill. She's taken over my life; I live her life more than mine.

On her eightieth birthday, I arranged for the entire family to come, I bought her a new dress for £30 or £40 – it didn't mean a thing. She just thinks it's what you should do.

I feel sorry that this has happened: up to the age of 79 she could do her own decorating. This is why she can't accept it.'

Her husband, who had had high blood pressure, died of a stroke: Delia had looked after him for the last ten years.

She'd have been a different woman if he'd have been here. He was a strong man, a determined man – she wouldn't get away with half of what she does now. She still treats me as though we're young children. I say to her, Mother I'm 63 you know.

We were never really close. I thought the world of her, but the youngest (sister) was the favourite and still is. My sisters do nothing; they come about every six weeks. One sister I see more often, but neither of them do anything. They wanted her in a home and I wouldn't. Yet my mother's smashing with them, it's: how are you Joan, lovely to see you. She's never asked me how I am.

The youngest has always been the favourite, she can do no wrong. It's mind how you go Joan, be careful Joan, thank you very much Joan. (She raises her hands in irritation)

She can be charming, and she's got a lovely smile. I have a hell of a job in the morning when I take her to the hairdressers – but when we get there she's lovely with the girls there. I suppose I've ruined her from when she first came, but I couldn't change it. I'm too soft, but I'll only go so far and then I blow my top and tell her she'll go into a home.

I never would, though. Having worked in a home, I said no way. I thought the world of my mother. I wouldn't do that to her – even now. I think it's dreadful when it comes to your own.

Delia retired from her work at the old people's home not long after her husband's death.

I was very involved – you can't help it when you're looking after people. I loved looking after them, I used to be in at seven in the morning and when my husband died I used to help out in the evenings. To do a job in a home you have to have it born in you. I've always been involved with sick people, I've always liked people, liked doing things for people. I'm very neighbourly; that's what people should be like.

This is one thing: I'm becoming cynical. My husband always said, never become cynical or bitter. I'm afraid I am; it's to do with human beings, particularly my two sisters. I've said, it's your mother too, but it doesn't seem to make any impact. I won't ask them to sit, it's such a fuss: it's always, I've got this and that to do. I said, just forget it. I wouldn't ask again. We're quite close but I have a go at them, I have to let fly. It's the same with their children: they don't come and see my mother, even the great-grandchildren.

Delia has a son and a daughter, both married with young children and living in the north: the daughter comes once a fortnight, the son once a year.

I love to go out, I like people. My social life's affected. That's one thing with Mother: if anybody comes, the atmosphere is so heavy, they just don't want to come again. Everybody says the same thing: why don't you go out. But last Friday, 11.30 at night, she fell; she was in a terrible state. I can't relax, if she'd had another bad stroke, if I'd been here I might have been able to avoid it. Supposing I come in and I find her dead? This is what frightens me, why I don't like to go out. It could happen anytime so quickly. She's had a lot of headaches lately; it could lead to another one. I try not to think about it – if she comes out of it she will be a vegetable. I've said, I'd rather she died.

She won't have anybody (to sit). One neighbour came in but she wouldn't come in again – it's the atmosphere: she won't have anybody here. I'm better off staying in than going out. Everybody says this, you're a fool. But when you go out you're on tenterhooks anyway. A prisoner of conscience. I've got a shocking conscience.

I've been doing my best for four years, I've got to be able to live with myself. If you give them the best you can live afterwards. It was the same when my husband died: you don't need to visit the cemetery every week if you do everything for them while they're alive.

I don't let it affect me. I'll be singing and I'll hear her talking to herself: I wish she'd shut up singing, or, she's a rotten bitch. My mother never swore, now she says I'm always out boozing and I'm a rotten bitch. When she said that, I opened the door like a tornado, went in and blasted the roof off.

I used to be happy-go-lucky; I like cycling, cooking, gardening, knitting. I'm like a canary. I sit and watch TV, knit, crochet and jigsaw. When my mother goes I'll be back to square one. From time to time I get depressed, but I think of other poor devils far worse off than myself. I shouldn't complain; I've had two good husbands. But it doesn't compensate any. I've told everybody, my sisters too. I've said I'd only do this once, if anything happens to you – no way. Once, and that's it.

18

I've always felt I should do it, it's because of Dad: when he was dying he said, would you look after your mother. Besides, she's got so incapable of looking after herself. I don't like to think of people, saying, you know, she smells – behind her back. (Karen Hastings, late 30s, married with two children, caring for a frail, elderly mother)

The neighbours were always saying he shouldn't be left on his own, the doctor said he was too old to move, the doctor said the best thing would be for you to get a little job down here, that would be the solution. I just felt I had to – there was nobody else. (Dorothy Preston, 52, former carer for sixteen years of a father suffering from dementia. He died a few weeks before this interview)

I was thinking of taking in a lodger. My mother said, that's my room gone. The next thing I knew, she said she would sell up and come to live with me. I was 33. I never wanted to do it, I never looked for it, I never welcomed it. (Dora Taylor, 57, single, who lived with and looked after her mother for eighteen years)

She came here permanently a year ago. Why me? Because I knew she would have done it for me. As a child I had scarlet fever, rheumatic fever, and St Vitus' dance. She never left me. (Joan Jarratt, in her sixties, married, caring for a mother with dementia)

I didn't even consider a home, time is the only thing I've got left to give her. If you ask most carers: would they do it again, they would say yes – because they are looking after someone they love. (Stella Layton, 47, caring for a mother with angina, arthritis, diabetes and partial blindness)

Most women take on responsibility for a parent for the most simple and understandable reasons: a mixture of love, loyalty, duty, guilt, the desire to do their best by someone who they feel did their best by them, a sense of moral responsibility, social pressure, even fear of what the neighbours might think.

Whatever their motives, most of these daughters have one thing in common: they are reluctant to see a parent – loved or otherwise – 'put away' in a local home or geriatric ward, and are forced into caring fulltime because that is the only alternative.

I couldn't bear the idea of her staying down there (the local geriatric home). I wouldn't send my cat down there. I went in one day and Mother was sitting in a plastic stacker chair – a frail old lady of nearly 90 in a plastic stacker chair. (Janet Bambry, caring for a mother disabled by a stroke)

Support from family and friends

Once a woman starts looking after a parent, she will get little help from anyone else, not even her own brothers and sisters, who, while they may have been involved at the 'crisis' stage – 'what do we do with Mother' – often tend to draw back completely thereafter:

It's not for me to say how the others should react. I said to them when she was in the hospital: we've got to do what we can each live with afterwards. One of my sisters opposed it all the way along the line; she believed what she was told in the hospital: that Mum would be better off in a home. It definitely has caused a rift in the family. My sister couldn't do it, so she feels guilty about me doing it. She will be devastated by Mum's death. (Joan Jarratt)

The reason why one child is selected to care – while the other brothers and sisters cannot cope, or insist their mother goes into residential care – are rooted in individual family histories and are too complex to deal with here; but many women spoke of a sister who had always been the 'favourite' or the 'spoilt one', who was horrified at the idea of having to look after a mother who had always looked after her – but who felt so guilty about anyone else doing so that she often withdrew completely. Whatever the pattern, the withdrawal of other relatives is a problem which causes bitterness among carers and enormous rifts within families.

I was the black sheep of the family; I was always different, always in trouble. I was always trying to get her affection. One sister, she was always very pretty. My brother was the only boy, the son Mum had always wanted. The eldest daughter was the mother figure. I was in the middle, the naughty child, always crying, always wanting something. (Tina Stanson)

I was an absolute horror, I led them a hell of a life, I wouldn't be told. I always wanted to do my own thing, would do it behind their backs if necessary. That's my guilt. (Joan Jarratt)

The isolation faced by these women is often made worse by the attitudes of neighbours and friends, who, while they may be willing to keep an eye open or do the shopping for an old person living alone, tend to withdraw once a daughter takes over. The evidence also indicates that neighbours and friends who may be willing to keep an eye open for someone a little unsteady on their feet, tend to withdraw in the face of dementia or double incontinence – especially where a female carer is present (men, whose experience of caring will be described in a later chapter, tend to be offered more help). Far from blaming the neighbours for their standing back, carers do not often expect involvement from outsiders, in fact most carers will try to protect their friends from the emotional and physical stress they themselves are under. The lack of help does mean, however, that the presumed existence of informal networks of support from friends and neighbours – on which so much 'community care' policy depends – is often illusory.

Before I came back home one of the neighbours would call in and have a cup of tea with him and bring him a pie. That all stopped once I got here. Nobody came any more – they didn't need to. (Dorothy Preston)

Support from the state

The social isolation which these women face is further rein-forced by the approach of those domiciliary services tra-ditionally aimed at supporting frail elderly people living at home: home helps and Meals on Wheels, for example. Not only are these services overstretched as a result of cutbacks in social services in many parts of the country in recent years; all the evidence indicates that they tend to be provided to elderly people living alone, unsupported by family members; and that they may even be withheld if there is a daughter in the house. Research carried out by the Equal Opportunities

Commission has shown that the presence of a carer – especially a woman – prejudices the likelihood of a dependant receiving statutory services:

It is clear from the comments made in this survey that dependants . . . are not expected to require residential or domiciliary care when there is a female relative at hand. In general, assistance from social services seems more likely to be available to dependants when their families are unwilling or unable to provide care . . . many of the women who have retained the responsibility for a dependent relative do not receive the level of support which they really need. It is these women who pay the price. (Equal Opportunities Commission, 'The experience of caring for elderly and handicapped dependants', March 1980)

Women looking after elderly persons with dementia are particularly badly served. One major study commissioned by the DHSS, and published in 1983, found, for instance, that just under two-thirds of those with severe dementia had never seen a psychiatrist; that around one-third had never received day or relief care; and that about two-thirds had no home help or Meals on Wheels. Not surprisingly, it also found that one-third of those supporting confused elderly relatives reported symptoms of such acute stress as to suggest that they themselves needed psychiatric help.

Over the last few years initiatives aimed at supporting carers themselves, rather than their dependants, have been developed. Often organised jointly by statutory and voluntary agencies, new projects such as day centres, 'sitting in' services and various kinds of relief care have been welcomed by many carers and have made a genuine difference to the quality of their lives.

Yet, like the traditional services aimed at elderly people themselves, the provision of these new services is at best patchy, and in some parts of the country non-existent. In addition, they tend to be used as 'crisis' services, aimed at keeping relatives going for as long as possible, rather than as a positive approach to genuinely sharing the burden of care.

Often the quality of the services which are provided makes them unattractive: they seem to be based on the assumption that elderly people no longer need to be treated as individuals, with their own likes and dislikes, but as part of a group, 'the elderly'. This view of old age is especially prevalent in the long-stay geriatric wards, which were in the past the dumping grounds for elderly people. But it is also present in more recent developments: even in the growing numbers of day centres now being provided for elderly people. In one way it seems churlish to criticise these, since they can alleviate so much loneliness and isolation among elderly people as well as give their carers a break, but a visit to one such centre – a model of its kind – in a new town not far from London proved a depressing experience. The place was warm, clean, and brightly decorated; the staff seemed kind and clearly proud of the food, the hairdressing, and the afternoon dancing sessions they were so enthusiastically organising; the old people themselves, ferried to the centre in fleets of ambulances, seemed happy enough – even if they were rather bullied into 'joining in' by numerous well-meaning volunteers. But they were still being treated as a helpless mass of dependency which needed to be serviced as efficiently as possible.

Getting worse with age

In many ways, the physical and emotional strain of caring for an elderly relative is much the same as that involved in caring for disabled people of any age. But looking after an elderly parent is made more difficult by the ageing process itself, not only because of the deterioration in physical and mental ability that it brings, but also because of our attitudes towards old age.

The physical strain is a problem: I've got arthritis and a slipped disc and I'm trying to lose weight; and I know I'm doing things I shouldn't be doing, given the state of my own health – I've put on three stone since I gave up work. She takes diuretic pills, so there's quite a lot of lifting – she's 12 stone. I'm always running up and downstairs with the commode. I'll push her out in the summer – and we live on a hill. (Stella Layton)

Wheelchair pushing – she's a dead weight. When it comes to the kerb it really puts your back out. It's not bad, but I get the odd twinge now and then. It definitely takes it out of you physically. (Delia Holland)

Caring for an elderly person is not a role which remains the same: growing older brings increasing disability, and the burden of caring is likely to get worse as the years go by. The common and chronic illness of old age are all likely to intensify with time and become complicated by other conditions, such as failing eyesight, forgetfulness, hearing problems, and incontinence. This means that what may have been taken on as a temporary solution – having a parent, to stay, for instance, after a stint in hospital – can easily become a permanent arrangement; that a daughter who had started out by giving an acceptable degree of support to a parent may soon find herself drifting, unwillingly, into a full-time commitment, and that what started out as help with the housework or shopping gradually becomes a routine of washing, feeding and dressing, leading eventually to full-time nursing care.

This burden of care is most often taken on by women who are themselves approaching old age; who will probably be getting slower and less fit; and who will themselves soon be facing the problems common to their age group – heart disease, hypertension, anaemia and the menopause. The 1983 DHSS study of those caring for confused elderly relatives found that almost half of these carers had to contend with disabilities of their own. For many, the presence of an elderly relative is also a constant reminder of their own mortality: they wonder who will care for them in their old age.

Up to now we've taken her on holiday; a year ago we went to Blackpool, but it was such hard work. There was bingo, entertainment – she lapped it all up. But everywhere she goes, she's got to have you hanging on her arm, putting her in the car; and everything takes time – washing her, getting her ready, getting the boys ready. By the time I came back, I was exhausted. (Karen Hastings)

Most of them are on the go most of the day, and for some of them most of the night. They feel that they are on call all the time, running backwards and forwards, checking all is well . . . straightening the person in the chair, fetching and carrying, supplying drinks . . . (Bristol, AK, Crossroads Care Attendant Scheme, 1980)

Until recently there has been little research into what carers do for their elderly parents or how long it takes. One study of families with disabled elderly relatives did find, however, that the average amount of daily care needed by a dependant was around five hours. But caring is more than a series of physical tasks, and by treating it as such one can only underestimate the real time and emotional effort involved. What most carers of elderly people find really wearing is that they are never free from caring, that they constantly have to 'see to' an elderly relative – a feeling which is as often generated by the growing frailty and vulnerability of old age as by a specific physical disability. Like Delia Holland most carers of elderly people feel far too anxious to leave them alone for more than an hour or so.

I don't go out, not unless I've really got to. I can get to the hairdressers and back but she falls so easily it worries me to death. (Delia Holland)

Incontinence and dementia

There are two disabilities common among elderly people which are major causes of distress for their carers, and which are more likely than anything else to cause a breakdown in care. One of these is incontinence, a problem now thought to be suffered by between two and three million people, most of them elderly. Incontinence in elderly parents can be the last straw for their carers; it is the one problem which makes them feel they have reached the end of the road. This is not just because of the unpleasant work which coping with either faecal or urinary incontinence involves, but because of the strain it puts on family relationships: whereas parents are expected to clean up after a baby, doing the same for an elderly parent breaks deeply-held taboos and does little for the dignity or privacy of anyone.

I was stripping beds all day, dumping them in the bath and shoving them out in the garden to dry, then rushing to get some lunch and off to an afternoon's work. You have to make up the bed with the normal sheet at the bottom, the drawsheet on top, pads with polythene under the patient. I would put the drawsheets in one bag, the pads in another, wipe down the mattress, remake the bed. The inco (incontinence) service would come every week; you'd put it out on your doorstep and everyone would know all about it. Bank holidays were a nightmare: you'd be left with a double load of soiled stuff until the following week. With anyone who's incontinent, it gets everywhere, especially with a stroke patient. The mattress gets rucked back when she's trying to get to the commode, it gets in her slippers, on the carpet, on the wall. You're very conscious of the smell all the time – it just goes right through the house. You think, I dare not invite people round. (Janet Bambry)

I can't describe it: it was in the carpets, the bedroom; the bed was always dripping wet, his clothes were filthy; the whole place was awash with disinfectant.

One day he came home from the day hospital in different clothes carrying a whole bag of his old clothes – which were covered in faeces. When I opened the bag I started to scream. I remember what I was screaming: is there anybody out there? I felt we were encased in this mess of faeces and disinfectant and anger. We were alone with it. (Dorothy Preston)

The sad thing is that much of what passes for incontinence is not caused by physical or organic illness, but by depression, confusion about the right place to go, inability to get to the toilet on time, and sometimes diet. Yet the few services which do exist – laundry services and the provision of pads – tend to be geared towards coping with rather than helping to prevent the problem, which is often presumed to be an inevitable part of growing old.

I tried to talk to the health visitor and the doctor about it, but all you get is the attitude: oh how tiresome, still it happens to elderly ladies – it's just waved away. There's no real advice about dealing with incontinence. (Janet Bambry)

The other major problem is dementia, one of the most feared disabilities of old age, and one which is now thought to afflict one in seven people over the age of 75 – most of them supported by their families in the community. An irreversible process which involves the death of brain cells, dementia may begin with small signs of confusion and forgetfulness, and end with loss of speech, mobility, faecal control, recognition of close family members, even the ability to swallow. For carers the illness means having to deal with sleepless nights, meaningless chatter, heavy incontinence, hyperactivity, violence, paranoia – and, sometimes, being followed around all day.

However wearing physical disabilities can be, there are few whose effects can match the distress felt by an adult child who witnesses the intellectual and physical breakdown of a parent who was previously a powerful figure in his or her life. The 1983 study of relatives caring for dementia sufferers found that one-fifth of these carers had been forced to put their relatives into institutional care within a year of the study – because of the strain involved in caring and the lack of support for dementia sufferers and their families given by statutory services.

It is now thought that many cases of confusion and mental disturbances in old people are misdiagnosed as dementia, when they may be caused by depression or even physical illness. It is also thought that, rather than being part of the natural process of ageing, dementia itself may be caused by specific diseases which could be treatable in the future. Even for those currently suffering irreversible dementia, the picture is not as bleak as has always been painted: with early assessment and professional support, and by maintaining the right kind of environment and stimulation, some of the worst symptoms can be alleviated.

Clearly, much depends on the current research into the organic causes of dementia; perhaps there will be successful prevention and treatment in the future. For the moment, though, most carers get little help in coping with this problem until it is too late – when they reach crisis point, and an elderly person has to be admitted to a long-stay psycho-geriatric ward or to a local authority home.

27

The GP said, learn to laugh at it, if you don't it will pull you down. Mum knows she does silly things, so we laugh about it. I say, you are daft. I know, she says. It lightens it for her and it brings out all the love. (Joan Jarratt)

He got terribly distressed and aggressive, banging his fists, breaking things. What is wrong with me, he'd say. It was the frustration of not being able to do things and not understand why he couldn't. He hated me. I was the jailer, the person making it impossible.

One terrible morning I came home from work and the neighbour said he'd been trying to climb over the wall, saying a man was attacking him. There was no sign of anyone. When I got home he didn't recognise me. (Dorothy Preston)

It's the aggression and bad temper which is the problem. I'll leave her a note saying your lunch is in the fridge and she immediately tears it up, saying, I'm not stupid. When I get home she's been up and down the road asking for lunch. (Jane Morton, 52, single, living with a mother with senile dementia)

There was only one way I could come to terms with this; my son was able to help me. My son's a nurse; he said: Mother, that is not Grandma, you're looking after a condition – the illness has taken over. (Joan Jarratt)

Dementia is a dismantling of the human being . . . a form of dying. It is an awe-inspiring illness; as those elements have been built up, so they are taken apart. (RL Symonds, 'Dementia as an experience,' Nursing Times *77,40,1981)*

Frustration and resentment

It is not just mental disorder in old people which can bring about changes in personality or reinforce character traits with which their children have always found it difficult to cope. The pain and discomfort of illness and disability, and the loss of independence which it normally entails, as well as the organic changes caused by strokes and other illnesses, can all lead to depression, frustration and resentment. For many, the process of growing older, and the approach of death, is a frightening experience which can make them seem selfish, demanding and egotistical.

She's very selfish, really selfish. Her attitude is, I'm her daughter and I should do it. I take her everywhere but you don't get thanked for it. They do become possessive, they think you should be there. I've shouted at her: I'm your daughter, don't treat me like a servant. I try to make conversation. When she comes back from the day centre, I say, have you had a good day, Mum? Huh, she goes, nothing ever happens there. After that she never speaks, never opens her mouth. I've said, I'm a happy person, you're making this house miserable.

It's probably due to brain damage, you make all sorts of excuses in your mind. She's not my mother I'm looking after. It's a complete stranger. Not my mother at all. (Delia Holland)

She's always there – waving me off when I go out to do the shopping, waiting for me to come back. It really started to get on top of me, all this waving me off when I went to the shops. One day I came home from the shopping, I said hallo and went straight into the garden – she came out and said, would you mind telling me why I've been sent to Coventry? (Julie Beale, 53, looking after a mother in her late seventies)

I didn't truly understand my mother's problems while I was away. I realised immediately I had him to myself what she'd been up against. He had a weak character, he was too dependent and cried too easily – one doesn't like to see it in one's own father. (Dorothy Preston)

The strain of this kind of behaviour is reinforced when it is directed solely at the child who is caring; when the elderly person puts on his or her best face to the rest of the world – even to the rest of the family.

My mother's smashing with my sisters, it's mind how you go Joan, be careful Joan, thank you very much Joan, how are you Joan, lovely to see you. She's never asked me how I am. (Delia Holland)

He had an awful lot of charm, he could charm the birds off the tree. He had a lot of nice qualities; if you weren't living with him you could be very fond of him. (Dorothy Preston)

She's much worse with me than other people. She normally keeps up all the social niceties, some friends have been quite surprised to see the other side. One friend came through the door when she was swearing like a navvy. Her own father was always swearing, always rough and ready and a drinker – now it's coming out in her old age. (Jane Morton)

The strains that caring imposes on any relationship are often exacerbated by the parent/child bond: this is the relationship within which we are most often expected to care, yet it is often the one which proves the most problematic. The emotions involved in caring for one's own parent, and the inevitable reversal of roles which this entails, are often the determining factors in whether a carer can cope, yet it is this area which gets ignored by the professionals: the hospital consultant who expects the middle-aged, married woman, with a family of her own, to take home a mother immobilised by a stroke, may tell her – if she is lucky – about the local incontinence service, but is unlikely to ask if mother and daughter 'get on'; the GP who presses a single daughter to come home and take care of her widowed father will not want to know about the rows which drove her out in the first place.

Even where a relationship between parent and child has been loving and open and where the adult child genuinely wants to care, it is difficult to adjust to the reversal of natural roles – the parent becoming child, and the child, parent – and to the loss of dignity and privacy involved in physical dependence.

It got to the stage where he couldn't get in and out of the bath. I was his daughter, he was very Victorian, he couldn't bear for me to see him, certainly with no clothes on. He didn't like me to have anything to do with his intimate care; he got terribly aggressive (about it). I also found it distressing. I could do it for anyone else, but I'd never had anything to do like that with my father. (Dorothy Preston)

The role reversal which caring entails can breed resentment and frustration on both sides. An elderly parent may understandably resist the loss of independence which ageing and illness can bring and fight against any suggestion that she might need help; while a daughter will in turn feel her mother is just trying to make life difficult. Some carers feel the only way they can cope is to 'baby' their parent, to refuse to treat them as equals or allow them to take risks – insisting, for instance that they never go out alone because the last time they had a bad fall – thereby creating even more resentment.

As her brother said, she won't accept there's anything wrong with her. If you say, do you want to go to the toilet, Mum? She'll always say no I'm all right, I'm all right, and then she'll sit there and do it in her pants. (Karen Hastings)

There's no way she'll do what she doesn't want to do. Sometimes you want to get her to bed and she'll say no; five minutes later it'll be OK – it's as if she had a need to assert her independence. The worst mistake people make is to say: you've got to do that now. That's when you get the real aggression. You've got to allow her to say no. (Joan Jarratt)

In other cases, an old person may find that disability makes him or her the centre of attention, especially after years of looking after other people, and becomes determined to hang on to that role.

Before I came home he was doing most things for himself, he could still prepare meals, he was coping. As soon as I got home he stopped doing anything. He wouldn't even boil a kettle. He was so clever in the way he became totally dependent. It's very hard to be assertive with someone who seems helpless and who everyone else thinks is helpless. It was always: the poor old thing. Never a word about what I'd sacrificed to come and look after him. (Dorothy Preston)

The barriers of a lifetime are hard to remove, and it is difficult for a child to tell a parent who retreats into illness that it would be better for her to dress herself, or to sit in a chair rather than stay in bed; easier to soften, to allow a parent to sink into dependency.

The dependency brought about by disability is not all one sided, though: carers can play as many emotional games as the parents they are looking after. They may fall into the role of martyr and struggle on without outside help – perhaps to make themselves indispensable or to earn the love they feel has always been withheld by a parent, or simply because they are incapable of breaking away.

31

In some cases, the tensions between parent and child may boil over into verbal and even physical abuse, a problem which has been termed 'granny battering' by one researcher. No one knows how widespread this problem is, but it is clear that carers sometimes feel pushed beyond endurance, and that extreme states of anger and frustration are hard to control. One study found that nearly one-fifth of carers had been reduced to hitting or shaking their elderly and confused dependants. It is even claimed that there have been instances of elderly relatives being killed by their children.

I used to get angry; I never actually did anything, but I know my anger probably came down through my arms when I buttoned his shirt or was tying his tie. (Dorothy Preston)

Unfinished business

We never got on very well. She was never a good mother to me when I was a child. I was a bright kid, won prizes, I'd be in the school plays – she'd never come to see them. I wouldn't say I like her or dislike her. I don't think I've ever loved her because she's never loved me. If she wasn't my mother I wouldn't want anything to do with her. (Jane Morton)

Someone said, years ago, you should get rid of that mother complex. I never thought of it like that. I gave her a promise to look after her years ago, when we were always having to live with other people. You make a promise within you – that you will try and make up for all the hurt.

Over the years I've hated my father. I've thought, damn my father. I've taken on all his responsibility. (Julie Beale, 53 and married, who has been living with and looking after her mother since she was 13, when her father left home)

The 'unfinished business', the emotional tensions between a parent and child – which may have been dormant for years while the child moved away from home to raise her own family or to build a career – may resurface and grow stronger when she takes over as carer. Illness and disability can provide the perfect cover for emotional manipulation, and a parent who has always been possessive and domineering may become even more so; refusing, for instance, to have a sitter – a 'stranger' – in the house. Conversely, a woman who has never really managed to break the parent/child bond and carve her own identity, and who still needs her mother's approval – even though she has perhaps left home and had a family of her own – may find herself returning to the same traumas she thought she had left behind in adolescence.

Few of us have perfect relationships with our families, and tension is present in most parent/child relationships; but for those who are forced into the intimacy and isolation of looking after a parent, there can grow a neurotic and destructive bond which neither side is able or willing to break. Some women feel they have cared for a parent – often a mother who lost a partner early on in married life and could not face being alone – ever since adolescence or childhood, when they became substitute partners and protectors; some have never managed to fight off a parent's emotional demands and have finally had their lives swallowed up in a relationship with a 'dependent' parent who may have little wrong physically. It is often the case that where such a parent does become physically ill, her daughter will find it impossible to cope because of her own unresolved feelings of resentment, or perhaps because real caring means taking real responsibility – the one thing she has never been allowed to do, in the past.

It could be said that these problems are primarily emotional in nature and have little to do with genuine disability or dependency. Yet most caring relationships – especially those between parent and child – are not based on physical disability alone, but involve a complex of emotions, one of which may be the need for parental approval. Many women feel guilty about drawing the line on care, and most relationships contain an element of what could be called 'compulsive caring' – where a carer refuses to take a holiday without her mother, for instance, or to accept help which she desperately needs. Most women have never been encouraged to assert their own needs or to put any limits on their caring, and feel they should give up everything for a parent – even if it means carrying on until they drop.

33

The emotions involved in a caring relationship are no different from those found in most relationships between elderly parents and their adult children; they include dislike, guilt, and resentment as well as love and affection. But the weaknesses in a relationship with which most of us can cope – perhaps by putting some distance between ourselves and our parents – are magnified and exposed by the isolation and intimacy involved in caring. As a result, carers are constantly confronted by these feelings; they rarely escape them.

The emotional education needed to give carers insight into their relationships, and to teach women to accept and assert their own needs, is an area which has so far been ignored by the professionals. Counselling a woman on how to cope with her mother is not easy; it involves coming to terms with your own mother first. Yet some understanding of the psychology of caring, and sympathy for the emotional dilemmas carers find themselves facing, is crucial to solving the current crisis. The emotional tension between dependent parent and caring child is the first factor cited by the carers themselves as causing suffering and misery.

The second factor is money.

Money worries

I think I'm paid a pittance. I don't know anyone else who'd work that many hours for £23 a week. I applied for supplementary benefit to top it up and all I could get was 60p. (Joanne Naylor, 18, looking after a mother with multiple sclerosis; the £23 she refers to is the Invalid Care Allowance)

It is difficult to generalise about the financial circumstances of adults caring for elderly relatives, as these will vary from family to family. Where a parent has moved in, for example, the carer may be able to use the proceeds of the sale of the family home, or the parent's savings, to pay for an extension, to buy in commercial caring services, or simply to supplement the family income. But there is little evidence to show that carers actually benefit financially from taking on a parent. There is far more to suggest that they lose out.

34

For one thing, the elderly are, as a group, one of the poorest in the country; and the majority of those being cared for are elderly women, whose own caring responsibilities for husbands and families have often left them dependent on re-duced pensions and supplementary benefit (income support, as it is now called). The result is that many carers of elderly people may find themselves subsidising the costs of disability.

Many women also lose out financially when caring for a parent because they either have to give up work completely, or go part-time, or take on casual, more convenient but less well-paid work to fit in with their domestic commitments. One study of married women who gave up work to care for elderly parents found that they had, on average, lost about £4,500 annually (1982 figures); while those who had gone part-time lost around £1,900 a year.

For a true picture of the financial costs of caring, however, the value of caring itself has to be taken into account. The same study found that these married daughters were every day putting in three or four hours caring; and it calculated the value of this work – at the hourly market rate paid to home helps and ward orderlies – to be about £2,500 a year. This sum, the researchers are quick to point out:

is of course a nonsense in relation to reality. Most families are doing what no-one else would come into the house to do, and as such it is priceless. (M. Nissal and L. Bonnerjea, Family Care of the Handicapped Elderly: Who Pays?, *Policy Studies Institute, 1982).*

Another study, published in 1984 by the Family Policy Studies Centre, puts the value of caring even higher: it estimates that there are about one million people with major caring responsibilities for frail elderly persons, and that on average these carers are putting in twenty-four to thirty-five hours a week. Costing this on the basis of the hourly rates for the home help service, it concludes that the annual hidden costs of caring lie somewhere between £3.7 and £5.3 billion. A similar study, published two years later by the Centre, estimates that the value of the work all carers do is between £5.1 and £7.3 billion annually.

Whatever the direct or indirect costs of caring for an elderly relative, they are rarely, it ever, offset by the only allowance available to carers: the Invalid Care Allowance (for a full explanation of benefits and allowances, see Chapter Eleven). Although in theory payable to all non-working carers as compensation for lost earnings, the ICA poses particular problems for carers of elderly people. There are thousands of both single and married women who are not working because they are looking after an elderly relative, but who cannot claim ICA because their elderly relative does not qualify for the Attendance Allowance.

The Attendance Allowance is the main form of financial help available to disabled people who need constant care: they have to be in receipt of the Attendance Allowance before their carer can claim Invalid Care Allowance. But many elderly people, who need a great deal of support and supervision – enough to warrant a carer giving up work – still do not satisfy the stringent conditions which need to be fulfilled for receipt of the Attendance Allowance.

Caring is washing clothing, making meals, feeding people, keeping someone warm and dry – but you need to be totally bedridden and doubly incontinent before you can qualify for anything. Cooking, cleaning, setting out someone's clothes – none of that counts. You have, to put it crudely, to be wiping someone's arse before you get an Attendance Allowance – even emptying the commode doesn't constitute.

The doctor who comes to visit (for assessment) is a total stranger. He doesn't know who you are; he's usually retired; he knows sod all about you and your patient; and he plays judge and jury – he could come when your patient is having a good day. He makes one visit for half an hour: he doesn't even have access to the GP files.

The Attendance Allowance wants you to make people into invalids – to qualify they ask you if you're feeding a person when you should be encouraging independence. When my mother-in-law gets out of bed, I put her on the commode and let her wash herself, but what they want is someone totally helpless.

I know cases where some elderly people have been so bad they've died before their allowance came through. It takes at least six months to get, even if you're successful. (Eliza Ray, 40, looking after a mother and mother-in-law)

There are also thousands of elderly people who have not even heard of this allowance, and thousands of others who may be reluctant to apply because they regard it as charity, or because they are too proud to admit the full extent of their disability. It is hardly surprising that out of an estimated 1.3 million carers in this country, only about 81,000 are deemed eligible for the Invalid Care Allowance.

Women who give up work or go part-time to care, face not only a poorer present but also an insecure future, since many of them will forfeit pension rights. The pattern of part-time, casual work, which so often fits in with caring, means that many are not eligible for private or occupational pension schemes; and despite moves over the last decade to protect female pension rights, many women who stay at home to care are likely to face a cut in their basic pension, and poverty in old age. Home Responsibilities Protection, for example, is the system which was introduced in 1978 to protect the basic pension rights of women not paying an insurance stamp because they are caring for someone at home; but in order for the carer of an elderly person to qualify for HRP, their relative has to receive the Attendance Allowance – again, not easy to get for some people. The same qualifying condition is true of the Invalid Care Allowance, the other means by which pension rights can be protected.*

The sweeping changes in social security provision which are being planned by the current government could in the future make the position of women carers even more precarious. There are, for instance, plans to modify SERPS, the state earnings related pension scheme, which has been of

---

* Women who began to care for elderly relatives before 1978, when the HRP scheme was introduced, will not have their pension rights fully protected by HRP. Those who used to pay the now defunct 'married women's option' of reduced insurance contributions while they were still at work will not have their pension rights protected for the first two years at home caring.

particular value to women carers with broken employment records, as it provides for an additional earnings related pension based on the twenty highest earning years. These plans, which will be looked at in greater detail in Chapter Eleven, will hit women carers of the future, despite government claims that special steps have been taken to protect them.

For years my father-in-law refused to hand anything over, either from his pension or his Attendance Allowance. He was incontinent, he had Parkinson's disease, I was at one point nursing him twenty-four hours a day; but he blankly refused to hand anything over. He might dole out £1 here or there, going back to what things cost ten years ago. I used to knit my mother-in-law's clothes – he never gave her any money either.

To begin with I was too wishy-washy; I expected everybody to be grateful for what I was doing and they weren't. You don't like asking, yet you know you can't manage on your own resources. I expected my husband's parents to be just the same as mine – to hand it over.

It nearly led to having to sell the house at one point, but then I managed to get control of his pension. Even then, he said: you don't have to get up in the night – so he only gave me half of his Attendance Allowance. (Eliza Ray, who cared for her own and her husband's parents for over twenty years)

Money is a subject which most carers – like most people – find difficult to talk about, especially with elderly relatives. Many feel reluctant to bring up the topic at a time of illness or upheaval, or are embarrassed about taking money from their own parents. Old people, in their turn, may be used to years of living frugally, out of touch with current prices and sometimes reluctant to pay their way once they have moved into a child's home. Like Eliza Ray's father-in-law, many are reluctant to hand over their Attendance Allowance, thinking it wrong that a daughter be paid for what they regard as a natural duty. Illness, confusion and depression can make the subject even more difficult to tackle; so that many carers soon find themselves out of pocket, or engaged in a painful struggle to wrest financial control from their parents.

When a parent dies

I feel enormous relief. For sixteen years I felt everything depended on him; I

38

never felt free at all. I felt it had an effect on everything: there was this great weight. For the first time in sixteen years I haven't felt, what is there, there's nothing to look forward to. I used to feel my father would outlive me; that he was sapping my strength. I miss him in a funny way. I get little shocks when I realise he's gone – a wave of feeling terribly vulnerable. I had an attachment to him, a mixture of intense dislike and compassion. It was all so ugly I tended to forget the positive side. In the last weeks I was filled with tenderness for him. I very much wanted his end to be happy – I'm glad it was. (Dorothy Preston)

People say I'm being too hard on myself, but I think, how could I ever get tired of lifting my own mother? How could I? I'm so full of (self) reproach. How hard and unkind to feel tired. I've been told I did everything possible, but you get this feeling as the years go by. You'd give anything to say to them, hallo, I never stopped loving you. I'd give anything to say to Mum, I'm sorry. It's easy to say, don't feel guilty; the books tell you not to feel guilty; but it's the carer who is emotionally involved. (Violet Brown, 63, who looked after a blind, arthritic and incontinent mother for eight years, until her death, at 89, in 1984. Towards the end she had asked for her mother to be catheterised because she could not manage to lift her onto the toilet every half-hour)

The death of a parent they have looked after, often for twenty or thirty years, brings for many women not only feelings of bereavement and grief, but also regret, relief and, sometimes, intense guilt – for not being the perfect carer they think they should have been. Many of these carers will be growing old themselves, will have sacrificed their work and friendships to their parents and will find it difficult to pick up the threads of their old lives. Despite the burden of caring, the death of a parent can leave many women with a gap, which they will find it difficult to fill; and sometimes with a life which seems empty and meaningless.

I'd take a bottle of paracetamol rather than have anyone looking after me. I've told both my children, if anything ever happens to me I want you to put me in a home, I don't care what you say. I wouldn't like for them what it's doing to me. (Delia Holland)

3

_____ • _____

Women in the middle: Married women looking after elderly relatives

The vast majority of carers in Britain were until recently invisible in the official statistics. They are married women, usually middle-aged and with families of their own, who are looking after one of either their own or their husband's parents. One recent survey found that more than one-fifth of all married women over 40 were, in addition to their 'normal' family responsibilities, looking after a dependent relative.

These women have to a large extent replaced the single childless daughters whose allotted task it once was to care for aged parents. They will often be in the middle of a threefold cycle of care: first for young children, then for elderly parents and finally for their own partners. They might well be multiple carers, looking after more than one dependant. They will usually have to combine caring with their traditional domestic duties; and, if living separately from their elderly relative, will probably be running two homes single-handed. As one researcher has aptly put it, they could be called the 'women in the middle': in middle age, mid-generation and in the middle of competing roles as wives, mothers, daughters and workers. As such they face a multitude of dilemmas.

Divided loyalties

I couldn't see my mum in a home – it would break my heart. My husband I love equally. Who is more important in the end? The health visitor said half of me belonged to my husband. He's always had to share me. (Julie Beale, 53, caring for her mother since she was 13 – through thirty years of married life)

40

I feel awkward with my husband, a little bit beholden to him for having her nere. (Karen Hastings, married and looking after a mother who lives with her and her family)

For most of these women, the stress involved in caring is exacerbated by their own sense of divided loyalties, to elderly parents on one hand, and to husbands and children – normally regarded as their primary responsibilities – on the other. The physical and emotional burden under which these different obligations place women generates feelings of guilt and conflict, especially when the conventional social roles expected in a marriage break down – when a woman is too busy to have her husband's supper ready, or too tired to listen to his business worries. If a woman has her own unresolved emotional problems, and is insecure in her relationship with husband or parent, she will feel torn in two trying to please them both.

It has placed a great strain on my marriage because she has never recognised my husband. The times she's taken badly something he's said; I remember sitting by her side trying to put things right, crying my eyes out, crying for hours. (Julie Beale)

The husband, in turn, may resent the fact that his wife no longer puts the marriage first and may feel left out; just as he may have felt left out when his wife was busy looking after the babies. A man's insecurities will be intensified if taking on an elderly parent comes at a time when he is himself going through the identity crisis which sometimes accompanies middle age, and is dogged by his own worries about work, the end of his career and the approach of retirement.

It is hardly surprising that many caring situations – especially where a parent has moved into the family home – lead to the emergence of a triangle relationship, where a woman feels torn between husband and parent and some-times has to negotiate between the two. One survey, pub-lished in 1981, of couples caring for confused elderly relatives found that several husbands were not even on speaking terms with the dependent parent and that the wife not only

41

had to mediate between the two but would be held account-able by both for the other's behaviour.

This is not to suggest that marriages which may have lasted half a lifetime and have survived other strains, including bringing up children, will necessarily crack under the tension of caring for a parent, when a woman no longer fulfils her primary wifely role; nor is it to suggest that all husbands are selfish, demanding and unable to offer love or support to a caring wife. But how well a relationship can stand the strain will depend on how flexible it is, how independent it is of traditional roles, and how much the caring burden is shared between husband and wife.

How husbands react

I felt sometimes my husband wasn't as helpful as he could have been. His attitude (towards his father) was: if he couldn't help himself, what did he expect? Father and son were not as close as they might have been. But men are like that, aren't they – different from women.

My husband started to stay out late at nights; he couldn't bear to come home and face it. He didn't want all the bother. He wanted life to be as it was before, and not have all these problems. I felt I did everything for his dad. The man doesn't really get involved – it was just left for me to do every-thing. (Alexandra Mills, 43, a former carer of both her husband's parents; the mother-in-law with arthritis and father-in-law with arteriosclerosis)

He doesn't like illness and has little to do with caring. I was the one who would have had to visit them in hospital every week of my life; I was the one who was visiting, washing their sheets, not Robert. There again, that is the Scottish thing: the wife visits the parents, the husband doesn't bother. It was my decision (to care); it was up to me to make it work, to look after them and to find the money.

My husband and his mother never have a conversation as such. I have got to fit in everybody, they can't overlap. My time with his mum has got to be different from my time with him. When he comes home, I'll be giving tea to his mum, so he'll report that he's in and go to the pub; then by the time he's back I'll have put her to bed and I'll spend time with him. Then at 9p.m. I'll make tea for her. It's very much sectioned out, like a clock – my time with her, my time with him. (Eliza Ray, 40, who has over the last years lived with, and looked after, both her own and her husband's parents. She is still caring for both her mother and her mother-in-law)

The evidence suggests that most married women caring for a parent get little support from their husbands – even where it is a husband's parent who is being cared for. While husbands may carry out traditional masculine tasks, such as picking up a prescription or sorting out pension rights, they rarely get involved in the physical side of caring: one study found that over half the husbands surveyed played no direct part in the care of the dependant living with them, even where the wife had a job outside the home. It also revealed that, whereas women spent on average over three hours daily on caring tasks, husbands spent an average of only thirteen minutes.

This lack of involvement is no doubt partly because caring for a parent is seen as an extension of women's normal domestic roles as wives and mothers: most men, especially if they are out at work all day, are not expected to help any more than they might be expected to make the beds or cook the evening meal. There are also social taboos that prevent men carrying out intimate physical care. On an emotional level, too, men are more likely to retreat – often into their work, or to the pub – in the face of illness and pain, and the demands which caring can entail.

Marital roles have begun to change, albeit slowly, and many younger men are becoming involved in taking care of their children and in domestic life. It remains to be seen how widespread these changes become, and whether they will affect the nature of caring, and who does it.

Forced to feel grateful

I couldn't have done it without my husband to help me – if he hadn't felt he wanted to do it. (Janet Bambry, who looked after a mother, a semi-invalid after a stroke, for twelve years)

I'm very fortunate – I couldn't do it without Harold's backing. (Joan Jarratt)

43

Most women looking after one of their own parents – especially if he or she is living in the matrimonial home – feel grateful to their husbands for 'allowing' them to do so; they say that their husbands are 'very good about it', and that they would never have been able to take it on 'if he hadn't agreed to it'. Some mention sisters who had refused to take on caring, because their husbands 'wouldn't stand for it'. Feelings of gratitude are understandable, given the sudden change in lifestyle, the strain on the relationship and the lack of privacy which caring for a parent can entail; but perhaps they also reflect women's sense of obligations to their husbands, their dependence and their relative powerlessness within marriage. It is as simple as the question of who pays the mortgage.

A similar sense of obligation makes many women take on caring for a husband's parent, especially where there is no sister available.

There's a bit of emotional blackmail here. His father died at home in his own bed and his mother wants to do the same. The emotional pressure is on me to keep going as long as possible. Sometimes I feel like the pig in the middle, and sometimes I feel guilty that I should be doing more for my own mother. If anything happened to me, she would immediately have to go into a home because he couldn't cope with her. (Beth Prentice, 49, caring for a sick husband and his mother, 82)

The effect on the children

I've got two children; you can't deprive them for the sake of her. The one thing I feel I couldn't cope with is if she became doubly incontinent at home. It wouldn't be fair on the boys, especially now they're getting older and bringing in their friends. (Karen Hastings)

It had quite an effect on my son, he never once went to see his grandad, he couldn't bring himself to see him ill, it upset him. He became like my husband – more withdrawn. (Alexandra Mills)

My son was very close to my mum, he absolutely adored her; but he now finds it very difficult to cope, going to see her. He hasn't gone since she's been in hospital. (Tina Stanson)

44

Some women find themselves torn between caring for an elderly parent and seeing to the needs of children who are still living at home. They feel guilty about neglecting children, who may themselves be at a difficult age – beginning to grow away from their parents, or facing the problems of adolescence, or unemployment. These anxieties are reinforced by the common belief that children should have an upbringing which excludes the pain, discomfort and embarrassment of old age and approaching death; the more so if their parents find it hard to come to terms with these issues and project their own fears onto their children.

For women whose children have left home, and started families of their own, the biggest regret is often that of missing out on their role as grandmothers:

The last time they came with the grandchildren it was dreadful. I said, don't come while she's here, she doesn't think anybody should be here. I wanted to see more of my children and grandchildren, and now this happens. (Delia Holland)

No privacy

Many of these women feel they are left with little option but to move an elderly or frail parent into their own homes – houses which are usually designed for nuclear rather than extended families, and where there is often little money or space available for adaptations or improvements. Moving a parent into the family home often happens when the husband and wife move to a different part of the country and can no longer keep an eye on things or pay a quick visit to make sure everything is all right. Yet this kind of move can often be disastrous for both adult children and their parents, especially where, as is usually the case, a separate space for a parent has not been established and where two or three generations are frequently eating or watching television together. Even where there is enough space to establish a separate sitting room for a parent, many families may feel reluctant to shut off an old person or make them feel unwelcome; in other cases, an old person may be too ill or too demanding to allow others any privacy. Generally this problem reflects the fact that modern family life makes little provision for, or acknowledgement of, the individual's need for privacy.

We all sit in the same sitting room at night, and maybe she wants one thing on the box and the boys want another. Sometimes I'll say to her, go and watch it on the other set . . . I wouldn't want her to feel she was shut up in a room like a prison. (Karen Hastings)

She has her own sitting room, she eats separately, it's something she has chosen to do. I couldn't have her in the same room. I (used to) always wonder what's going to be said, what's going to put her out. (Julie Beale)

It's like living in a goldfish bowl. Your home doesn't feel as if it's your own – it's like a public place. (Joan Jarratt)

The lack of privacy and space involved when a parent moves in can put an enormous strain on marriages, families and old people themselves, most of whom would probably prefer to keep their independence for as long as possible. Many old people are forced into even greater dependence on their children if they have been uprooted from their friends and familiar places to live with families in a different part of the country. Yet the growth in the numbers of the very elderly is far outpacing the development of suitable housing – such as sheltered flats – or the community services needed to support them in their own homes; and many families will at some point have a handicapped elderly relative living with them.

The loss of privacy – you've no married life, you can't settle down to do anything. You can't even talk on your own together because Mum doesn't realise you're talking to each other and she'll chip in. In the end you give up – you lose a lot. (Joan Jarratt)

Giving up work

I gave up my nursing career and now in a way I'm nursing both of them, but it's not a fulfilment. I was different when I was nursing. I was totally in control. I knew my job and I loved it. (Beth Prentice)

For most married women, middle age is a time they can look forward to: they are free after years of raising a family, and they can return to work – the largest increase in economic activity in recent years has been among women aged 45 to 59. Yet this is also the age when women are most likely to find themselves looking after an elderly parent. Many find themselves torn between yet another, often unexpected domestic responsibility – one which is not chosen in the same way as are children – and the social involvement, sense of identity and the extra earnings which a job can bring. While some women will give up work altogether, others will take part-time, usually low paid, jobs which fit in with caring – a familiar pattern of employment for married women, for whom paid work is still a secondary consideration. Unlike single women carers few of the married women interviewed for this book had at any time had what might be called a career.

Some married women carers may try to continue working full-time, only to find themselves attempting to be 'super-women', juggling with an unprecedented number of roles and responsibilities; they may even be made to feel guilty for ignoring their family duties. Married carers who want to continue working are unlikely to get the support they need to do so, since their jobs are still regarded as dispensable and their earnings seen as pin money; research indicates that married daughters looking after their parents are less likely to receive the help of statutory services than any other group of carers.

In a sense, these women face a similar dilemma to that faced by the younger mothers of a generation ago, for whom the problem has at least been partially solved by improvements such as childcare provision and maternity leave – services which may not always be available in practice but the need for which has at least been recognised in principle; such provision has made it possible for younger women to juggle the demands of families and working lives. Yet the dilemma between the demands of work and home which faces these older carers has so far been ignored. Perhaps similar arrangements – more daycare provision and more statutory rights to leave from work – are needed.

The Invalid Care Allowance

Giving up a job, of course, also means giving up earnings which are more than just pin money: they often make a significant contribution to the family income. Until recently, and despite being the largest group of caregivers in the country, married women were in the unique position of not being able to claim any financial compensation for lost earnings. This was because they were ineligible for the Invalid Care Allowance (for full details of allowances, see Chapter Eleven).

Introduced by a Labour government in 1975, the ICA was originally aimed at helping what was then thought to be a fast vanishing species: the single middle-aged daughter who had sacrificed both job and marriage prospects to look after ageing parents. Married women carers were, at the time, specifically excluded from eligibility for the ICA on grounds which have been used to justify discrimination against married women through every phase of the development of Britain's social security system; they did not need compensation for lost earnings, it was argued, because they had husbands to support them and 'might be at home in any event', as the 1974 White Paper on the ICA put it. This assumption was to prove not only unjust, but misguided; it completely misjudged the significance of married women's growing participation in the labour market. From 1961 to 1981, for example, among married women aged 45 to 59, participation in the labour force jumped from 32.6 per cent to 61.8 per cent.

Thanks at least partly to a long and bitter fight against the DHSS which was waged by one married woman carer, Jacqueline Drake, the government in June 1986 extended eligibility for the Invalid Care Allowance to married women;

the announcement was made only hours before the European Court of Justice made a final ruling on Mrs Drake's case, in which it reaffirmed that the UK policy on ICA was in breach of a European Community directive on equal opportunities. (Mrs Drake, who had given up her job in June 1984 to care for both her parents, had originally taken her case to a British social security appeal tribunal, which ruled, in March 1985, that she was eligible for the allowance since UK policy was in breach of the EC directive. This judgement was later upheld by the European Commission, and finally by the European Court of Justice.) According to government figures, 70,000 married women – still a tiny proportion of the total numbers of married carers – are now eligible to claim the Allowance, at an additional net cost of about £55 million.

Back into the home?

In the current climate of high unemployment, cuts in public spending and fashionable policies of 'community care', fears have been expressed that married women will be forced back into the home to provide a cheap workforce of carers for elderly and disabled people. Yet powerful social and economic forces have led to radical changes in both the role and expectations of married women, in marriage, the family and in the workplace – changes which it is difficult to imagine being reversed. The image of the model nuclear family, where the wife is at home and available to care, no longer fits reality. High rates of divorce, the breakdown of conventional family patterns and changing lifestyles threaten to make the future role of married women even more uncertain. Will divorced women, looking after children and holding down jobs, have the time, financial resources or even inclination to take on their former parents-in-law, for example? Will they be prepared to give up work to do so? As men are affected by unemployment, will there be a new division of labour; will husbands take a greater role in caring? Whatever the answers, it seems highly unlikely that married women will willingly return to their traditional caring role.

Karen Hastings

Karen Hastings is in her late thirties, married, with two teenage boys. She and her family share their semi-detached London home – which she keeps immaculate – with Karen's mother: a frail, deaf, and slightly forgetful old lady of 73 who has stayed with her daughter most weekends since her husband's death and who moved in permanently two years ago.

Her mother, she says, is 'quite a character' who loves going out to clubs and day centres: 'I'll be all right, she says. She still thinks of herself as reasonably young. But she falls over easily, she's fallen over the couple of times going to get her pension. She wanted to go to the hairdresser but I put my foot down.'

We had eighteen years of marriage on our own, I always steered clear of having her to live with me. I was 24 when Dad died; if she'd had her way she would have come then. She's no bother in her personality. She's not a person who interferes, she's very easy going. She more or less just sits there, she doesn't interfere with the children, I can't complain about that. I suppose it's the extra responsibility – bringing food into her, taking her coffee up in the mornings – it's all extra work.

She's got this habit in the mornings – she takes her wet pants off and puts them on the radiator in her room. It reeks and the pants have all gone yellow, where they've dried out. And then this morning first thing, she hadn't got any pants on – she doesn't like wearing pants at night, she really should wear them because she dribbles across the landing. I don't think she can be bothered: they get lazy. I'm washing about three pairs of pants a day – it's all her washing which is out on the line. With old people they wear two of everything, two slips. You change her and everything's got to be washed, otherwise the slips begin to smell. This was what was happening when she was at home; she wasn't bothering to look after herself.

As her brother said, the problem is she won't accept there's anything wrong with her. If you say, do you want to go to the toilet Mum? she always says (she imitates her mother's high voice), No I'm all right, I'm all right, and then she'll sit there and do it in her pants. I'm all right, she'll say. It would be easier if she would do the two things I ask – leave her pants off the radiator and put her pants on at night.

I look upon it – I try to take it as it comes. You've got to wait and see how she goes. If it got beyond me, if she had a very bad stroke. I'd have to weigh up . . . with my husband as well, we've got two children, you can't deprive them.

I will try to look after her, I feel I can't do anything more than that. I don't think she'd like to go to a home; she would find it very difficult to accept; but probably she would settle. She's very easy going and if she struck up friendships with people, she does row in.

I feel very awkward as well with my husband, I've got a responsibility to him and it's my mum. I feel a little beholden to him for having her here. I do feel that sometimes. My husband gets a little bit annoyed, the invasion of our privacy, I would say that. She has got this habit, if we're talking, she'll look at us both, one to the other (she imitates her mother's squint).

I do feel a little bit awkward with my husband at times; he might say something to make me feel a bit guilty. He's been under a lot of pressure in his job, worried about the future and how he would get another job now he's over 40. So he comes home and wants me to give my attention to him, he wants my support; so he might object a bit to my mum here, taking my attention. He looks on her as a bit of a rival (laughs). Sometimes he'll say, come on Esther, off to bed, I want to talk to Karen.

We're thinking of moving. She owned her own house and the money should be invested; so if we had a bigger, older house with a bedroom on the ground floor . . . although I wouldn't want her to feel she was shut up in her room like a prison. At one time she talked about getting married to an old gent; I said (laughs), you must be joking.

We aren't alike, not really. I'm much more houseproud than she's ever been, but then she was always in the position where she had to go out to work and there was no money. I worry about things more. She's always been the sort of person who as long as she can go out and enjoy herself, she's OK. I'm much more homely.

When I was much younger I didn't get on with her very well, she was always nagging and telling me off. I got on with my father very, very well, he was a very easygoing man who everyone got on with. It's because of him, I've always felt: when he was dying he said would you look after your mother – I've always felt I should do it . . . (*She is almost in tears.*)

It would upset me, if it came to a home. I would feel a bit guilty, I suppose. I feel she hasn't got a great life at the moment. She's got her clubs and her daytrips and up to now we've taken her on holiday – a year ago we went to Blackpool. I came home worn out. My husband has stipulated, we must have two weeks holiday on our own. I might take her up north, to the rest of the family, if my husband will say yes.

If it got to the stage where she was so difficult to look after and the rest of the family were suffering, I'd have to let her go because I must put them first in that way. I feel that while she's all right . . . it's more personal for her to be here. At least it's her home and her family.

Harold Jarratt

Joan and Harold Jarratt share their spacious and comfortably furnished home in the Kent commuter belt with Joan's mother Vi, who suffers from dementia and who has been living with them for the last year. Vi, 75, has a private nurse to look after her during the day, paid for out of her pension, the Attendance Allowance and her life savings.

Joan – like her husband, originally from the north – took over the care of her mother completely when the rota system of care shared with her five brothers and sisters broke down. A forceful, organised woman who runs the local self-help group, she says she knows her husband isn't able to cope as well as she is. 'I was brought up in a big family, so I'm used to having people around. He isn't'. They have one son, now married, and living away from home.

Harold, 51, has his own business as a paper merchant. It's 8 p.m.; Vi has gone to bed and Joan to a meeting. He's finishing his dinner.

I feel increasingly resentful, not against Vi, I think the world of her, but that we've got to take this on at our time of life. And all the restrictions – our house is like a public place with all these third parties calling in.

I sometimes feel Joan gives a greater priority to it than to our married life. I don't always feel like that, but if she was truly putting the marriage first . . . I've said to Joan she should be putting a time-limit on it; at the moment it could be until she dies.

Joan hasn't had good health herself – she's had heart trouble, she's had major heart surgery – so we've already had restrictions on our married life. So just at a time when we should be enjoying our freedom we have this.

I'm more conscious of this than Joan, of the fact that our home isn't our own with Vi here. She prowls about, comes into the bedroom. There's no privacy in our marital life, she's always there. I put my foot down recently about never going out together – now we do arrange it, but you can't come home and think it'd be nice to go out for a drink You can't do it, everything has to be planned; we've got a caravan by the sea we haven't used for two years.

I keep financial records for Vi, administer her pension. When I look back over the records, I think to myself, will I be doing this in five years time? I'll be 56. I can't see the end of this.

What I've said to Joan is that we can only go on doing this for so long, and then we'll have to think about care. But Joan won't hear of that and I can't force her. Well I could but it wouldn't do me any good – I'd get the backlash, because Joan's mother would probably deteriorate and I'd get the blame for it.

The business is comparatively new: his last company folded about two years ago.

I did say to Joan when I started afresh, it shouldn't be allowed to inhibit the workings of the business. It did do until recently because when Joan was working, I'd have to stay here until the nurse turned up, so effectively I was an hour late for business; I didn't get in until nine o'clock. I was losing an important hour of work. Indirectly it began to have an effect. I also had to spend a fair bit of time sorting out her mother's life savings because by this time we were running on a £50-a-week deficit. That meant a huge battle with Joan's sister.

He and his wife row frequently, he says.

That's when it comes out, when we row about something else and I'll say something about 'your mother'. I feel not so much bitter as resentful, that our home's not our own. It's a question of when Joan puts her mum to bed. We might be here all evening on our own, have a chat and watch the telly, if we're lucky. But you get very resentful of your home being taken over with a nurse all day long. I've nothing against Carol (the nurse), she's a great girl, but sometimes I go past two or three times a day; I feel I can't come in and have a cup of tea.

It's not as bad now as it was when we were involved with community care through social services: it was dreadful. I would walk in and find three ladies in here with Mum, holding a meeting in my front room. I almost flipped my lid.

I don't have anything to do with any of the personal physical care, although I give her her medicine – she seems to take it better from me. Occasionally the three of us will go somewhere together at weekends; one of us does the shopping while the other navigates Mum. This coming weekend we're going out to a social do and Joan's made the necessary arrangements. But usually we're just starting to enjoy it and it's about time to come home.

Joan and I haven't had the easiest of marriages; it's been quite turbulent in the past. This has happened just as we're getting our house and our lifestyle together. When her brothers and sisters dropped out because they couldn't cope I could see what was going to happen. I understand why they dropped out, all three have got children at home, let's face it, the children must come first. I feel they did what they could do. At least they tried. But when they couldn't do it, I didn't see why we should be left to cope with it all the time. There was always the option, with Joan's brothers and sisters, to say no, we can't carry on. It's Joan who can't say no.

I'm inclined to agree with Joan that if her mother did leave here, where she's been well looked after and accustomed to a one-to-one relationship, if she went into a home, she would deteriorate rapidly. We're in a Catch 22 situation. If we take the selfish view and say to hell with it, she would deteriorate.

I do feel we've given her an extra span of life. The fact it could go on indefinitely, that's what I find hard to cope with. There are times when you get compensation: she's so cheerful, she does appreciate what you do; she is grateful, so there is a rewarding aspect.

I grit my teeth and get on with it. There are times it gets out of proportion. I must say I'm not looking forward to another summer. The doctor said to Joan he would give her a couple of years. You can't tell, can you? She could slip away tomorrow or tonight or be here in four or five years time. She's been well looked after.

Joan is a very determined lady; this is why it's so difficult because she's committed to it. But they've both been good parents-in-law to me. When we were younger and struggling for a home they never bothered to count the cost.

4

---- **.** ----

Dutiful daughters:
Single women looking after parents

Until recently, the traditional carers of elderly people were single women – often the youngest, unmarried daughters who were expected to sacrifice job and marriage prospects to ailing parents. The rise in marriage rates over the last twenty years, and the consequent decline in the numbers of single, childless women, has meant that it is now married women who have largely taken over as carers of the elderly; yet the role of their single sisters should not be underestimated. It is thought that there are over 300,000 single women living with – and to some degree or another, looking after – elderly and handicapped relatives, and 156,000 for whom caring is a major responsibility.

Expected to care

Today's typical unmarried women carers, mostly in their forties and fifties, will have left home for a period – even bought their own home – and carved a life and a career for themselves before becoming carers; many have travelled extensively and held down prestigious jobs, in fields such as social work and teaching. As a result, they feel more conflict about caring, and have more to lose, than the previous generation of single women.

Even today, however, single women are regarded as living on the periphery of a society which is rooted in marriage and children. Unlike their married counterparts they are often seen – and see themselves – as having no 'real' responsibilities, no domestic roots and no genuine role in life, no matter how important or demanding a job they may have held down. Consequently, the single daughter in a family is still expected to become the carer if necessary, by both professionals and other members of the family, but also by herself: she may feel she has no choice but to return home to look after an elderly parent, or to move that parent in with her, especially if her sisters have the responsibilities of husbands and children.

The evidence also indicates that single women carers tend to take on their caring role early in life – earlier than their married counterparts, who may have raised children and be approaching middle age before taking on a parent – and that they will often go on caring for a lifetime. Even single women who have moved away from home and tried to establish their own lives tend to feel responsible for their parents early on in life, especially if they are only children. Such women are often pushed into becoming emotional and social carers, sometimes substitute husbands and wives, for parents who become extremely dependent after the loss of a partner and who never really get used to the idea of being alone. Of course, the care and protection which all adult children provide for elderly relatives most often begins with the onset of the loneliness and sense of vulnerability which losing a partner entails. But if a single daughter is available, especially if she is an only child, she may be under strong emotional pressure to go beyond the normal caring role and to step in and take that partner's place. The relationship which builds up between a lonely parent and a caring child may well, if it happens early in life, have an influence on whether that child goes on to create a partnership or a family of her own.

There have been occasions on which I might have married; I did live with somebody for a while. My father was terrified I might get married. He used to say I was a great disappointment because I hadn't given him a grandchild, but he didn't even want to mention my boyfriend's name. The neighbours used to say, he dreads the idea you might marry.

He had always depended on my mother to the extent that she found it suffocating. He transferred that dependence onto me. (Dorothy Preston)

I do think about marriage, but it seems an age, another lifetime away. With dating, you have to explain right from the outset: I've got these responsibilities, are you prepared to put up with it? Put like that, a lot of people aren't. (Joanne Naylor, 18, caring for a mother paralysed by multiple sclerosis)

The dutiful daughters interviewed for this book included one or two, like Joanne Naylor, who had been looking after their mothers from childhood, and whose schoolwork, social life and career prospects were all drastically affected. Little is known about children under 18 who have major responsibility for caring for a disabled parent, but their numbers are thought to be somewhere in the region of 10,000.

Emotional traps

There are no secrets between us, we know everything about each other. We've got our own brand of humour, we like the same sort of programmes – we've been together for years. We talk a lot. We're together all day. We don't have to say anything; we can sit here some nights and not say a word but feel companionship. (Joanne Naylor)

We're very alike, we talk a lot, that's one of the problems – it's very much like a marriage. The sort of relationship I was living before was a normal, independent adult life, even though we were in the same house. The emotional relationship was not so intense. I'm worried about whether I'll be able to cope when she dies. (Stella Layton, 47, caring for a mother aged 79)

Single women, without the support or distraction of their own family lives, may be more vulnerable to the emotional traps which caring can involve, because they so quickly find themselves facing isolation. Of course all carers, whether single or married, face some isolation and lack of freedom; but at least married women have other social roles to perform. Indeed, for married women, the problem is rather one of being torn between different sets of domestic demands and responsibilities. A single woman, on the other hand, is in danger of losing the things which form the lifeblood of her independence – friends, hobbies, travel, culture – precisely because they are regarded as dispensable.

57

You try to normalise this life as far as possible but it isn't normal. It isn't normal to get invited to a New Year's Eve party and ring up seven sitters who can't do it and end up thinking it's not worth going out. If I want to get out I've got to find a sitter; it gets to the point where it affects your relationships with friends. I don't want my friends to think I only want them because they'll come and sit. (Stella Layton)

Single women easily become martyrs, totally subservient to a parent's demands, refusing help because they think that no one else can care in the same way that they can. Indeed, some may use their caring role as a cover for other problems, and as an excuse to retreat from a world – whether of work or relationships – that they have always found it difficult to deal with. In some cases, this mutual dependence can, develop into a neurotic, destructive relationship which has little to do with physical need, and which can lead to growing bitterness.

Dora Taylor

When her mother first moved in, Dora Taylor was 33; she was a successful professional woman with a promising career in social work ahead of her. Eighteen years later, at the time of her mother's death, her independent life and career were finished, destroyed by the relationship which had grown up between them. 'I never did anything physical for my mother, in fact she was my carer from time to time. It was her personality. That's what it was, that's all it ever was.'

Now 57 and single, she lives frugally in a cold, uncomfortable rented flat – reminiscent of an institution, like the children's homes she once worked in – in the bedsit area of a large provincial town. Forced into early retirement from her last job as a medical social worker because of back problems, she still exudes the qualities which used to be associated with people 'from the Welfare': brisk, sensible, and slightly moralistic. People – including carers – are in her eyes at least partly to blame for the predicaments in which they find themselves. She is also kindly, well-meaning, lonely, and in chronic pain most of the time.

Her story is one of an unhappy, lonely childhood, a stormy and unsuccessful marriage between her parents – an 'emotional hot-

*house' – a cold, dependent, possessive mother, and a father whom
she clearly adored: 'He wasn't an easy father but I admired him.
He's the one I'd have liked to be close to, but she came between us.
She was terribly threatened by what he and I had in common.'*

*After that came a university education, social work training, a
promising career as a child care officer; and later, while living with
her mother, a nervous breakdown which wrecked her career. Her
father died of cancer at the age of 59: it was at this point she says,
that the problems started. 'I felt stifled from the moment I knew my
father only had a year to live. The night he died, I said to my aunt,
there goes my life.' Five years later, her mother moved in with her
permanently.*

I was going to buy my first house and was thinking of taking in a
lodger. My mother said, that's my room gone. The next thing I knew
she said she would sell up and come to live with me. She was 66
then, but she was managing. I was 33. I never wanted to do it, I
never looked for it, never welcomed it. I would never have wanted to
join forces with her – not at all.

I'd done very well; I was an area children's officer by the time I
was 28. Once she moved in, my career went downward. I started to
take less responsible jobs with shorter hours. I moved around the
country, taking her with me – I kept thinking it might be different
somewhere else. By the time she died I'd gone down from the very
senior to the quite junior jobs.

She was very jealous of my work. She grew up in a family where
the father thought it wrong for women to work: the attitude was that
his sisters hadn't worked and his daughters weren't going to
(either). They lived and died with the idea that they were really upper
crust; her father gave her no education. My mother thought that girls
should sacrifice themselves for their mums.

She affected my social life drastically. I didn't feel comfortable
having friends in – it restricted the conversation, you couldn't be too
work oriented. She didn't have many interests or a lot to talk about;
she wouldn't clear out when friends came.

My mother was hopeless at decision making. Even when my
father was dying she asked him how much coal to have delivered –
when he was dying. She made it impossible for me to see him alone
in hospital. I remember wanting to talk to him about his diagnosis
and the future – she wouldn't leave us alone. She was terribly
threatened by what he and I had in common: intelligence, ambition,

a desire to learn. She had come from a different drawer; born with the ideas that she didn't need to strive.

When I went home after eighteen years away, I was appalled; she would come into the bathroom without knocking and all the mail would (be opened). I used to see father as ruthless before I had her, now I see he had to be.

She was so charming to other people, very ready to smile. All the shopkeepers thought she was marvellous. She could be very pleasant, very hospitable, quite affectionate with strangers; she reserved all the other side for the family. She could act injured, go very quiet; she was very good at making others feel guilty towards her. She could turn quite nasty. I pitied her, felt sorry for her. I understood what had made her what she was.

After she died I felt very guilty. I think towards the end you build up so much resentment, you're just absolutely full of it – you go on letting it out when the dice are loaded, when somebody is older and really threatened by the thought that you might go and leave them. You can't stop hitting back when, probably, you should (stop).

We argued a lot anyway, but towards the end there were massive rows. By that time I should have seen her arteries were going and she hadn't got the judgement, and she was getting paranoid; but you don't make allowances. Just as a mother sees her daughter as always 16, a daughter sees her mother as always dominant. She had got arterial sclerosis, she was arthritic, but with someone who has always been awkward, you don't make allowances.

All the traits which were troublesome in the middle-aged woman were heightened. She got moodier. She was always a very, very insecure person; I didn't have the knowledge to understand all of it.

I'm not entirely over her death; there are a lot of regrets. You wish you'd been nicer. The last month was particularly difficult, an awful lot of rows. It was probably organic in my mother's case – if one had known one would have let it ride.

Perhaps I could have had a happier relationship with my mother. I wish I could have seen more of the good in her, more of the qualities she had. She was a bit of a trooper, she kept going, she was an optimist; she didn't worry about material things. She took each day as it came and she was cheerful.

I miss the presence of someone else. I miss my father more. He made an unfavourable marriage and he stood by it; he never said a word about her to me, ever. He was terribly loyal. All his faults were faults of strength, whereas hers were faults of weakness: unreliability, buying friendship, being untruthful. She had no self-confidence, her upbringing hadn't given her any. I think that's what's at the bottom, of it; she couldn't stand close relationships, people being close to her.

I don't know if she loved me. I'm sure she behaved to others as though there was great affection. But very rarely did I pick up any indication that she did. There must have been something in me which wanted this bond. No one is tied unless they want to be.

I was an appalling carer. On the few occasions my mother needed physical care, I couldn't give it. There was nothing to give. Mainly because there was never a very deep affection, not on my part. I took it on never out of love but out of a sense of obligation and responsibility. Never out of love.

Loss of career

For the professional single woman, the most devastating loss which caring can bring in its wake is the loss of a job and the end of a career: one recent study of single female carers, by researcher Fay Wright, found that one-third of those below retirement age had had to give up work, while half of those above retirement age had given up work before reaching retirement. (It also found one woman who had scarcely worked outside the home at all: she had been persuaded to give up work at the age of 14 because of her mother's poor health. At the time of the interview she was 75 years old and still looking after her mother – by then 99.)

My mother wasn't well. I was in the middle of a crunch job negotiating – you can't do that kind of work when you're near bursting into tears in the middle of it. I remember sitting in the chair in that room saying I'm so tired. If I'd stayed I would have been earning £16,000. I've sacrificed financially, I've sacrificed socially. Public life will probably go by the board altogether. I'm very unlikely to get back into youth work at 50, there are too many young people coming in. (Stella Layton, who resigned from her job as general secretary of a national trade union to look after a mother with heart trouble and arthritis, and an aunt who was dying)

The main effect is the loss of ambition. When I started senior school I was

61

very serious about what I was going to do. By the time I left school I didn't give a damn. Sometimes I think, it's not fair, why me and all this rubbish; but it would have been far worse if I'd got a job and given it up. (Joanne Naylor, 18. She does not expect to go to work while her mother is still alive)

Research has also found that single women carers typically gave up white collar jobs in areas such as social work, the civil service, teaching, nursing and local government – fields which have traditionally been the preserve of single rather than married women. On the other hand, single women carers are not under the moral imperative to give up work to the same degree as they might have been twenty or thirty years ago: on the contrary, those with mortgages to pay may well be viewed as the essential breadwinners, and be expected to struggle on at work for as long as they can – often under great emotional strain and sometimes with little sympathy from their employers or colleagues. As one single woman commented in Fay Wright's survey:

None of the women (at work) gave me any sympathy. They turned round and told me to give up my job! Really, it was a big mistake talking about my problems at work. All they wanted to talk about were husbands and boyfriends. (Fay Wright, Left to Care Alone, Gower, 1986)

Even when single women carers do not give up work completely, caring is likely to influence their career development: few can cope with the dual pressure of caring and a career. Many are likely to move to easier jobs with flexible hours, where they can take time off when needed.

For a single professional woman, giving up work means losing the one thing which may have enabled her to lead an independent life – the main channel for expressing herself and her talents; and as has been described earlier, it may also mean a loss of, or reduction in, both basic and occupational pension rights. Those in their forties and fifties will find it difficult, if not impossible, to return to their chosen fields. Work plays a crucial role in giving women economic freedom and an ability to develop social relationships outside the home; giving up work usually has the effect of increasing their social isolation. There is evidence to show that many parents who have accepted a daughter going out in the evenings – because she goes out to work during the day – will, once she has given up work, become stubborn about being left at home alone at all.

Jane Morton

Jane Morton is 52 and single. She is a cheerful woman who looks younger than her years. She is obsessed with computers, and totally uninterested in the domestic side of life. Three years ago, she was forced to take early retirement because she could no longer cope with the demands of the job – a junior management post in the computer department of a large British firm for which she had worked for twenty years – and those of her increasingly confused and forgetful mother. 'I'd run into difficulties with another manager at work who was making life difficult,' she says. 'I was coping with problems at work and then going home and having problems with Mother. The only time I felt free was in the car on the way home.'

Her subsequent efforts to build a career as a freelance in the computer field have also failed for the same reasons. She now works as a local authority lecturer. 'The freelance work is very high-powered stuff: you sign a contract to produce results within a time limit, which can mean working long hours and weekends. I felt I couldn't commit myself: if there was any problem with her, I would have fallen behind.'

I quite enjoy the teaching but working in a local authority college doesn't pay as well. I could be earning £500 a week if I was teaching in the commercial field, I'm lucky to earn £100 where I am. Also the computer industry is moving very quickly and I'm not keeping pace. It's very hard work, trying to keep up to date.

I do feel resentful a bit because it's upset my provision for old age; I took a lower pension because I left my company early. The theory was that I could do enough highly-paid freelance work to make it up, to get a nice bit of capital to invest, but it hasn't worked out like that.

Her mother has lived in a granny flat in Jane's home for the last thirteen years; she is reasonably physically active but has been diagnosed as having dementia.

She cannot cook for herself. Meals on Wheels would help, but she won't have it. This is the aggressive, unco-operative side. She'd probably grumble about the food. She said she didn't want all these people coming to the house. She probably wouldn't answer the door.

We've never got on. She was never a good mother to me when I was a child. I was a bright kid, won prizes; I'd be in the school plays but she'd never come to see them. I never felt she took any interest. I don't particularly owe her anything, to repay what she did in my childhood.

She's always been a bit inadequate; she used to nag my father all night in bed. He carried on work after his retirement – died while he was still working. He used to take more interest in me as a child. I've inherited his temperament more than hers. He had a sense of humour. He would have been a lot easier to look after, I could have had some fun with him.

Last night, she said there's two things under my bed. I looked: there were two chamber pots. She said somebody's been in here; she wouldn't laugh about it. Now if it had been my father we'd have had a joke about it.

They get very suspicious – it's part of the senile confusion. Mine thinks I'm having men in, going upstairs and drinking all her whisky. She's starting drawing lines on the side of the whisky bottle. I said to her, chance would be a fine thing.

I get all the shopping. I put £5 in her purse and the rest in the drawer. The next thing I know, she's shouting down the stairs saying I haven't left her any money. But sometimes she'll go out with £20, come back £15 lighter and only £3 worth of goods in the bag, I keep having to stop her taking money out. She thinks I'm robbing her when all I've done is lock it away in the savings bank.

She never takes the initiative. She keeps on saying: I never see anyone. I say, ring them up, go and see them. I have to organise it. She's always been like that: sat back and waited for everyone to organise her life.

I don't take her out socially. I can't stand being with her in a restaurant. We've got absolutely nothing in common; it's a super-ficial relationship. I can speak to her reasonably about practical things but we are never able to discuss anything serious. She sits and watches her TV and I sit and watch mine, in separate flats.

I used to go about with the Scout crowd; they were quite active

64

socially – various dinner parties and so on. It's affected that to a certain extent. I'm always having to refuse invitations or come away early. I used to be in the Sea Rangers; they have reunion weekends rowing boats on the river. They had a great weekend recently but I couldn't go to it.

I was recently asked out to a supper party. An old friend of hers suggested bringing Mother round, but she wouldn't go; she said it didn't matter how late I was. I said to her, why don't you go round to Mary's? She said, why should I go out, just because you want to go out? So I had to be home at eleven, I'd only just had coffee by then.

A friend says she's jealous of me because I've had a good independent life which she's never had. She said: that's the reason she's nasty to you – she's jealous you're enjoying your life. She resents me enjoying myself now. I'm determined not to let her stop me; there's this constant battle of wills.

Just before this job, I had a really bad spell – tense all the time, churning stomach. I always swore I'd never let her get to me. She wants to row all the time and I walk away. But it gets to a point where you can't walk away. Good thing I've started this job; when I leave the house, I've trained myself to completely switch off.

I wouldn't say I dislike her or like her. I don't think I've ever loved her, because she's never loved me. If she wasn't my mother I wouldn't want anything to do with her. If anything I pity her for being so inadequate, not being able to enjoy life. She moans about everything. I think she nagged my father to death; he died of a stomach ulcer. But she's my mother and I'm stuck with her.

The risk is that she'd have a big stroke which would leave her paralysed and largely speechless and incontinent, and I would have all the physical problems. I don't want to cope with that. I'd want her to go into a home; but if there's a daughter living at home it's incredibly difficult. So it would have to be a private home and I'd have to go back into full-time highly paid work.

I'm just not the Florence Nightingale type. I've chosen not to get married and not to have children because I couldn't face the thought of nappies and endless housework. I've never wanted it. The thought of looking after her physically horrifies me; I would fight tooth and nail to get her taken off my hands. I would even put her in a home temporarily and emigrate. The thought of being stuck in that situation with someone you don't care for a great deal – it's intolerable.

Her mother, she adds, was the youngest of six children.

Auntie Doris – my uncle's widow – says she was always spoilt, always got her way. Maybe that's it. Always whining and moaning.

Lack of support

As far as help from statutory services is concerned, single women carers are subject to the same assumptions made about all women: that if a woman is around, she should be able to cope. Research has found that, overall, single sons caring for a parent receive far more help from local home-help services than do single women: 55 per cent of house-holds with sons have a home help, compared to 22 per cent of those with daughters. The difference is partly explained by the fact that single women themselves are less likely to expect or apply for help than their male counterparts.

The district nurse looked into the kitchen, she saw the unwashed pots and the beds not made. She called me down, caught me in the hall. The next thing she said was, you'll have to do less outside the house, otherwise you'll have a nervous breakdown. (Stella Layton)

Financial hardship

For these women, giving up work will also be a major financial blow to a household in which they are usually the sole earner: many will find themselves having to use up their savings or early retirement sums before going on to the state's safety net for those without an adequate income – supplementary benefit, or income support.

For single women living with a parent, even getting the income support for which carers are eligible without signing on for work can prove a problem if their dependant is judged by the DHSS to have sufficient resources to pay for private help. The Carers' National Association knows of cases where, because a parent has her own savings or a private pension, her carer has been unable to claim any benefit whatsoever and has been forced to live off her parent. Whether a carer gets benefit depends on an individual judgement from the DHSS, which can only be made after a carer has given up work – so a daughter may find herself out of a job before she is told she is ineligible for benefit. This problem is made worse by the fact that many old people are reluctant to disclose their financial circumstances to the DHSS, and also by the ignorance of many carers about what they are allowed to claim.

The Invalid Care Allowance, which was originally introduced to help single women and to protect their pension rights, goes nowhere near making up the income which a single woman will have sacrificed to care (for fuller details of allowances, see Chapter Eleven). And, like all carers, single daughters are anyway eligible for the ICA only if their parents are in receipt of the Attendance Allowance. Before eligibility for the ICA was extended to married women, only 11,000 people were claiming it – a fraction of the numbers of single women who have given up work to look after a parent. Fay Wright's recent study of fifty-eight single carers and their dependants found that nearly one-third of old people who met the criteria for an Attendance Allowance had not applied. The position over ICA was even worse: of these fifty-eight carers – the very people whom the ICA was originally designed to help – only one woman in the study received it. Most depended totally on supplementary benefit.

Single women carers living on means-tested benefits face even more daunting financial problems in the future: it is this group which will be one of the hardest hit by the government's Social Security Act, which in April 1988 abolished the long-term rate of supplementary benefit. Although existing benefits are to be frozen until the new rules catch up, this change, according to the Carers' National Association, will eventually mean a loss of 23 per cent in the income of the 11,000 carers previously on the long-term rate of supplementary benefit, many of them single women (for full details of the Social Security Act, see Chapter Eleven).

I know of one woman carer in her mid-sixties who is looking after a mother in her nineties; the mother gives her £5 a week – and fines her for extravagances. A lot of old ladies don't believe their daughters can deal with finance, so they may give financial control of the household to a son living miles way and not doing anything to contribute to care. They may even leave all their money to someone else – to a son because he was 'such a good boy'. A major problem with old people is that they don't hand over the money when they move in, they may well hang on to their Attendance Allowance and their pensions. Carers can be made destitute by their parents' refusal to contribute to household costs. (Judith Oliver, Carers' National Association)

The reluctance of many old people to hand over money for their upkeep, or to contribute to household costs, can, in the case of single carers, mean real financial hardship – especially where, as has been described above, they cannot claim benefits in their own right because their parent is deemed to have adequate financial resources to pay for care.

Worse, a single woman carer often faces real financial hardship when the parent dies: she abruptly loses both the Attendance Allowance and the Invalid Care Allowance – even though her fixed outgoings may be the same as when her parent was alive, and the likelihood of her finding work is minimal. After years of caring, she may be unfit to register for work and will therefore be unable to claim unemployment benefit. If she has been living in the parental home, and has brothers and sisters with a share in the parental will – or if a parent has died intestate and there has been no legal agreement drawn up with her carer – there is even a danger she will have no legal rights to stay in the only home she has.

Death and bereavement

One of the problems will be to find a replacement when she dies – a way to help me get back into life. (Stella Layton)

For a single woman, the death of a parent for whom she has been caring for years – often at the expense of all other interests – will come as a blow rather than as a release, and may leave a void which it is impossible to fill, whatever had been the quality of the relationship between parent and child. Too old to find another job or to recreate the lives they have sacrificed, and left without other family members to turn to,

68

single women carers often look forward to an old age of poverty and loneliness.

Caring for brothers and sisters

There exists another smaller but significant group of dutiful daughters: those who have remained at home and sacrificed their own lives to look after a disabled brother or sister, sometimes as well as an elderly parent.

Nowadays, most parents of younger disabled children would not expect other children to take on the burden of caring after their own deaths; if they are lucky, their disabled child will be found a place in a community unit rather than be expected to go and live with a brother or sister. But twenty or thirty years ago, the only provision for a disabled child whose parents had died was a 'subnormality' hospital; if that was to be avoided the burden of care would have to be undertaken by a member of the family, usually an unmarried sister.

It was often the oldest daughter in a family who took on this responsibility; the one who never left home to get married or get a job. Many of these women are now elderly; and, because their dependants are of the same generation, the responsibilities they took on have often lasted a lifetime.

Hannah Gaskell

If there is a God he's not all-powerful and omnipotent and all-loving because he wouldn't have produced someone like Lil. Her life's been hell on the whole.

Hannah Gaskell is 58, single, and lives with Lil, 56, a brain-damaged sister with a mental age of four, whom she has looked after for nearly forty years. When Lil was two, she contracted cerebral-spinal meningitis, an illness which left her retarded, epileptic and mildly psychotic. These days she is heavily tranquillised.

They're very heavy drugs and they help a lot. She is vile when she's not on the right drugs. She can be very nasty in a very adult way –

really aggressive – although she's never actually hurt anyone. She used to throw things, but always past people. Her worst violence (now) is spitting. But the extremes of vile nastiness still come out.

Hannah is the eldest of seven sisters and two brothers, and her father, a self-educated man, was a wealthy company executive. In the end, however, the property deals he was involved in backfired and the family home, a large country house in the south of England, had to be sold on his death.

Most of the time we were very well off: we had a nanny, a governess, a cook. At other times, Mother was alone. It was a very stable background, on the whole very good. Everyone has some horrors in their background; ours was Lil, poor soul.

I can remember being told not to sing in the middle of the day; we all loved singing, but if Lil didn't like it Mother would ask us to be quiet. I must say I adored my mother. The only thing we quarrelled about was how I would look after Lil. I told her I wouldn't be turned into a cabbage like she had been. Mother would allow Lil to talk to her as though she was dirt, and to swear; I said Mother, you are mad. Lil never did any of the jobs we did. She was never taught to be polite to any of us – but if we were impolite to Lil, that really got Mother's dander up. She and my father were the perfect couple; they adored each other, it was love at first sight. When he died, if Mother hadn't had Lil, she would have died – she would have refused to eat. It was looking after Lil which got her through it.

Father was affected (by Lil) hardly at all; he wouldn't allow her to get away with things. Mother àcted as protecter for both Dad and Lil; she was in the middle, she kept them apart. Once you start down that slippery slope . . . She used to get the most appalling migraines; after his death, she never had another.

Hannah has never had a proper job, nor ever left her parents' home apart from a short spell as an au pair *in Paris.*

My father did not do well by his daughters, I have to say it. We all ought to have gone to university; we were all capable of it. We all resented Mike (a brother) going to Oxford – it was always: tidy the house up, Mike's coming home. Every one of my sisters should have had a chance of college. He made us all think we were stupid – the one thing I find difficult to forgive. We weren't. I didn't think for

70

myself until Father died, but that didn't mean I was stupid. He should have known. He would call us stupid when he lost his temper. That was terrible, terrible, terrible. We all thought we were.

She started to take over responsibility for Lil when she was about 22, her mother 55, her father in his seventies. The rest of the family had left home.

It was my own choice quite definitely. I was stuck with it, but if I had to make the choice again I would, there's no doubt about it. The alternative was to put Lil in some sort of home, which would have been unthinkable, especially fifty or so years ago.

The two sisters now live in a small village near the south coast, in a spacious, relaxed, pleasant and very English house which she loves and is determined to keep – despite her much reduced finances. It has Virginia creeper on the walls, leaded windows, a well-kept garden and a view overlooking the Downs. They manage on about £7,000 a year, a sum made up from disability benefits, help from Hannah's sisters and brothers and the rent from another house bought by her father as an investment for Lil's future.

I think Father probably knew I would look after her. He bought a house in both our names seven years before he died; he used to call it my old age pension. It was never discussed, just presumed. I presumed it too, when I made up my mind to come home from abroad. Father bought the property as an investment in Lil's and my name in case either of us died. He worried desperately about providing enough; as things turned out, he didn't. Hannah does bed and breakfast to supplement their income; she runs a car and manages to pay a cleaning lady and a gardener – both 'absolute musts'.

One of her brothers is a scientist, the other a doctor; her six sisters, three of them nurses, are now living in different parts of the world –

I think to be anywhere where Lil isn't. I don't feel resentment against them, or if I do I don't know it. They come home fairly frequently, so we see plenty of them. The boys are out of it; they do what they can financially, but the girls help out. Sometimes I get annoyed with my brothers and then I think: they're not capable of looking after Lil. They do their best financially. Some people can do much more than others, there's no doubt about it. It's nearly always women, isn't that true?

71

Hannah herself is not in good health: she is very overweight and several years ago suffered a stroke which left her vision impaired – although she still insists on driving a car. She seems calm and relaxed on the surface but says this is because she has found ways of relieving the stress. She finds it hard to talk about the worst years, before the advent of modern drugs, when her sister had so many fits and was so aggressive that she needed constant restraining.

Lil, she says, is very retarded in some ways – her drawing, for instance, hasn't got beyond the matchstick stage – but the strange thing is that she can talk like an adult; partly, Hannah thinks, because she comes from such an articulate family.

One specialist said that if she'd been born into a working class, into a poor environment, she would have been dumb. We have always talked to her, me and my sisters. If we're watching TV together we will always talk; it's almost a tutorial, a one-to-one relationship. For example, she has very strong views on capital punishment: she's against that now. She could probably tell you about nuclear disarmament. So she is mentally retarded but she mustn't be spoken to in a childish way: intellectually she can hold her own.

She has never been to school, there were no special schools then; she had a governess who taught her to knit, and Mother taught her the alphabet. She's hardly ever been away from home – except when she was sent to a mental hospital for six weeks at the age of 16, she was having so many fits and the family could no longer cope. It was supposedly one of the finest hospitals in the country; there was a locked ward, a padded cell, God knows what else. Very occasionally something floats up from Lil about that time and I can't bear to think of it.

Lil can't be left alone. I leave her if I go up to the shop, for fifteen minutes at the most, but I don't leave her in the house alone. I wouldn't leave a four-year-old child in the house. The others say, she mustn't bind you like that, but if there was a fire she couldn't get out of the house by herself.

She has all her food done; she can make tea and just about do toast. She washes herself very well, but she might go on scrubbing the same bit for forty-five minutes. She can now bath by herself, but she floods the whole place. Sometimes I let her wash her hair by herself. She gets dressed by herself, although I put her clothes in order. It's like having a four-year-old child. She is always demanding,

72

but you can't say: leave me alone. You can't say: no not now, as you might to a four-year-old, because she's also an adult.

It's very difficult, this adult/child business. Our nieces and nephews are growing up; she remembers them as children and suddenly they are taking charge of her – it's tricky.

Emotionally she is very aggressive, although since the new drugs there's been a great improvement. Now it will all go into slamming doors; after half an hour she might come down and say she's sorry. It took me years to get her to say sorry.

Mother spoilt her something shocking; it almost spoilt my sisters' lives. They're very ambivalent about her: they're marvellous to her, they take her on holidays, they're nice to her, but they hate, hate, hate. All my sisters are very good indeed but it's hiding a lot.

When she's nice, she's sweet. I don't love her, I couldn't. The frustration of the old days, when she had one of her fearful tempers, when she would go gently beserk – there weren't the drugs then, she would have to be restrained; I would have to do it, hold her wrists behind her back – I have a feeling she's never forgotten that.

Compassion yes, but not love. This was really brought out about four years ago when we were given a cat. I adore the cat, I notice myself in the mornings saying hallo *darling*; and then, hallo Lil – the difference in my approach between Lil and the cat has rather shocked me.

I show verbal affection, but I have to *make* myself touch her; and I'm very much a touching person, but I have to make myself, literally. It's deep-seated, it's just there. The other sisters, I hug them, bite them. It's made me feel so guilty, I feel it is important for Lil to touch.

When she is suddenly being obstreperous or almost evilly nasty, I feel sometimes these stabbing feelings of hate that frighten me so much. But then it gets out, it's over, it doesn't stay.

If life could have been different?

I don't know what I'd have done. I probably would have gone jogging about, from job to job, rather than build up a career. I think I would have gone abroad. Even now I feel the urge to travel; it never really leaves you.

It's hard to say if I would have married. I was already 22 by the time I discarded my first two proposals! I had one lovely affair, not a one-night stand but a ten-night stand. We picked each other up in Paris – he was French. We had ten days together and we didn't even exchange addresses. It was sheer utter gorgeous, and then we split. It was rather a case of wham, bang, thank you, ma'am – absolutely lovely. Any time!

Shortly after that I came home. I didn't carry on as I meant to.

Does she have any regrets?

Children. Not so much a man, although of course it would have been lovely – but it's the children most. Now of course it's grand-children; I was working out the other day, there could have been a grandchild by now. I'm drawn to babies terribly, I go all stupid over them; I still feel broody at my age. That's my only real regret. And the thing I miss most is laughter – someone to laugh with.

And someone to talk to. Of course I talk to Lil, that's my job, but when I find myself saying something to her which is more on my own behalf, something, like, oh look, isn't that pretty – where I feel the real me is talking – I feel dreadful and I'll have to stop.

I regard what I do for Lil – to the best of my ability – as my job. When I'm off duty – even when I'm sitting with her – if there's no one there to share the real me, I'll keep to myself. I feel terrible about this sometimes. Sometimes I will ask her opinion – if we're watching something on TV and I'll forget it's her and say something, and she'll give an answer. Then, when I find it's Lil replying I feel so angry with myself, I feel as if I've let myself be invaded again.

Talking to someone – telling them things, even simple things – it's one of the most important things in life; normally it's something you do with your partner, someone special, your husband, lover, mother. I hope she doesn't notice. If I start a sentence and get this feeling, I will carry on with it. I'll go to great pains to hide it. It's a very deep feeling, this one I get – very deep.

She has been taking anti-depressants – on and off – since about eighteen months after her mother's death twelve years ago.

When Mother died they all came home, and then when they all left, when the last car had driven out of the gate and Lil and I stood standing – I shall never ever forget that moment, I thought it was the worst moment of my life. It was the inevitability of it all. Because it's forever, you see. Now that's a very depressing thought.

There's also the terrible worry – what happens if I die first? The rest of family have said – and I quite understand – that they couldn't or wouldn't take her, why should they? They're three-quarters of the way through their lives. If it was me I'd take her, but that's different.

74

What is the alternative? Employing a carer would cost much more than Lil will ever have through her trustees; the rent, the house, still wouldn't pay for it. The alternative would be to go into care – I don't think she'd survive. Even if it was a tiny little unit. I rather hope she wouldn't survive. She would know perfectly well she has brothers and sisters and has just enough logic to ask: where are they?

I often think how wonderful it would be if Lil could have a heart attack in the night; I would be thoroughly delighted. Of course I would grieve, but it would be lovely to have some years to myself.

I always come back to: I chose to do it. And I would choose again. I didn't have any choice in a way, if you see what I mean – the others wouldn't have considered it.

The greatest strain, of course, is keeping her on an even keel and trying to deal with it in a firm way when she isn't. That's where all the stress comes in. Friends say, why don't you say shut up. I say well do you say shut up to your annoying toddler? Not if you can help it you don't. I don't condone losing your temper.

One of her fads will start it off – if her age is mentioned she'll go haywire: she associates death and age ever since Father died. She doesn't want to remember how old she is. I do mention it though; I even discuss death with her now. Again, I feel I have to. 'We all die when we get to a certain age' – that's dangerous ground. I said (to her), I personally will be cremated, she says, I'd like to be buried down at the swimming pool, I say, well I'm sure that can be arranged.

She does believe in God and heaven and I encourage it, because for a child to know about death and not believe in heaven would be too much.

She uses aggressive, violent language – she picks it up from the TV. She will work herself up into a most extraordinary state. Sometimes I can stop her: if I catch it I can switch her off; if she doesn't feel like being stopped, she'll just go on and on and on. The effect is devastating – there's so much *venom*.

I'm explaining it very badly, it's almost impossible to explain Lil to anybody. Ask any of my sisters and they wouldn't know what they were describing, it's the *horribleness* which comes out which is so offensive. It's a very adult nastiness. Not long ago, she said: 'I wouldn't mind if you had another stroke and lost the rest of your sight anyway.'

We all said she should have been put in a home when she was little, but I said they (her parents) didn't damn well know in time. How do you put a four- or five-year-old in a home when you've had it that long? It would be different if it was a baby, and even then it would be difficult. They all say it should never have been allowed, or that Mother should have made her take her normal place in the family.

I think I've done what I should have done, I very definitely think that. I don't think it's wasted. No, I don't think it's wasted. I come back to this business – I really had no choice and yet I definitely chose.

Lil's room is a child's room, full of toys and mobiles. Lil is in hospital, where she is being treated for a stomach blockage: a small, gaunt, middle-aged woman, she is well spoken and prim in front of visitors. It is difficult to imagine her as the little monster who took all the mother's love in a family of nine and inspired so much hatred in the others.

5

·

In sickness and in health: Women caring for husbands with disabilities

When you get married and you take the vows: for better, for worse, in sickness and in health – no one thinks about those words when they're actually saying them. It's only after, you go back over them and it makes you stop in your tracks – what your marriage vows really mean. It makes you more aware: nothing is a bed of roses. It's not happy ever after. (Kate Sugden, 31, looking after husband Terry, almost totally paralysed after breaking his neck in a fall three years ago)

Most wives caring for handicapped husbands are middle-aged or elderly women whose partners have been disabled by the major illnesses common to their age group: stroke, dementia and Parkinson's disease. There also exists a smaller, and so far neglected, group of caring wives: younger women whose husbands have become unexpectedly disabled by accidents and injuries, or who are victims of crippling and progressive illnesses, such as multiple sclerosis, which strike early in life. These women face not only the loss of a partnership which most of them had hoped would last for life, but also the end of the emotional, social, and financial support which they had expected from their marriage. All idea of an equal relationship, and the sharing of responsibilities on which they had hoped their marriage would be based, has gone, destroyed by the burden of their husband's disability and dependency. Many speak of their husbands – sometimes in their presence – as if they are spoilt children, to be watched over, indulged and constantly cared for.

I grieved for the husband I had. I went through all the symptoms of widowhood when he had the stroke. I am virtually a widow without a widow's freedom. (Pam Purdy, 61, caring for a partner of 76)

The disappointment in marriage which these women express, and the way they treat their husbands, is similar to what sometimes happens in a marriage between able-bodied partners: many middle-aged and elderly women treat their husbands as if they were demanding and dependent children – and the husbands act as such. The role of wife as carer, and disabled husband as dependent, is thus in an important sense an extension of 'normal' marital relations and obligations.

When a husband becomes disabled

It was just desperate. There was a very grim period in hospital, with very little social support. The immediacy of it almost numbs you – I was told immediately he would never walk again. Then, when he came out, it became horribly real what disadvantages he was going to face. I just remember day after day, desperately, trying to change beds because he couldn't control his bowel movements. His distress was awful: there were long periods of wondering whether he should commit suicide. Everything seemed to be heavy going; even getting incontinence sheets meant going from one place to another. People didn't seem to have the information at their finger-tips – to say, what you need is a ripple mattress or a sheepskin. It took me two years to get the physical side settled. (Anna Fields, whose husband was paralysed from just below the arms after an accident in his early thirties)

When he first came out of hospital it was very hard. I didn't have a clue what it would entail. In hospital he had nurses there to do it all. It isn't until someone comes home that you realise how totally dependent they are on you to do everything. (Kate Sugden)

Few carers are given much option about caring, but because of the nature of the marital relationship and the role expected of a wife, women whose husbands become disabled are probably given the least choice of all. Theoretically at least, other carers have the options of sending an elderly parent or a handicapped child to an old people's home or a residential school. But a husband who has had a stroke, or become paralysed in an accident, will automatically be discharged home to his wife, who will be expected – by professionals, family, friends, her disabled partner, and not least by herself – to look after him.

Few women would want to 'put away' or forget about a partner with whom they have shared most of a lifetime. Most would not dream of doing anything other than trying to care for a husband who is disabled. But, as Judith Oliver – herself caring for a disabled husband – makes clear in one of the few surveys to be carried out on caring wives, there is often an automatic assumption that a wife should *completely* take over the care of a handicapped partner, and will be able to cope without support or preparation:

A very frequent comment heard from wives in this situation is that 'I was never asked if I'd be able to manage'. This seems to encapsulate the attitude of professionals: the assumption that the ability to cope is bestowed with the wedding ring. (Judith Oliver, 'The Caring Wife', A Labour of Love, Routledge & Kegan Paul, 1983)

From partner to patient

At 7 a.m. I go into Jocelyn and turn him – he's usually spent the night on his back – and I'll go in to turn him onto his other side. Some days I'll give him a bowel evacuation and put some suppositories in. I'll help the district nurse wash him, and get him up at 9.30. Then it's a case of meals, feeding, shopping. I can leave for short periods to do a bit of shopping but by the end of an hour I'm on pins to get back, because he hasn't had his drugs or he might have had a coughing fit. It's like having a baby really. It does change your relationship and it takes time to adjust. It's something someone like Jocelyn will never be happy about – the loss of dignity. That's the worst part. (June Gaze, whose husband Jocelyn broke his neck in a car accident three years ago and is now tetraplegic – all four limbs are paralysed)

The physical care these women provide for their husbands is much the same as that taken on by any other carer, yet it carries a special significance within a relationship which is meant to be based on equality, sexuality and partnership between two adults. The intimate tasks involved in looking after a disabled husband can cause feelings of embarrassment, resentment and shame in both partners:

You might have a blazing row but you can't just walk out on each other – the next moment he's on the bed and I'm taking off his clothes. You can't go away and fume, you have to keep caring. If he told me he'd taken up with another woman, I'd still have to do his bowels. (Judith Oliver, married to Mike, paralysed from below the shoulders)

Not all women object to caring for their partners in this way. Many would say they could only take it on precisely because of the love they feel for their husbands. Yet most women find that this physical dependence alters their relationship profoundly: to one which bears more resemblance to that of a nurse and her patient – or parent and child – than to a partnership between equals.

Matt was a very active man, very practical, he could repair anything: he was a wonderful carpenter, he used to spend hours on the car. I miss that side of him. I miss Matt as a husband, I miss him as he was, as someone who could take over. I'm always the one who has to cope, who has to do the bills, who has to fix the curtan rails. (Mary Bardon, 49. Her husband is paralysed by multiple sclerosis)

You have to do everything, the map reading if we go out in the car, change the plug, the washer on the tap, see to the bills. I have to take full responsibility for the maintenance of the home. (Madeleine Harris, 58, looking after a husband with Alzheimer's disease)

Apart from the physical drudgery common to all carers, women looking after their husbands also face what sociologists call 'role overload': the exhaustion and sense of isolation which come from taking over tasks previously performed by their partners. This can be especially hard for older women in whose marriages husband and wife had previously taken on conventional masculine and feminine roles; where a woman had little to do with paying the mortgage or mending the roof. Some women who have been dominated all their lives by their husbands, may welcome the sense of release and power which taking over gives them; but for most, having to 'see to everything', to take over responsibilities which have always been shared, is a major burden. Some women in this position face a double burden: having to 'see to everything' while still trying to please their husbands – to 'do things his way':

80

We're opposites: I'm very easy going and he's the organised one. He still likes things to be organised, he likes things done the way he would do them if he was walking around. So you always have to think of how he likes things done. (Kate Sugden)

Rosa Petro

Rosa Petro is 74 but looks younger. Her husband Bill has Alzheimer's disease, one of the major causes of senile dementia. They live in a large converted ground floor flat in a north London suburb, run down but friendly and full of old people. They moved here around four years ago – before he became ill – from a three-bedroomed house in the same area.

It's 10 a.m. and she is cooking him breakfast. She is still in her dressing gown. 'My only time alone is late at night after he's gone to bed, so I tend to stay up.'

In her sitting room, where she also sleeps, the put-you-up bed is still unmade, the curtains half drawn, the room disordered.

She is Jewish, self-educated, interested in art and politics – in their younger days they were both in the Communist Party. She has two grown up children: a daughter, living in California, and a son, married, a schoolteacher, living in Essex. She speaks slowly and deliberately.

His illness has developed gradually over the last three years. First he started to lose the use of words, then his memory went. The short-term memory went first, the long-term came later. The hospital did a brain scan and said the cells affecting memory and communication had gone and that the process would continue.

At the moment he still shaves himself, washes and dresses himself. I let him do it but he has developed odd behaviour patterns: he'll put on two pairs of trousers, two ties, a pullover back to front. I've had to hide all his clothes because he puts on two or three of everything. He won't look for a proper toilet; the only way I can get him in the bath is by getting in myself and then saying to him to get in after me. It's a ritual. He hates having his head washed, he screams at that, or if I go near him with scissors.

With Alzheimer's everything changes places, so instead of going into the bathroom, he'll walk into the back garden and go behind a tree. He's not incontinent, he's careless, he can't always control it

81

easily; but at the moment it's on a small scale. At the moment I can make a sort of joke of it: I say, you smell, you must let me wash you – I help him wash his back.

He's not as clean as I'd like him to be, even now. I haven't been used to dealing with him on a personal level; he won't let me come near him, he gets very angry if I come in to dress him. We've always been like that – the generation which undresses in the dark.

He will cut up the clingfilm into bits, he'll cut up the cheese, the fish, butter – he'll cut up anything. He'll pour his orange juice into his tea; he'll cut up a banana with his fish and chips and eat it all together. He has changed so much. You don't even notice because you're living so close to it. But when my son comes he says he's quite mad. He says, Mum, you don't notice it.

Then there is this great anxiety and aggression. Apparently the pattern of behaviour in this illness varies: it depends on the individual's former character. Bill has always been an aggressive, dominating man, very anxious, conscientious, with an unreasonable temper – now it's taken over.

I have great difficulty in coping with the aggression. I become very weepy and scream back, which sometimes frightens and controls him, and sometimes makes him worse. Also he is hyperactive, he can't sit still.

I can't leave him very long. I can't give him keys because he loses them. I will open the door for him and he'll go out; he'll be missing for a couple of hours. He has a strong geographical sense, he knows his way back – I don't know how long that will last.

I've gone in for medication now; he has a drug which is used for schizophrenics, the lowest strength, to calm him down. How long it will work I don't know. We started off on one tablet, now it's gone to two. You become tolerant of drugs. I *could* cope without, I could cope with it by just bearing it; but I have no intention of becoming a martyr to this man. If anyone dies first it's going to be him, not me.

The worst of it is the things we used to do together. We always went to the theatre together; he wants to go now but as soon as we get on the bus the anxiety takes over, he sits forward and grips the seat. He won't sit through a performance. We used to go to the cinema; we got free entry because he was in the film business, but the last three or four visits, half-way through the programme he'll start pointing to the screen, the anxiety will take over and we'll have to walk out. We still go to the museums and galleries. We went to

82

the National Gallery yesterday. It is one of the few things left to me; the bus route was familiar so he sat with it. He's very visual, he stood in front of one of the Turners for a long time.

He doesn't speak at all to me. Not voluntarily. If I say, how are you, are you cold, would you like to eat, I can draw him out – but he doesn't voluntarily start a conversation with me. He'll point – to the birds, the sky – if you say you can't understand him he becomes impatient. But a lot of this is a matter of will. The young girl who lives upstairs – she's been a good friend to me – he will make an effort to smile and talk to her, try to make himself agreeable. A lot of it is in the man's nature.

The worst part of it is I have no privacy. He harasses me. If I'm sitting here writing a letter, reading a book, watching television, he walks in here and wants to know what I'm doing.

And I'm bereaved. I am a widow. If he were to die, the grief and loss would be terrific, but most of what he is has gone. He was a good professional photographer, we travelled a lot, he was a political animal, we would have been active politically at this point. Now I can't even go to a meeting.

I haven't got a companion. This is the man I've got; a man who pees in wastepaper baskets, who uses the washbasin instead of the toilet. If I say, don't do that, he'll get angry. I can't reason with him, there is nothing there to appeal to. Consequently I'm . . . '

She is crying.

He was an aggressive man, but in the last ten years, since he retired, he mellowed. I began to assert myself: the children had left home, I didn't have to worry about the effect on them. I should have done it years ago, but I didn't, I just suffered, like a lot of women do. In the last ten years we've been very happy. In the last ten years we travelled a lot, met a lot of people, did a lot together.

In a sense he was a very shy man. The anxiety and aggression spring from fear. He had a very unhappy childhood: a *wicked* mother, I knew her. The man is a very frightened man, he always has been. Now, it's come out on top. Now he's regressed. He makes animal noises, he growls; it's quite atavistic. He's gone back to his deepest primitive instincts.

He's not physically violent, not yet. He has lifted his hand to me. He's verbally aggressive; he calls me names he has never called me in his life.

83

We have a whole life we shared together, sometimes flashes of it come back to him. The other night, watching a film about the Holocaust, he took my hand. We both knew exactly what we were feeling. I haven't got that with anybody else. I've still got that with him. He loves music; when we play it it takes us back to our young days. This is the hard part; you're a half-widow, you can't grieve for a death. It's a part-death. And sometimes he knows that his mind is going, and that's terrible.

Bill is trying to control me. People do, they use the disease, not deliberately, but as a means of possessing. That is one aspect that unless you're very strong . . . I know carers where the husband, the madman, is in control, not the wise one – where she will follow all his crazy instincts.

Whatever happens I must not let Bill control my life. He did it before, when we were married. He was possessive, I always had to be there. I did it, I shouldn't have. He did it in the name of love; it was the only way he knew how to love. Now it goes on, but now it's crazy.

You mustn't go along with their confused way of thinking, with the madness. If he mumbles, you must tell him, you're talking rubbish. Or when he behaves badly, you must tell him, hard as it is. You must use the right tone of voice. You must say (her voice hardens): I'm not going along with your rubbish.

Sometimes Bill won't go to his bed. He opens the door and disturbs me. I shout very loudly, get out Bill, go away, I don't want you, I need to be on my own. You must not be too sorry for them: you'll go down, you'll go right down, you'll be submerged.

And don't give way to your worst fears, keeping yourself immured for days because you're afraid of what they might do if you leave them. Keep your inner self intact if you can. Keep yourself intact.

And take risks. If I go with my son to the theatre I will cut myself off completely. I say: whatever happens, it's not the end of the world.

We went for a walk; there's a lake near here, a beautiful park; he was being very difficult. I walked to the edge of the lake and threatened to throw myself in. I said, if you don't calm yourself and behave reasonably I will kill myself. His whole face cleared: don't do that, please, please, don't do that. I used that scene to re-establish my dominance. Once before he was refusing to get on the bus to do the shopping. I clasped my throat and said I'm dying, I'm dying. He got on the bus.

I'm very cruel all the time. I'm forcing my will on him. I've taken away his money, his bus pass. I'm applying to the Court of Protection to have control over his money. What am I saying, *his* money? It's our money, our house.

I will not live with guilt. I was always a victim of his unreasonable rages. The children used to go up to their rooms and shiver with fear; my son now says he was terrified. I think I was afraid of him because he was my only security.

In some ways it has made me very different. My daughter says it's what I always was. I'm taking hold; I'm controlling him, controlling our finances, I take all the decisions about investments, spending money, buying things for the house. I enjoy that.

If it came to putting him into a home – I've only got ten years of life left to me: what am I going to be at 84, looking after an idiot? The children are suffering on my behalf and I won't have that. I will not sacrifice all our lives to this man. He can't help it, and I'm sorry for him, and it will break me up, but I'll do what I have to.

I had my father living with us for six years before he died. He was very lovely, intelligent. He developed cancer of the bowel in the last year of his life. He went into hospital and I refused to take him home. He was 89, incontinent, his bedroom was at the top of the stairs, my husband had had a heart attack. The doctor at the hospital said, it's your moral duty to have him. I said, don't tell me what my moral duty is, I've been doing it for the last six years. I said: you must find a home for him, you have no right to tell me – my husband has a heart condition and I've had my father for six years – you've no right to tell me what my duty is. They found him a home.

I know what I want to do. I want to join the University of the Third Age, do voluntary work, develop friendships with the people around me. There are so many things I don't do any more. I discontinued my creative writing class. I did an A-level in art history and architecture a few years ago and I loved it.

My God, I know what I'd do. I haven't got much time left and I've got so much to do.

I moved into a separate room about a year ago. I couldn't sleep next to a man whose mind I couldn't touch, even whose body I couldn't touch. Not only that: he was wandering about at night. He has no sense of time and will get up at three in the morning, dress and shave and walk out.

It's funny, he didn't even remark on it; it used to be a thing so

85

important to him, if I went into another room to sleep. But when I moved out he actually helped make up my bed. He's accepted my dominance. He's like a child, he brings everything to me.

Sleeping separately was something he would never have accepted in the old days. It would have been an insult to his manhood, even though we weren't having sex. We haven't had sex since he had a heart attack sixteen years ago, which has been a great deprivation for me.

I have known times when he'll spend the whole day in bed, completely depressed, unwilling to eat. He'll smile and talk to the neighbour, but he relapses when I come in. He uses me. You have to use your discretion about how much you allow yourself to be manipulated: you mustn't let your love and grief take over.

When he sits and holds my hand after the TV programme, I think, how could I ever let you go into a home? I'm told this is the worst stage of the disease because he still retains part of himself, and I've got to deal with that as well as with the irrational. I talk very tough about putting him away. I don't know how tough I would be if it came to it.

My husband used to be a great reader, now he tries to read but it makes him depressed. He said to Patricia, the girl upstairs, I'm no good, I'm stupid. He used to write me little letters and leave them about the house: I'm so sorry Rosa, I know it's difficult for you. That's the part which is holding me. What do I do with that? They told me, at the first meeting (of the Alzheimer's Disease Society): this is really hard for you, the man is not completely gone, with Alzheimer's this could go on for a long, long time.

I'm obsessed with this, I can't think or talk about anything else. I was prepared for physical disability: he'd already had a heart attack, I thought he would have a stroke. This is the terrible thing: the difference between him and people suffering strokes, they still have a mind.

Bill knows around here, it's very important to him where he is, he knows the faces. There was a lot of pressure from my son to move near him. I refused because I've got an instinct about what's right. I told him, his father wouldn't survive; he knows this area, he can walk up to Sainsbury's, walk to the post office; he knows the neighbours.

This is why we can't go on holiday. We went to Rhodes in August with my son. He wandered about in the hotel room all the time, extremely distressed – I was glad to get home.

This can happen to anybody; it's almost like a plague, you have no idea it's going to happen. Very often it hits the most privileged: people in authority, with money, men in complete control, in executive positions, people who've retained a tight hold. Who come from an office where they're at full stretch, and who flop in front of the TV and the wife can't get a word out of them. I've had all that.

His last rational words were: don't ask me to make decisions, about lunch, about holidays, we'll go wherever you like. This was before this happened, when we were retired and going abroad. It was then he started to give up his decision-making role, not concentrating on what was happening to the children, or the house or what we bought. He always kept control of the purse strings – that was the last thing to go. He had charge of all the investments – I wasn't interested.

I've tried to redirect all the mail for the house; if he finds anything with money in it, he just takes it. I'm going to the Court of Protection because I need authority over our insurance bonds. He has to sign for one in January; I don't know whether he'll sign or not. I've taken him up to the office and they've seen his condition, but they still won't let me take them out without his signature. He's signed so far. We're joint owners of the flat, the building society; but the bonds are in his name.

I've got to break out; it's sheer will, the only way to survive. People who are caring are surely and steadily dying themselves. In the end the state will have not one in a ward but two. This is what happens.

I'm strong but I'm having a hell of a job not to take to drink. I have the money, I can easily buy a bottle of gin or whisky. I smoke more than I ever did. I discipline myself, but how long can you live with that kind of discipline? How strong do you have to be to survive it? I know men who drink in order to live with their demented wives – it's very dangerous. I have to say: all right, no more cigarettes, no more spirits. Never in my life have I been drunk. I've always had an aversion to drunkenness – being Jewish is something to do with it – but it's there.

Pam Purdy

Pam Purdy's husband suffered a severe stroke which paralysed his right side just eleven months after she had left her first husband to live with him fifteen years ago – he was 61 and she was 46. They then spent the statutory five-year period separated from their respective husbands and wives before marrying – 'It never entered my head not to marry him.' She had to feed him with a teaspoon at first and it was five years before he managed to form a sentence. 'But it was his lack of speech which was the biggest thing – that and the fact that he couldn't walk. I used to drag him about.' Now, his speech is still slow and sometimes muddled, and although he can walk a few yards, he can never go anywhere unaccompanied. He is able, awkwardly, to wash and dress himself, except for putting on his shoes and socks. 'He can undress himself, but I have to lift his legs into bed. He has a urinary bottle for the night.'

Pam and her husband, David, both had to leave their jobs – they'd met working in local government – after his stroke. Having done forty years, he got a good pension: it was her salary – and her loss of pension – that they missed. 'I get the Invalid Care Allowance but it's no good to me now; I should have had it then, to replace what I earned.' Six years ago, she also started to look after her elderly parents: her mother – who has since died – had skin cancer, and her father – now in residential care – dementia and cancer of the larynx. She has two grown up sons and a stepdaughter, living in Norfolk, whom they visit for holidays.

They live in a small town 50 miles north of London, in a sheltered flat they got when she took a live-in job as warden for disabled elderly people living in the same block. In one sense, her worst days – when her husband was totally helpless and they were living in a furnished flat – are over.

'I cried for about three months after his stroke – the sense of loss,' she says. 'I used to look out for him; used to see him. I ran after someone (else) once when he was home in bed. I looked at all the people that looked like him – it's a typical widow's thing. I grieved for the husband I had. I went through all the symptoms of widow-hood. I am virtually a widow – without a widow's freedom.'

Small, calm, self-controlled, an old hand at caring, she has, she says, managed to create another life for herself; writing a column for the local paper and helping to run voluntary and self-help groups. She describes her life in flat, detached tones, with no heroics and no drama: 'I'm resigned and composed because I've done it for so long. I've learned that awful detachment that nurses have, when they're accused of being hard.'

Her day begins at 9 a.m. when she gives her husband breakfast in bed, reads him bits from the paper, brings him his razor, treats the eczema he gets on his feet and head, puts ointment on his leg and helps him get to the side of the bed where he can shave.

He shaves while I have a bath. Then he goes to the bathroom and washes himself – well, he calls it washing, it's very sketchy. He dresses himself, except his shoes and socks. By that time it's 11.30. We don't have much of a morning, which is deliberate: it would be such a long day.

I go out once a day on the bus or into town, while he sits in the chair and watches TV. He watches TV all day. The first thing he does is get up and put it on, and it's on until he goes to bed. It just goes over me, I've got used to it. It's a godsend, it occupies him.

He couldn't answer the door or phone. We have a late lunch. In the afternoon I'll read or write a letter and he'll watch TV, or he might stick stamps in his album.

It's changed his personality: he's passive, like a child. You can go all day without exchanging even a word or two. Unless it's something about stamps – then he'll never stop. Or sometimes he's worried about something – I used to think it was something important – but he'll worry, he'll ask me, have you put the scissors in the bathroom for the nurse coming on Friday? When it's only Monday. It doesn't occur to him I might want to cut *my* nails, that doesn't even enter into it.

The nursing auxiliary comes once a week to bath him – that's all the help I get. The health visitor never comes; she won't come unless you summon her. I could do with help on transport – I pay out no end in taxis. If I go to see my father, it costs me nearly £4, it's not worth the money.

Her husband goes into the same home as her father, to give her a break occasionally.

He goes twice a year. He isn't any trouble for them; he's not incontinent, he can wash and dress, he enjoys it. They like him coming.

I had to have a respite; you can't go on indefinitely. At first, when the doctor recommended two breaks a year, it filled me with horror – I said, you couldn't put him in there. He said, I'll tell him for you. I thought, I really must do it: I was constantly ill and miserable.

89

I went away this year for the first time in fifteen years, to friends in Hove. I daren't go any further than Brighton – I know I can get back from there. I've a friend in the Lake District, but it's too far and I haven't got enough energy.

I've had nervous exhaustion, I get terribly tired. And all the lifting and pushing the wheelchair has give me uterus problems, a mild prolapse. All the pulling and heaving was too much for me. The gynaecologist said I couldn't get a repair; the gynaecologist said it was no good because I'd be coming back to the same situation, I would have to wait for a repair until I was on my own, until my husband was dead. He gave me a ring (for her uterus), I said I didn't want a ring but he put it in anyway. The ring's a damn nuisance, the ring's no solution – it sets up infections.

I'm always run down. I'll have had a fortnight's break but what I need is six months to make me feel better.

Every day I feel I've got to get up and do the same things, they never go away. You can't do anything, even lie in bed: if I lie in bed he'll come to see if I'm better. It's a very rigid life. You can't say you'll do something different, every day's just the same as every other day. It becomes meaningless. You can't go and leave him without first thinking: how long will I be? Has he got everything? Will he set fire to anything? Will he let the budgie out with the window open?

We're very close in the sense that I know what he's thinking – I know when he's worried. It might be about the scissors, the nurse, the butcher. He has a constant fear he'll not have food, it's of prime importance: if I have to go out early, he'll ask, does it mean he won't have breakfast? He doesn't know I need breakfast too. His thinking is all about *his* breakfast. Like a child.

He's mellowed, though. At one time he couldn't bear me out of his sight. When my parents were getting old it was dreadful – he'd sulk if I left him. This is common to all dependent people, they want you there all the time.

I have taken him to restaurants and hotels. People look at us but I never worry about it. But it's a strain for him, the eating; he can't concentrate, it wears him out, having to think he's in a strange place. Anyway, hotels aren't built for wheelchairs.

It's a very odd life you live. For three years we both went to bed at nine o'clock because he couldn't go to bed by himself. I used to lie there thinking, what am I doing in bed at my age, but I did it. Lights out at 9 p.m. I learnt to be absolutely rigid in bed, till he'd gone to sleep.

There's no night sitting service for people like him. Suppose he had pneumonia? If he has a temperature he would be incontinent, if his temperature goes up he loses bladder control. I've nursed him through that twice. One night I was too tired to get up any more; I lay in the wet bed, wet with urine from head to foot. He went to sleep. That night, I wanted to die. I thought, there's really no point in us being alive. I couldn't do that again – I'd be straight on to the doctor.

I'd like a nurse all the time, to get him up, so that I didn't have to do anything. This half-way help is never appropriate, never at the right time. If the nurse is two hours late, that's your bad luck.

When I cleaned my husband up for the first time, I remember thinking, well, no one ever told me. Of all the people to be a nurse. I never wanted to be one. I hated the smell and the sight of hospitals. My husband used to cry so, he used to be so sorry. I realised he couldn't help it. Physically he has improved, but even now he has accidents. I don't take any notice, I have special rubber gloves and disinfectant.

I used to clean my father up – my mother wouldn't go with him (to the lavatory). She opted out completely. Once I asked, where's Dad; she said, in the lavatory. I said, well how long's he been in there. I found him in the lavatory covered in faeces. I realised she couldn't cope at all. There seemed to be years with my parents and my husband – I was either cleaning up here or cleaning up there. I did all their shopping and washing – the washing I did was fantastic.

He was 76 in February, when I'm 70 he'll be 85. What then? He's very likely to live to that age because he's so well looked after. He's fed well, kept warm, given his tablets, never at risk. He doesn't have high blood pressure, he has no stress because he never worries. His stress was with the job in his late fifties – like me now, I can't take the stress on me.

I would only put him into care if he was unaware where he was, otherwise it would upset him terribly. If anything happened to me he can't live with them (his or her children). I've told her (her step-daughter), not to take him and I've told him (her husband) not to go. He might be tempted. But she wouldn't be able to cope.

I don't wish he'd die because we've had a very happy marriage. We've been very happy. Sometimes I wonder why I work so hard to keep him alive, because it'll lead to him being like my father and living till he's 92. You have to go day by day and hope for the best.

91

Social isolation

I miss the freedom, being able to say to myself I'll go out for the day. The children had got to an age that when Jocelyn was away I'd be able to go and see friends, do a little painting, or have a day's sewing. Probably the clockwatching is the thing which gets to you. It's totally altered our way of life – no question. We had finally got to the point where we were beginning to do things for ourselves rather than being totally based on the children. That's all gone: everything centres on looking after Jocelyn. (June Gaze)

I don't get out at all. Mr R [her husband] has got his disabled club and goes out with his old comrades in the navy. The only time when I get out is when I go shopping with one of my daughters. He sits with his telly and his crosswords – he's all right for a time. I don't go out all; I don't have a social life as such. I think that's my problem. The more I'm in the house, the harder I'm finding it to get out. I don't have an escape valve. (Madge Redbridge, looking after Ted, a husband paralysed by a stroke)

Like most carers, women with disabled husbands lose the freedom to get out of the house when they want to, a loss which hits them especially hard if it comes at a time when the children are finally 'off their hands' and they are looking forward to a new lease of life. A further strain for these women is that they cannot do the things which 'normal' couples do, like going for a drink or a meal together. Going out with a disabled partner can involve such a mass of arrangements – such as checking if a pub or restaurant can accommodate wheelchairs – that many couples just give up the idea, especially if the husband has always taken the lead socially, or now feels embarrassed and ashamed of his disability.

We'd love to go out as a family – Matt would love to take me out. We miss not being able to live as a family, to get out as he would like to, to do the simple things which every family does, to go to the park at weekends. I wouldn't know what it's like to go out for a meal nowadays. (Mary Bardon)

I used to go out to the pub, play darts, go to dances with my husband. He doesn't like going out now because he's so embarrassed: he can't cut up his food, and it dribbles down the side of his face.

92

We can't walk anywhere – he's dead slow, stopping and starting; and you can't get out at all if it's cold and windy. (Madge Redbridge)

For these wives, arranging holidays, and packing all the necessary aids and equipment, can turn what is meant to be a rest into a nightmare. Yet while other carers – of elderly parents, for instance – might be encouraged to take a break, wives caring for husbands are never expected to go away by themselves; often they will feel too guilty to do so.

I tried to take him to Jersey last year; it was a nightmare. If you're out of sight, he panics. You can't relax. The social worker suggested taking him to Canada; I said it wouldn't be a holiday. (Madeleine Harris, 58, looking after a husband of 59 with Alzheimer's disease)

In many cases, the family car gets sold once the husband becomes disabled, either because the wife has never learnt to drive, or because the husband cannot now tolerate the idea of her doing so. This means that wives who previously relied on going everywhere in the car with their husbands become even more isolated, dependent on grown-up children or the vagaries of public transport to get them around.

I learned to drive, but then I had to lift him in and out of the car and on to the seat – I can't do that any more, I can't lift him now. (Mary Bardon)

The obstacles to these couples going out together are reinforced by the difficulties of maintaining previous social relationships, especially if friends and other couples, who may have been used to playing certain roles with each other, find it difficult to cope with disability and the changes it entails. Disabled husbands may find that their men friends draw back, embarrassed and unable to deal with illness, while wives may find they no longer fit into the normal social life of their circle, and will rarely be invited anywhere alone.

We have friends in – I try to keep that up, otherwise I'd go barmy. They are quite understanding but you can't fully appreciate what it entails unless you're there for a while. I don't bore other people with it – they get fed up with listening. We are going out for a meal this Saturday (with the people from work). The supervisor said, you will bring Fred, won't you. He'll be in the loo every five minutes; how it'll work out I don't know. They'll all be strangers to him.

He's OK if we go out for dinner in a foursome, with friends, but he's scared of having an accident. It's pathetic to see him, scared to have an accident. He'll ask his men friends: do you find your underpants get wet? He's gone childish, like a baby. They're very tolerant; he bores them to tears talking about the war and India. It bothers me: I get embarrassed for him when he comes out with the same tales over again. (Madeleine Harris)

It does damn your social life. No other man will come in here because he can't have a conversation with him. (Pam Purdy)

Loss of family life

Middle-aged and elderly women also tend to lose out on the more relaxed activities enjoyed by couples with adult families, such as visits to the grandchildren and invitations to weddings; while those with younger children may find themselves torn between the husband and the rest of the family.

We'd only been here six months, so my daughter had changed schools. She was at a critical stage with her O-levels; she hadn't had the chance to get herself settled in. We had a very stormy relationship for quite some time. In hindsight, I didn't shut her out – but I didn't give her quite the understanding. It was very difficult being split two ways. Everybody suffered. (June Gaze)

Some younger wives with disabled husbands face the prospect of a future without children; others have to bring up their offspring singlehanded.

Mark was two when the accident happened, so he didn't quite understand. He and his father have a good relationship but in lots of ways he's missed a dad who can walk: they can't play football and do the normal things. Mark needs a lot of attention – I can't give it to him all the time. And I feel he's missed out a lot on not having a brother or sister. (Kate Sugden)

The social isolation facing these couples can be made worse by the attitudes of their own families. Clearly, the support adult children offer will depend on their previous relationship with their parents: some older women with disabled husbands seem to get regular visits, especially from married daughters, but others feel bitterly neglected.

My husband was ever so bad Sunday week, I really felt I'd had enough. I was screaming, I couldn't do it, the mess. I rang my son. He said, oh dear. He never rang back to see how I got on. He's a district organiser for the T & GWU, everybody thinks he's marvellous, doing everything for everybody. But when you see how little he does for his own mother and father.

He (her husband) had had sickness and diarrhoea three times: it was all over his clothes, over everything. I'd changed him three times from top to bottom. And my son says, oh dear. That's all he says, oh dear. (Betty Hampton, 75, whose husband has a disease of the colon)

As the social and family life they shared with their husbands becomes eroded, wives may find it impossible to create a separate life of their own: going out, or doing things alone, is something that many of them have never done before and they may feel guilty and awkward doing it now, especially if the husband is opposed to the idea.

I did start going to darts evenings on my own once a week, but I stopped that, I felt so guilty about it. I needed that time to myself – leaving him alone. He tried to persuade me to go, but it was his money and I felt guilty using it. You get so lonely and so trapped – it's a horrible panicky feeling. There's nothing you can do. It's very isolating, a loneliness you can't describe. (Madge Redbridge)

I do try to get out but there's always this feeling of guilt: that I can go out and be involved in social life and it excludes Jocelyn. (June Gaze)

The few women who have managed to build up something of a new and separate life for themselves are those with the most detachment from, and insight into, their relationship. It takes strength and courage to break the habits and traditions of a lifetime; and to break with the custom of always being in a couple.

I realised I'd have to start a new life for myself. I couldn't rely on our life because our life consists of watching TV, even children's programmes. You simply cannot live on the shrine to the life you once had. (Pam Purdy)

Even putting their husbands into relief care for a couple of weeks so that they can have a break is a big step, one which many women feel too guilty to take.

He went into care while I went to Canada to visit my daughter. The first week of being away, I did find it difficult; but it got to the state where I thought, to hell with it. I dreaded coming back. (Madeleine Harris)

I'm always frightened when he goes into respite care, we're on the ground floor – it's the safety. When he's away, I feel lost, I'm really relieved when he comes back. (Mary Bardon)

Not the man I married

It frustrates him terribly, being a very bookish man. He'll be alert and interested but then his eyes will start hurting and he'll get frustrated because it means a wasted day.

He's not the same person I married. People change through ill-health (Beth Prentice, 49, looking after a 55-year-old husband who was retired from his job at 49 because of a disease of the colon and failing sight)

Many of these women are looking after husbands whose personalities have been changed, sometimes out of all recognition, by illnesses such as stroke and dementia.

It has changed his character terribly; he gets very contrary. Several weeks ago, he got up in the night to go to the toilet but the door didn't close and he was banging around. Eventually I walked onto the landing. There was something in his face, a look; I knew it wasn't safe to touch him. He is (normally) a gentle, a mild man. He was fully dressed; he came out on the landing, didn't say anything, just stood. I immediately felt my stomach knot up: I knew it wasn't safe. It took forty minutes of gentle talking – I used every method under the sun – to convince him it was night-time.

I know if I'd have touched him that night something would have happened. You keep your nerves; you deal with the situation. It was only after I shut my door and got into bed . . . I was shaking all over. I came out afterwards; I came downstairs and stayed here all night. (Winifred Rivers, 65, whose husband, 72, has had Alzheimer's for the last four years)

His memory can go back pre-war, but he can't tell you what happened yesterday. He still eats his food, but his conversation doesn't make sense. He wanders round the house, up and down like a yoyo. It began to get me down. Last July I got really ratty: so much so that I actually hit him. (Madeleine Harris)

It is not just the physical changes which affect husbands. Many men cannot cope with the destruction of their previous roles, whether as fathers, partners or breadwinners. Disabled men who have to give up work find it especially difficult to come to terms with the loss of a job and the sense of identity and social and economic status it gave them.

My husband was a manager with Lloyds, a professional man with quite high aspirations, a member of the Rotary Club. He was always very keen on sports – golf, cricket, snooker – always more inclined to sport than a book or TV. Now, TV is his life. He's lost the motivation to try, to get involved in anything else. (June Gaze)

He's still a clever man, he's got all his faculties, he's still got a head for figures. Now – to just sit doing the crossword and watching telly – he can't even have a hobby: most of them need two hands. Even to try and do the jigsaw puzzle – his hand's a dead weight. (Madge Redbridge, whose husband, now 55, was forced to give up work after a severe stroke which paralysed his right side six years ago)

Many husbands in this position become depressed, frustrated and unable to make any sense of their new lives. Some seem to become trapped in a double bind where, on the one hand, they resent being so dependent on their wives:

He is very bitter and he takes it out on me – to get rid of his frustration. It's not deliberate. He says, it's my money keeping you now. (Madge Redbridge, who stopped work to look after her husband and so is forced to live on his invalidity benefit)

and, on the other hand, are unable to achieve the degree of emotional independence which might allow their wives some freedom. Many husbands, for example, would absolutely refuse to tolerate a sitter – a 'strange woman' – in the house, and seem to have a real, and understandable, fear of being cared for by professionals. While some – often younger – husbands do encourage their wives to go out, many expect their wives to be there all the time and the marriage to continue as it always has done.

97

If I went for, say, a small part-time job he gets frightened, panicky, though he won't say it, he never has done. If I go out in the evening he gets irritable and picky; he's always picking on me, talking about how fat I am. He looks at me disgusted-like. One day I mentioned I was on a diet. The next minute, he walked round to the shop – it's not very far and he can just about get there – and he bought me a bar of chocolate. I thought, is it fear: worry that I'll get nice and slim again and want to go out? I still wonder. Perhaps he didn't mean anything by it; perhaps it was me being mean. (Madge Redbridge)

Many wives can cope with their husbands' anxieties and their own guilt feelings only by refusing to recognise their own needs and opting instead for the 'quiet life'. The result, especially where neither husband nor wife is at work, is that many of these couples spend 24-hours a day cooped up together, in a relationship without any of the external supports on which most marriages depend for survival; a relationship which can become increasingly bitter, claustrophobic and destructive, but from which neither feels able to break free.

The emotional side is terrible at times. You get to the stage . . . being cooped up together isn't natural. I feel it's Matt's fault and he feels it's mine – you have to keep up a brave face even though you feel like screaming. (Mary Bardon)

Sexual problems

He would get terrific muscle spasms which were triggered if I touched him around the chest, so it was even difficult to cuddle him. Then we had all the problems of having to wear leg bags for the incontinence. And when I got to bed I would feel just about exhausted, while the drugs had knocked him out. Sex is very important – you don't realise how much until you actually lose it. (Anna Fields, whose husband was left paralysed by a car accident)

The sexual difficulties which are caused by disability, especially where a husband can no longer assume the traditional dominant role, are not easy to overcome. They may mean that a couple has to 'learn new tricks', or that a woman has to take the initiative or use a sex aid, changes which many couples – even younger ones with less traditional ideas about sex – find impossible to accept, often because they

98

make sex 'too mechanical'. Sexual problems can be aggravated by disability aids which take little account of marital relationships – the special ripple mattresses used to prevent pressure sores, for example, are often available in single size only, making a woman feel even more like her husband's nurse than his sexual partner.

When Terry first came home, he had the single electric bed – it wasn't natural. I would ask: what am I doing here, just looking after him? So we got our own double electric bed – it looks normal but it elevates from the floor. (Kate Sugden)

Sex, of course, cannot be seen in isolation from the rest of a relationship, and physical problems are only one factor affecting our feelings about sexuality. While a woman may simply be worn out by the job of looking after her partner, a man's sexual confidence may disappear along with his loss of work, his ability to have children, his control over his body and his self-esteem.

It's difficult to switch roles from being someone's nurse to being their lover; difficult to see the person whose bottom you have to wipe as a sexual partner. (Judith Oliver)

In her survey, Judith Oliver found that many women felt 'de-sexed': that they had lost their femaleness through caring and had no sense of being a woman any more:

One woman cried because she thought she looked so physically repulsive now. She said she had huge muscles from lifting and pulling, damaged fingernails and a bad complexion from too much cheap, starchy food. (Judith Oliver, The Caring Wife)

It has to be said, however, that for many middle-aged and elderly women, the lack of a sexual relationship with their husbands seems to be the least of their worries, perhaps because sex had anyway ceased to be important in their marriages. It is common even in 'normal' marriages for the sexual element to be gradually replaced by a more childlike relationship: there are a good few able-bodied husbands who take to calling their wives 'Mum' in later years.

It's non-existent. Sex was never the great centre of our whole existence. We'd got to the age where we'd both lost interest, and I'd had gynaecological problems. We did used to share the same room but I found I wasn't getting a good night's sleep. He has a ripple mattress: some nights all I could hear was this motor. (June Gaze, who now has a room separate from her husband)

We have to share a bedroom – that's the worst of it. I've never slept with him in the same room before. It's better in the sense that I can see to him – but he's up and down all night for the toilet. (Betty Hampton, who started to share a room with her husband when they moved from a larger house to a small sheltered flat for disabled elderly people)

The feeling that sexual problems are unimportant is also common among younger women, perhaps because sex has to take a back seat when it comes to preserving a marriage:

It doesn't bother me. I still feel we've got enough love between us, and I've already got two children. If he can just be affectionate in a loving way, it's enough. We've got a strong enough relationship. As well as being lovers, we were friends. (Eva Wilson, whose husband John has severe head injuries after a motorbike racing accident)

We compensate in other ways. (Kate Sudgen)

Money worries

We're now living on a pension which is much lower than his salary, although we had a cash payment which we invested. We're not on the breadline, but nevertheless, there's not the increase in salary I would have expected. He was due for quite a substantial increase in his salary. (June Gaze)

Financially, he had done forty years in local government so he got a good pension – it was my salary we missed. I gave up two jobs to look after him and my parents – and two pensions. I get the Invalid Care Allowance but it's no good to me now: I should have had it then, to replace what I earned. (Pam Purdy, caring for a husband who suffered a stroke fifteen years ago)

Early retirement and the dependence on Invalidity Benefits, which disabled husbands face, mean that most marriages are the poorer for disability, particularly where the wife has also been forced to give up work to look after her husband.

This loss of income is reinforced by problems over the Invalid Care Allowance (for full details of allowances, see Chapter Eleven). Originally introduced to compensate those single women who had been forced to give up work to look after their parents, the ICA was until recently not payable to married women carers, whoever they were looking after. The assumption was that married women would not be working anyway because they had husbands to support them – clearly a nonsensical assumption to make about married women caring for husbands who are disabled.

Thanks to Jackie Drake's battle with the government in 1986, all this has now changed, and married women carers are eligible for the Invalid Care Allowance. But wives caring for their husbands face a further injustice, one which has so far received little publicity: if they claim the Invalid Care Allowance, the money they receive is deducted from any claim their husbands make for them, as dependants, in their Invalidity Benefit or pension. The same thing happens where a husband is on supplementary benefit or income support: any extra money he receives on behalf of his wife as a dependant will be deducted once she claims ICA.

Since the ICA has always been an 'overlapping benefit', designed to replace lost earnings, and since it could be argued that when a wife claims this allowance she is no longer dependent on her husband, such deductions may seem to have logic on their side. Nevertheless, the regulations have disappointed and angered thousands of wives who had expected to receive a carer's allowance in their own right, and who have found instead that if they claim it, the same amount of money will be deducted from their husband's benefit.

I don't claim the Allowance, because it would come off his invalidity benefit. It's all wrong – there's no justice in it. And I won't be entitled to a pension because I won't have the stamps. But if it's left on his book it helps him psychologically. The fact that he can still support me – I didn't want to take that away from him. Anyone else could come into my home and earn this care allowance by looking after him – I could get my daughter to do it – but they won't give it to me. (Madge Redbridge)

I have so much difficulty in getting out of bed: I get so much pain in the night that by the morning I can't move – it's agony. It takes around two hours for me to feel better. He could do with someone to dress and wash him in the mornings. Up until now I have, but I'm getting so much pain round the middle. The worst agony is trying to tuck in the bedclothes. (Betty Hampton, a 75-year-old woman with a disease of the bones which makes it difficult for her to walk; she is looking after a husband, 83, with a disease of the colon which gives him diarrhoea, sickness and emphysema)

Many older women caring for invalid husbands are chronically ill themselves, so that sometimes it is hard to distinguish between the carer and the cared for. The roles are determined by gender; by who became disabled first; even by which disability is the most dramatic, according to Judith Oliver. In her survey of caring wives, she says she came across one example of a woman looking after a paraplegic husband who is now both mentally and physically more capable than his wife – yet this couple could not reverse their caring/cared for roles.

One cannot expect, I suppose, that one day, after thirty years, the husband will leap out of bed and say, 'Stay there! I'll look after you now!' (Judith Oliver, The Caring Wife)

Sometimes, where an elderly couple are both ill, the caring/cared for roles are determined by personality: in the case quoted above, for instance, husband and wife were in similar physical condition, yet it was the wife who acted as carer, perhaps because of her greater stamina, her personality or her own self-image.

I've always had someone to look after since I was a tiny child. My mother was always ill, and my sisters both epileptic. I can never sit still; I can't sit down if something wants to be done; if it wants to be done I've got to get up and do it. We were brought up like that. (Betty Hampton)

Elderly couples who are both in ill-health face other problems too. Like the couple above, they may be encouraged to move from a home they have lived in for years to smaller, sheltered housing in a different part of town, or even a different part of the country. Moving house can bring an even greater sense of loss and isolation: it means that a wife not only loses her friends and neighbours but sometimes even her pleasure in domestic life.

We were there seventeen years. I miss the house, the neighbours, the lovely big garden, the fruit and vegetables I used to grow. We had everything, I was always making something, chutneys, or cake. I regret the move, I really do. We had to get rid of all the furniture. It was the toilet more than anything: we had a curved staircase, I fell on it twice. If the stairlift (we asked for) had come first . . . we had been trying to get one for two years. (Betty Hampton; she and her husband had moved from a large three-bedroomed house to a sheltered flat in a different part of town eight months before this interview)

On the rocks

It has completely changed my relationship with my husband – in every way. We've just drifted apart, there's nothing. (Madge Redbridge)

It is hardly surprising that the strains of disability reveal in a relationship the cracks which could previously be ignored, especially where a marriage has got by in the past by depending on traditional roles and expectations: of man as bread-winner and woman as wife and mother, for example. In some ways, the effect of disability on a couple resembles the crisis which can occur in any marriage when the children have grown up and husband and wife suddenly find there is little left between them.

We don't manage to talk to each other about our feelings. I suppose we never really did talk in that sense: you get involved in normal day-to-day living and the children, and you don't always get the chance to talk. There have been times when he's told me to bugger off; told me to take my miserable face somewhere else. I have said to him at times, I'm not the right person to be looking after him. In some ways it's brought out our worst characteristics to the front which otherwise wouldn't have surfaced. There have been times when I've taken our son back to school and wanted not to come back here. But I always feel – Jocelyn's dependent on me and I couldn't do that to him. (June Gaze)

Despite the difficulties, few women consider leaving husbands who are so dependent on them, or abandoning marriages which in many cases have lasted for years. Domestic and financial ties, feelings of affection, guilt and obligation, a home and children shared, as well as the fact that there is often no alternative, mean that most wives tend to soldier on after the onset of disability, however hard to tolerate the situation becomes.

Sometimes I get terribly depressed, I go upstairs and have a good howl. I think: pull yourself together, you've got to get on with it. (Madeleine Harris)

Making it work

Many younger women with disabled husbands seem determined to make their marriages work; more so than some of the older women who are more or less resigned to the fact that the partnerships they had known are over, even if they have no intention of leaving their husbands. Perhaps this determination to make a go of it in a younger marriage is because so much more seems to be at stake, both financially and emotionally: there are young children to bring up and years of caring, sometimes for a partner they have only known for a few years, ahead. Or perhaps this difference in attitude between older and younger women is just one of age and experience.

I feel I don't want to give up. I want him back. I have days I don't know if I can take any more, when I want to run away. But I'm not going to give in without a fight. If I don't have him at home where does he go? There's nothing in this borough for head injuries.

The type of guy he was before – he'll get better, I thought. But obviously if that part of the brain is damaged, he won't have the same drive. I do think back to before the accident: he's changed a lot. At times a lot of him still comes through; at times you think the old John is still there. He's very different with me than he is with anybody else, he's quite loving; there's obviously still something special between us. My feelings haven't changed: I don't feel sorry for him, I don't want to mother him or have him as a child.

I've always said I don't want a child, I want my husband. I won't accept him as a child.

I'm determined to make it work. I want it to work. I know I won't have John as he was, but I'd rather have him as he is than not at all. (Eva Wilson, talking about her husband John, who 18 months ago was involved in a motorbike racing accident which caused severe head injuries; it has left him permanently without speech, depressed, apathetic, aggressive and unable to concentrate. She has two young children)

I get my down days – so does he. But we have our ups too. It's made us more close. I always felt I had to give it a try, and if it didn't work out – I can say I tried. (Kate Sugden)

Putting him away?

You've got to think of the years of marriage when you're thinking of signing your husband's life away to a home – it's a very, very hard thing to make a judgement like that. I said no for so long. (Winifred Rivers, who has decided on residential care for her husband)

Few wives consider residential care for their husbands: social attitudes and marital loyalties are such that 'putting a partner away' is seen as even less acceptable than 'putting away' an elderly parent. Unlike our blood-relationships with our children and parents – which exist whether we live with them or not – marriage is based on a chosen domestic arrangement. Giving up that arrangement is equated with failure and with divorce. As Judith Oliver has pointed out:

Other caring relationships can better stand separation than can marriage. The parent of a very handicapped child can see him go off to a residential school knowing that she is still his mother. Your parents remain your parents, even when they are living in an old people's home or hospital. But your husband seems to be a different matter. (Judith Oliver, The Caring Wife)

Oliver also believes that disability in a husband is actually likely to keep a failing marriage going, with wives staying with their partners out of feelings of guilt and obligation rather than love. This could explain why divorce rates among wives with disabled husbands are lower than the national

105

average – a fact which it is interesting to compare with the higher than average divorce rates among men with disabled wives.

Of the women interviewed for this book three were considering alternative care; all three were looking after partners suffering from dementia, an illness which had virtually destroyed all vestiges of their previous relationships.

I've accepted the possibility of him going into care. How he'll take it when the time comes . . . You're bound to have regrets because he's such a pathetic creature. Yet you can only do so much for them. No, I don't love him. No, it's more pity. The Fred I knew has died. (Madeleine Harris)

Break-up

Whether two people stay together or separate will depend not only on the strengths and weaknesses within their relationship, but also on such circumstances as their beliefs about marriage, and whether they have the emotional and financial resources to separate.

One woman to whom I talked had been married for ten years when her husband had a car accident which broke his back and left him in a wheelchair; they split up nine years later, after months of bitterness and antagonism, and following her husband's relationship with another, younger woman. One of the reasons behind their separation, she believes, was his growing resentment at his dependence on her.

Like most men he sees himself as independent – so having to rely on anyone else was very difficult. What he felt was that after the accident I was in complete control – although I didn't feel I was. I feel the control he gained from being a paraplegic was very strong: it was difficult to deny anything he wanted. I felt responsibility for him totally – as though I had to keep him happy; I took that as my burden. I felt he had gained control over me. He's got emotional control now (in the new relationship). He's the organiser; she's younger, like I was in my early twenties, and more compliant. He takes more responsibility with her. I still very much regret splitting up, it had lasted nineteen years and I always hoped he would work through the depression and antagonism. I always believed it would be possible. But he

106

felt so angry with me. There was this expectation that I could make everything better. And I felt inadequate because it was never enough. I felt as though I did everything I possibly could. I don't feel guilty, I feel sad. I feel I helped him quite a long way along the road. (Anna Fields)

Is there a future?

His death? Yes, it would be a release. I know that sounds horrible but you wonder when you're going to be an individual in your own right. You've been mother and father for so many years, and then this. You wonder when you're going to start living. (Madeleine Harris)

Sometimes I feel: I've had my life, I've lived it. But I know there's so much more to do. (Madge Redbridge)

I think the future for the next ten years looks pretty bleak. I suppose, I feel time is running out. (Beth Prentice)

Many women looking after a disabled husband have already done a substantial caring stint, bringing up children and caring for their own or their husband's parents. Facing up to disability in their own partners often comes at a time when they were hoping to start leading a life of their own. For many, it can be a bitter blow to realise that the rest of their lives may be swallowed up by caring.

And yet:

I'm sorry if I've been whingeing on. I feel I haven't mentioned all the love. (Beth Prentice)

I feel so guilty and bitter – sitting moaning about it. (Madge Redbridge)

6

_____ · _____

A normal family life?: Parents bringing up children with disabilities

Don't ever have a handicapped child – I wouldn't wish it on anyone. It destroys you. (Louisa Price, 42, single parent of five children and mother of Matthew, 10, brain-damaged at birth)

Up to 130,000 parents in Britain are thought to be looking after severely disabled children, many of them suffering from conditions which are mentally or physically crippling, and sometimes both; these include spina bifida, cerebral palsy and mental handicap. Half a century ago, many of these children would not have survived the first few weeks or months of life; those who did so would have had a life expectancy of only a few years and would, in most cases, have been condemned to a long-stay ward or residential home. Today, developments in medical science mean that children with severe disabilities can survive into adulthood and beyond; while the recent moves towards 'community care' mean that most of them will be brought up by their parents rather than in institutions. At home they will be supported – supposedly – by community services.

In practice, what 'community care' usually means is that the care of these children – whose physical and emotional demands can be enormous – falls almost exclusively on their parents, and particularly on their mothers. It also means that many of these parents – and their other children – will never experience a normal family life.

The issues which dominate the lives of these parents, and the hopes and fears they have for their children, are much the same as those which are important to every other parent: they want to see their children have a carefree childhood, a decent education and develop whatever potential they might have; they want to prepare their children for an independent life, with fulfilling and meaningful work, companionship, and financial and emotional security. But the parents of disabled children face some formidable obstacles in trying to achieve these ordinary goals: discrimination, lack of resources and ignorance and fear, all of which turn disability into a social handicap.

The situation of disabled people has improved over the last half-century and social attitudes to disability have radically changed: we no longer regard mentally disabled people, for instance, as 'defectives' or 'subnormals' who need to be separated from the rest of society, or as 'vegetables' who have no needs other than to be humanely treated. In the last few years, even the language of disability has changed – for example, learning difficulty instead of mental handicap – in an effort to distinguish intellectual impairment from wider concepts of intelligence, perception and sensitivity. Disabled people themselves are increasingly speaking up for their right to an independent life. These changes, as well as improvements in our support services, mean that parents of younger handicapped children will have a different, and better, experience than those whose children were born twenty or thirty years ago.

Yet despite these developments, most disabled people still face life-long disadvantages, especially in areas such as education, employment, housing and income, which rebound not only on themselves but on their carers. And despite some increase in tolerance and understanding, the stigma which surrounds disability, especially mental handicap, is still strong. There is an underlying suspicion, even now, that handicapped people are lacking in normal human responses, perceptions, emotions and thought processes.

Finding out

As soon as I saw her I knew there was something wrong, although you couldn't put your finger on anything. There was this shock of hair and long

109

poking tongue; she was very floppy. One sister said: there are places for these babies; put her away and forget about her. You live your own life as if nothing had happened. I was finally told – by a paediatrician I'd never seen before – that she would be a vegetable, ineducable, and that the best thing would be to place it in an institution before I became too fond of it. (Margaret Tass, mother of Rosa, now 19, who has Down's syndrome).

His appearance: he didn't look like my other children, he had very glassy eyes and his tongue was sticking out. He was a floppy baby, very floppy, not a lot of muscle tone. He didn't smile at six weeks or make any noises like the other children did. I kept taking him back but nobody said anything. (Louisa Price)

The medical people always say: forget about this one, have another child. I was once told, 'If we were in China, we would take him to the top of the hill and forget about him – there's a lot to be said for that way of doing things'. (Bella Clifford, mother of Peter, 39, diagnosed as spastic diaplegic)

The sister told me to put him in a home and forget him, he's a vegetable. (Meg Townsend, mother of John, 32, brain-damaged at birth)

For most parents, finding out that their child is disabled means not only having to confront their own feelings, but having to face the incompetence, embarrassment and even callousness of those whose job it is to tell them the bad news. Many parents are never told properly what is wrong with their child or why; rightly or wrongly, many feel suspicion and resentment over the circumstances surrounding the birth of their child – nagging uncertainties which often remain for years afterwards.

They wouldn't admit brain damage at the beginning and we hadn't the money to fight in any case. My husband blamed the lady doctor; my husband always felt that more could have been done. (Patsy Brown, mother of Simon, 21, brain-damaged at birth)

No one said why it happened; it could be toxaemia. I recall when I was pregnant I was having a lot of Valium to lower the blood pressure. I wanted to know why, I still do; I will want to know why until the day I die. (Louisa Price)

It was such a difficult birth over such a long period of time, they pulled her out with forceps. It wasn't until she was 18 months that we were told she

110

had massive brain damage. The doctors: they said that, in their opinion, it was not due to environmental factors; they were shrugging it off, from them to us – that we were deficient in some way. It's been put down as a genetic condition. It wasn't until we saw some American doctors, who told a different story, that we realised it was birth trauma. (Edward Oliver, father of Annette, 19, officially described as spastic quadraplegic)

Sometimes it takes weeks, even months or years, before a disability can be diagnosed with any certainty: this leads to a genuine professional dilemma about what should be said and when; and, in consequence, a tendency to fudge the issue. Parents are often traumatised and confused, unable to take in a lot of information or to remember what they have been told. Most professionals are rarely equipped or properly trained to counsel such parents, and may only be able to cope with the situation by distancing themselves from it; while those who used to advise parents to 'try for another' or to 'put it away' were only carrying out the policy whereby, until recently, the mentally handicapped were automatically assigned to residential institutions.

Professional attitudes have changed during the last decade, and most parents who have a child with disabilities are now expected and encouraged to take that child home; indeed, those who do not wish to may be seen by the professionals as failing to 'come to terms' with disability. Despite this change in policy, many doctors and nurses are still dismissive, sometimes even brutal, in their explanations and assessments: the attitude tends to be that parents should not expect too much of a handicapped child. It is an attitude which parents have to confront throughout their lives, one which emphasises the limitations of disability rather than the potential of the individual child.

First reactions

I had this awful guilt, the family were ringing up and asking about the baby; there is this great guilt if the child isn't normal. It's as though it's a reflection on you – you wonder if others will see you as inadequate.

Everyone has a period of grief. Mine was that I'd spent hours knitting a romper suit; my first reaction was, she'll never be able to wear it. You go through a period of mourning for the kid you might have had. (Margaret Tass)

It was difficult to accept, particularly for us, because, although he was only ten months old when he had meningitis, it was pretty obvious that he was a bright child. He was quite a show baby in fact, very fat and bonny and always laughing. That really was what we found difficult: the transition from appreciating his potential and realising all that had gone. (George Burford, father of Charles, 39, who suffers from cerebral palsy)

My wife and myself – we blamed each other for the fact that it had gone wrong. (Edward Oliver)

The parents of a child born with a disability may wonder secretly whether the disability was their fault, and whether future children will be disabled. They may also have to deal with conflicting feelings of love and rejection, feelings which few are given the opportunity to talk about with trained or sympathetic counsellors.

Once I felt like killing Matthew – something I never want to feel again. I wanted him to be dead: I went into the room and got a pillow, a voice was saying, suffocate him. I knew I would go to jail, it was only that that stopped me. If I could have got away with it I would have done it. I literally had the pillow, my hand was shaking; I must have been desperate. (Louisa Price)

The reactions of families and friends to the birth of a disabled child is of little comfort.

When I'd had the other two children, all my friends came with cards and flowers. When I had Mark, nobody came. Nobody came to see me at home to talk about it. When Mark was two weeks old, one very good friend saw us coming and crossed over the road. I crossed over and said to her, he's alive, we don't know how long we've got him, but for God's sake don't ignore me. I ended up having to say goodbye to fifteen to twenty friends. They don't know what to say or how to cope. (Christine Martin, whose seven-year-old son has brain and spinal damage)

My father-in-law blamed by family: there's no mongols in my family, he said, it must be yours. My husband did the same thing – he blamed my family. (Margaret Tass)

Don't ask me where he went – I haven't seen or heard of him since. I'd still have him back if he walked up the garden path. It was once explained to me that in his position he could control everything he handled; what he couldn't control was a handicapped son. He didn't blame me, but he couldn't accept it. The doctor told me: the more intelligent the man, the harder it is. We'd been married six and a half years, there were no problems – that was why it was so hard to take. (Meg Townsend, whose husband, a university professor, walked out when their brain-damaged son John was three years old)

When Matthew turned out to be the way he was, Mr P [her husband] couldn't handle that. I had had this fool, as he put it. He never blamed himself, just me. Men can't cope with that sort of thing. When the other pregnancy came along he told me that if I had another one of those he wasn't going to be around. Even now he refuses to accept paternity for Matthew – he calls him funny.

My husband loves Terry, loves my last child; he makes a fuss of Terry and not Matthew, because Terry's normal. He would accept paternity for Terry but he asks me, who is Matthew's father? If I could have turned the clock back, I would. What I have learnt about men. I don't regret it, but I had to do it all alone – and I didn't get the child alone. It made me sort of anti-men. If two people go into something they should stick it out. These men, why do they have it so easy? (Louisa Price, who is bringing up Matthew and four other children after separating from her husband)

One of the things which happen when you're told your child is less than normal – you tend to drink too much. Once you get through that there is the temptation to have affairs. The third stage – if you get through that – is to throw yourself into your work. Because I think it questions your belief in all the things you expected. But along the way, people don't get through the drunken stage, or they run off with 18-year-olds: not because they want to, but because they can't face themselves. (Edward Oliver, 51, single father caring for daughter Annette)

Men have particular difficulties in coming to terms with a disabled child, perhaps because it is a blow to the ambitions they may have had for their children and to their own self-image and self-esteem. Many husbands are unable to come to terms with their disappointment and finally reject their child completely by leaving the marriage. Others stay, but never get over their feelings of failure and are never able to love their disabled child as they can their other children. Some fathers adopt an authoritarian role with a disabled child; while mothers compensate by becoming overprotective.

I think my husband's a bit strict with Simon, on the whole he's quite well behaved. I would have liked more children, but my husband didn't want any. I think an only child is a lonely child. I think he was afraid it might happen again. (Patsy Brown)

He used to say I wasn't stern enough with John. We used to – not fall out over it exactly – he thought if I'd been stricter things would have been better. (Olive Wylie, mother of John, 14, mentally handicapped)

Although no official statistics exist, it appears that a high proportion of marriages do not survive the birth of a disabled child, and that many women are left alone to bring up their families in poverty and isolation, dependent on handouts from their husbands or means-tested benefit. Marriage break-ups, of course, are not confined to families with disabled children: the demands of able-bodied children, especially in the early years, can prove a strain on any partnership. But the problems which any child can bring to a marriage are intensified in a family with a disabled child, because of the overwhelming physical, emotional and mental demands that he or she can make. Sometimes the only way a couple can cope is by dividing up the family and taking on separate roles, with the wife looking after the disabled child while her husband concentrates on the others.

Literally from the time Mark was born, we've had no life together. You tend to be . . . you're tired, irritable. He [her husband] dreads the mornings, he knows exactly what I'm going to be like. Mark is very possessive: if he sees me cuddling my husband he will throw a tantrum. You can't go to bed and be together – you're up and down, up and down. (Christine Martin)

It has made a difference. The very first holiday we ever had after our honeymoon was to celebrate our silver wedding. (Bella Clifford)

How partners react to the birth of a disabled child is something which depends on how strong the relationship is in the first place. Thousands of fathers learn to love and care for their disabled children; thousands of marriages survive and grow stronger, and the marriages which fail may well have done so in any event.

We often talk to each other, comfort each other; say, we're only human, we've done our best. (Bill Clifford, Bella's husband and father of Peter)

Hannah Weill

Hannah Weill is originally from Finland; she has three children – Nina, a Down's syndrome child aged 10, Daniel aged 5 and Leila, 5 months. Divorced from her husband, she lives with her boyfriend in a flat in Chelsea.

Most people call her high grade, she's a very bright Down's; she can read a little bit, write, knows her alphabet and numbers. Socially she's very acceptable because of the way we've brought her up – she knows how to behave outside the home. She can dress herself, choose her own clothes; she knows when her clothes are dirty. She takes great pride in her own appearance. She can eat at the table: we can take her to a restaurant and she doesn't embarrass us, but she does need reminding not to stick her knife in her mouth. If she's really enjoyed a meal – she does love food – she forgets and eats with her mouth open.

She's a great mother to her little sister, she mothers her, smothers her almost; sometimes I just have to stop her because she just goes too far, she wants to cuddle her so much, she squeezes her so hard and the baby can't defend herself, so she needs watching. Daniel will push her away or even whack her, that upsets her. People say Down's syndrome are very loving, I don't like to generalise like that. Nina doesn't love everybody, she won't hug everybody, there's people she doesn't like, things she doesn't like.

How is she different? She doesn't speak like a normal ten-year-old – but she's got speech. We're always correcting her, so is Daniel, but in such a nice way; Daniel will translate for her, he does it so nicely. Last night she said what she had for lunch. She meant to say spaghetti but she kept getting it wrong, so Daniel goes: 'Nina may have had spaghetti, but I had such-and-such'. He's very

115

mature for his age. He's never asked us why Nina is different or why she can't speak properly. I'm sure it will come.

She's quite different. I think her mental age – I would put it at about five. Everything Nina is able to do has taken her a very long time; nothing comes automatically to her. You have to push, push, push the whole time.

She gets frustrated; I couldn't say she knows she's different: she's not bright enough or old enough yet. But at times she'll see other children doing something she can't do – she get really frustrated. She's as clumsy as anything: if they're playing hopscotch she can't do it.

I have to make myself believe she'll keep learning as long as she lives, otherwise what is the good of me trying. I don't kid myself she'll be normal one day, she never will be. But my other choice is to give up right now – I could send her away to boarding school.

When she was born that was the first thing they offered. There was no advice on who we could contact, they just had this folder full of residential places. The doctor was encouraging us to send her away. He said: there's no shame, lots of people do it, you could go and see if you like. I decided (not to) there and then.

The doctor was a paediatrician at a large London teaching hospital.

I hate him, hate him, hate him for what he said to me. If I'd have been a weaker person . . . lots of people regard what the doctors say as right. He's told parents the highest hope for their son in the future is for him to go and make cardboard boxes. What a thing to say. One of the things he said to us which hurt, he said: don't ever leave her in the house unattended because she'll let all the burglars in. He tells you things which are totally irrelevant when you're holding a couple of weeks old baby in your arms. It's wrong that anybody should take it upon themselves to start talking to anyone like that.

At first I didn't react at all: I didn't know she had Down's syndrome until she was six-weeks-old; I couldn't see it, I suppose I could say I didn't believe it. I just didn't acknowledge it for a few weeks. I didn't even know what Down's syndrome was; I thought it was a form of jaundice. When they told me, no, it's a form of mongolism – that word.

After they told us we went home from hospital, my husband bought me a bottle of Bacardi, I think I must have drunk three-quarters of the bottle. I just sat there.

Slowly it began to dawn on me – I couldn't look at her without crying. I remember I was breastfeeding at the time and I had a really good friend who'd say, shut your eyes, I'll put her to your breast.

I went through this process – I think it was almost grieving. I know it wasn't a death, but I was expecting a child for nine months, and the child I had wasn't the one I expected to have. It was something else. So I think I grieved.

I always loved her. I think that's stopped me from even considering . . . people say you love that child to madness. I love them all the same, but Nina's more hard work than the others.

I'll never accept my child is handicapped, I'll never ever accept that. Acceptance means it's OK; to me it's not OK – I don't want a handicapped child.

Her former husband is twenty years her senior, an Englishman born in Hong Kong, whose family were wiped out during the war.

He was very good and supportive at the beginning, the first three months. Then it sort of hit him; he's not really a child oriented person. He was very good from the practical point of view. I really don't believe our marriage went wrong because of Nina, it was just other things. He was very upset – he had no family, he didn't have anyone to support him. He'd speak about it to close friends but I don't think he's ever worked through his own emotions.

My mother was absolutely devastated, she was. She told me later that she cried for three years. But having said that, she's been so good to me. After I had Nina, I've become so close to her.

I've got a father, I'm not very close to him, I never have been. He always said: if you need me I'm here. He knows I never need him.

I'm the eldest of five. The sister after me can't have children. The first time I went back to Finland, when Nina was born, my sister, who is very bitter she can't have children, and who doesn't know what it's like to have a handicappped child, said some quite cruel things: 'I'd rather have a mongol baby than no baby.' I wanted her to listen, not to say anything; I just wanted to talk to her about everything I felt. I couldn't talk to my mother at the time because she kept bursting into tears – I thought Paula would be the one I could talk to. I said: I wish I hadn't had this baby. She said: stop whingeing and get on with it, I'd rather have a mongol than no baby at all. She's very bitter. She lives in Finland. Over there adoption is very difficult.

117

My mum is absolutely fantastic: she writes letters to Nina, Nina is very special to her. I think they're very, very close.

They've done a family tree, my mum and my dad. It was started off to see if there were any other Down's people. And my mum started a great big research in Finland: what was happening to mentally handicapped people over there.

When Nina was born I had nothing, no help. They made me feel like I was the only person in the world with a Down's kid. Now we've got pretty good services, but we wouldn't have them if we just sat on our arses and waited. We've had to really fight for them.

All these allowances: they never pay, they're just not sufficient. She goes through more clothes than a normal child, because she's so terribly clumsy. Educational toys, they're always much more expensive; you want them to learn as much as possible, so you get the best, but they cost more than the ones you get down the market.

Nina wanted a camera for her birthday, then she wanted a walkman; so we gave her a walkman. We spend a fortune on batteries because she always leaves it on. She wears glasses: she's always breaking her glasses. When she was younger she would throw her shoe out of the school coach: I would be buying her three pairs of shoes a month. In those days, when Nina was young, the health authority didn't provide free nappies. She was in nappies until she was three.

She has caused so much physical damage. I used to have shit all over the walls; she used to poo herself in bed and play with it – so I'd have to wash it all down and paint the walls. The carpets: we went through loads of carpets because she would just wreck them with glue, anything she could get her hands on. She set the place alight on New Year's Eve; we weren't insured so that cost us £3,000.

When I had Daniel, Nina was four. People used to look at Nina's face, then look at the face in the buggy, then look at mine, as if to ask, are they all like that?

My mum always said, don't look and don't stare – that was *my* education about disabled people. The things which stick in people's minds are the old wives' tales and the myths.

It doesn't worry me any more. The other children outside – they let Nina play with them. All the kids in this street are younger than she is, except three girls who are older. They started this business calling her spastic, but Nina doesn't understand what it is, so she used to laugh at them.

If we hear that kind of stuff, either Dave or I will go down and talk to them − in a way it's not our business and in a way it is. We explain: she's mentally handicapped, she's slower, she does understand but it takes time. When you start doing that you get a whole crowd of children standing there with their mouths open.

The kids in this street are fine now. They come into our house and Nina will show her things; but they're not very interested in her for any great length of time, I think because of Nina's concentration. If they're playing Had, for instance, she doesn't know who's It, she thinks anybody's It. Or if she's It she'll run round saying, touch me, touch me.

We've tried to teach her. It's such a simple game, it takes two minutes for a normal child; with Nina it will take a month, oh my God. But it's worth it, if she can go and join in with the other children.

She's in a school for severely mentally handicapped children; they've just had an integrated teacher appointed after the summer holidays, they're trying to integrate some of them with normal primary ones. Nina could cope in a reception class in an ordinary school, but she wouldn't cope with a whole lot of ten-year-olds.

I don't want Nina to go to a normal school, the way the system is now. I don't think very many teachers are around who've had specialist training. They would never be able to give Nina what she gets at her school, where they're specially trained for children with 'severe learning difficulties'. That's what they call it now: severe learning difficulties, not mental handicap. My boyfriend prefers severe learning difficulties, he's quite into the language. We have quite heated arguments. I say, what does it matter if people say mental handicap or severe learning difficulties, or any other fancy word ILEA has? Let's just get on with it.

All these professional people − now they go to the other extreme of being so sensitive they make parents feel uncomfortable. They're so supersensitive about what they say to you, and what they write down now we've got access to the files. Sometimes they're so sensitive what they write doesn't mean anything.

Hannah is not happy with Nina's education at the moment.

She's got a really deadbeat teacher at the moment; she had this really good teacher for two years, but she is one in a million − she believes Nina and others like her are totally capable of being educated, of learning to read and write. She started her programme with that at the top of her list, and Goddammit she's done it.

Now with the new teacher, I said to Nina: what did you do today? She said she was cutting up catalogues. We work so hard with her at home; we don't have her cutting up catalogues.

I'm a real fighter – I won't keep my mouth shut. She's learnt nothing new from September until now. Her teacher's got a play centre mentality; I doubt if she really believes the pupils are capable of learning anything academic. I've been up to see her a couple of times; I just get so angry. The teacher takes them ice skating on Mondays, swimming on Tuesdays, adventure playground Wednesdays, Thursday the roly-poly club and Friday, drama.

I think she should be carrying on with reading, writing and maths. To me these must be the important things. I do think she should have the chance to go swimming and ice skating and everything else, but I think they're really secondary. I don't think she should be cutting up pictures out of catalogues, doing puzzles. OK yes, do them – but let them be time fillers.

She's capable of doing other things, they interest her; when she's doing reading it's stretching her. Since she's been in this new class – the first couple of weeks she started wetting herself (she was dry by the time she was three). Then she's become the playground thug: she cut up a boy's shirt; it's just not like her, pushing people over. She's bored out of her mind.

My end goal with Nina: I would like her to be a young lady who knows what she wants within her own limitations. I want to bring her up to be as independent as possible. I don't think she could live totally on her own – but I don't want to bring her up with the feeling that she's totally reliant on me, Dave or her brother. I want her to believe she's able to leave the nest and make it on her own.

I'm never going to expect Daniel or Leila to take over when I get old. They've got their own lives to live, they're entitled to that. If they choose, if they want to, it's different. But I'm not bringing them up thinking I've got any expectations of them regarding Nina.

I'd love her to be able to work – some kind of job – but I don't think that's possible. I'd love her to have a relationship, a loving relationship with somebody: let her have sex, live with somebody, even get married to somebody; I don't care, it would be nice.

I would hate to ever think of Nina having a child, I couldn't bear that. I don't think she would be capable of bringing up a child. If she had a baby: I don't want to look after her baby, and I don't think she should be put through the trauma of being pregnant nine months and then having the child taken away. Her hormones and her emotions are just the same as yours and mine – she would feel the same as if somebody did that to us. And the children: would it be fair?

I know a lot of mentally handicapped women who say, I want to have a baby. One girl has just got married: she's already had one abortion; she's now had her coil removed – they've taken it out because she wants a baby. If she had a baby, she wouldn't be able to look after it. And her husband is violent – he's not handicapped but he's very simple. The husband only has to lose his temper and he'll whack that child and do damage or even kill it.

It may sound a bit cold, but I think it's realistic. The whole time, though, I'm questioning: what right have I got to say this – because it's not me, it's somebody else. I believe I don't own my children. I wouldn't dare say to Daniel and Leila: don't have children. But I'm saying that about Nina. After she's 21 she can do what she likes – that is the law. I feel, just because a person is mentally handicapped, they should have the same rights as we all do. But it doesn't quite work like that, because they're not the same. It's good to say: let them vote, get married, have sex. I think yes, let them. But I think – even the smarter ones who do get married and want children – they don't totally understand why they can't look after someone else. They think they can, but the reality is they can't.

Hannah belongs to a group of parents of children who discuss issues such as sex with a psychologist.

I'm the youngest mum in that group; one lady has a son of 32, one a daughter of 26. They should have had help a long time ago. The psychologist said that in some cases it's too late to start teaching some of these things to adults. The lady with the 32-year-old son: she's believed that the side of the brain to do with sex is damaged, so he has no sexuality. This is what she believes. He lives with them. Now he's going one night a week to a hostel where's he's got a girlfriend who he cuddles and kisses. In this hostel they let them do what they like, which is OK in one way, but not OK if he's had no education about their bodies and their hormones.

She (his mother) says, he's never masturbated. I say, how do you know, you're not in the same room as him? The lady with the 26-year-old girl thinks you shouldn't tell them anything in the first place and they won't have any sexual feelings. I turn around and say, I think you're wrong.

Now with Nina – she's showing really great awareness of her own body, she wants breasts like me to breastfeed her little sister. She knows she hasn't got a penis. I'm really straight with my kids: they know the baby came out of the vagina, they know it hurt, I was crying, there was blood, I had stitches.

I have to say I am worried if my children sleep around with all these diseases and now this AIDS and everything. To Daniel and Leila I can say: there's this AIDS going around. To Nina I can say something, but I can see I'll have to drum it in much more.

There's a boy of 15, he's at her school, he's after her body, we talk about it to his parents, it's because she's always kissing and cuddling him. I say, Nina. don't let him kiss so much, give him a kiss when you say hallo and goodbye. And she'll say, why? I have to say, in really simple terms: he's bigger than you, he knows more of what he's doing.

Nina just thinks you kiss somebody to be really nice. Daniel knows there could be more to kissing and cuddling.

They don't see their father; he doesn't want to. He had access but he forfeited it. He doesn't want photographs; he never rings up to ask. He came here once – he was following me around. He doesn't know what to say to them, he's not into children at all.

Dave (her boyfriend) adores children. He's great with her, he's got so much more patience. With homework and things like that, he'll sit for hours and hours. He calls her creepy.

What I appreciate is, he says: I'll never know 100 per cent what it's like to have a mentally handicapped child, she's not my flesh and blood. Which I think is honest. I appreciate that.

Having Nina has really enriched my life. I'd have quite a boring life if I didn't have her, because having her I've met some really lovely people who've become great friends. You know she was in 'Crossroads'. (Nina was written into the serial for three months.) We've got it all on tape; we just lived a life of luxury for six months, all the TV interviews, meeting Duran Duran. Also it gave us – the most important thing – an opportunity to tell millions of people what it's like to have a child with mental handicap, the effects but also the positive points.

I don't think Nina is a big negative in any of our lives. She's different in what she requires – but she's so lovely.

With a normal child, at the age of one they start to feed themselves:
Matthew didn't do that. At two a normal child is practically out of nappies:
Matthew was in nappies until he was four. These are the things. Even now
his food has to be cut up and you've got to supervise him. He can't clean
himself – I've got children younger than Matthew who can wash. A normal
child you might let go to the park: Matthew can't because he's no sense of
danger. He's hyperactive; he sleeps very little. He's a compulsive eater, he'd
drink anything in sight; he drank sulphuric acid when he was about five.
He just has to be watched all the time.

Odd words started when he was about five. He's now ten and he can
make a sentence of two or three words. He's a very excitable child, he
stutters a lot; you've got to listen very carefully to hear what he's saying. He
gets frustrated and so do I.

He behaves like a four-year-old, who needs supervision, who will have
tantrums, who needs to be washed, who seeks attention all the time. He's
no concept of writing and reading – nothing. (Louisa Price)

Someone's got to be with him every night, someone's up all night; he
catnaps a bit, twenty minutes at a time if you're lucky. It's my husband or I
who sleeps in with him; you can't both go to sleep at night because he's very
alert. If you fall asleep and he knows, he'll go to find something
immediately you've got to attend to. You can tell him off, smack him, he'll
do it again. He doesn't accept sleep; he takes a packed picnic to bed. He has
to be changed four or five times a night.

There's no one to share things with. Most friends with babies: when
Mark would do something new, I'd phone up and say, Mark smiled, and
they'd say, mine did that at six weeks. There's no one to share it with.
(Christine Martin, whose seven-year-old son Mark is hyperactive)

In the first years he was very destructive; he was always swinging on the
curtains, pulling down the rail, tipping up the furniture, upsetting the gas
cooker. He still has mood swings, gets aggressive or distressed quite easily –
the slightest thing will trigger it off. Also obsessions – with household
sprays, he'd want to spray them everywhere.

He talks constantly, repeats things, repeats questions; asks me to do
things again and again – it was getting out of hand. In this situation you
very often appease. You shouldn't, but you'd do anything for a bit of peace
and quiet. (Olive Wylie, who has just been persuaded to send her son to a
residential school for behavioural training)

123

As Hannah Weill's story illustrates, women with disabled children experience the same kind of pleasures and frustrations as any other mother with young children. But bringing up a disabled child involves a far more wearing routine, and one which goes on for much longer: disabled children will continue to make physical and emotional demands which 'normal' children have long outgrown.

Mothers have to cope with hyperactivity, or with aggressive, chaotic and sometimes socially embarrassing behaviour, which may make it difficult to take their children anywhere. The fact that many physically disabled children – those with spina bifida, for example – suffer constant health problems means for them a life built around hospital appointments.

It is difficult for any mother to combine bringing up a family with paid work, but at least women with able-bodied children can expect to return to a job when their children go to nursery or school. The mothers of disabled children often find this impossible, partly because there is so little pre-school provision for disabled children; but also because the prolonged dependence of disabled children means they never feel free to go back to work. This makes these women even more financially dependent on their husbands, not only for a few years but for a lifetime. It also leads to a social isolation which can be intensified by the attitudes of others to a disabled child:

He's very affectionate, he's also very friendly – people don't like that, they can't cope with it. They don't like handicapped children.

If a neighbour comes in, Matthew would run and cuddle him. You feel the withdrawal; they think it's catching, like a disease. If normal children come, they don't want to know. They'll invite Terry [her youngest child] but not Matthew. He stays home with me; he doesn't play with other children. He has no friends. He's not invited to parties. (Louisa Price)

A lot of people don't understand, because he looks normal; they just think he's very naughty and you're hopeless and can't cope. You always feel very edgy about taking him into someone's home, he's very destructive; as a young child he would whizz round smashing ornaments.

The woman in the shop across the road told him not to come in again because he threw the sweets across the counter. She said: my grandchild wouldn't do that. I thought, you should thank God your grandchild is all right. (Olive Wylie)

The fight to develop potential

The early years are when parents sacrifice all their time and energy to the painfully slow process of developing their child's potential, often with little help from our statutory services, and without the intensive physiotherapy which it is now thought can radically improve the prospects of brain-damaged children. The parents of a profoundly handicapped young woman, officially diagnosed as a spastic quadraplegic, who was totally paralysed, who could not speak, smile or feed herself and who had no sense of balance, spent time and money taking her to a clinic in the USA for intensive retraining, which was based on the idea that the undamaged parts of the brain could be re-educated or repatterned to take over the functions of the damaged parts. It was, her father believes, through the efforts of this clinic that his child, who spent her time lying on the floor until she was about ten, was finally able to sit up without being strapped into her chair.

What to other people is not even noticeable in terms of achievement, to me is a tremendous victory: getting her to lay her hands flat down on a low chair, for instance, so I can wipe her bottom properly rather than having her lay down, and all the indignities of her legs splayed out everywhere. (Edward Oliver, father of Annette)

It is the feeling that too little is being done by conventional services, which leads other parents on similar, often expensive and time-consuming quests. Some British parents of cerebral-palsied children, for instance, have moved more or less permanently to Hungary to be near the Peto Institute, in Budapest, a centre which provides specialised intensive retraining. These programmes have been successful for many, but they can take over the lives of both parents and children, and may prove heartbreaking if they do not work.

125

These parents' efforts are sometimes dismissed as obsessive, as a refusal to accept the limitations of disability; and as similar to, for instance, the behaviour of parents who push their 'normal' children too hard academically. But it is difficult to live with the knowledge that your child may have potential which is not being realised – simply because the services are not available.

He argues, he complains, he helps himself to biscuits, he steals, he lies; he's got a mind of his own. If he can do those things, why can't he read and write? It would take longer, but it could be done; I'm convinced of that. If he sees me coming and he's taken a few biscuits he will hide them; so if his brain works for that, why can't it work for something else? He likes fashion; he wouldn't have clothes from the jumble sale; he goes in the shop and shows me what he wants – he's got sense for all that. If he can think to do all that, why can't he read, why can't he write? (Louisa Price)

Brothers and sisters

It has altered my relationship with my eldest daughter; I don't think I've as much time to sit and listen. She takes part in a lot of activities at school, and she misses out: other mums and dads go and watch the netball or the play: we can't go because if we take Mark he'll only get wound up and frustrated. There's also the fact now she wants to sit and talk. She's growing up; there are lots of little emotional things, but there's never the time when we can be together on our own, because Mark is always in between us. He's very possessive of me. She turns to my mother, or others – I get very upset by that. She went to one of her schoolteachers with some problems and told her, 'Mummy didn't have time.' I know she didn't mean it, but it was very hurtful.

She is 10, but far advanced for her years because of what she's had to do. If Mark gets very mad he convulses and gets incontinent both ways. She cleans him and bathes him – even my little one has done that. My middle daughter was one year when Mark was born, so she lost out; the oldest was four and she's never been allowed to have a childhood. It's always been: you'll have to get on with it, I'm busy. We've tried to compensate by buying loads of toys, rabbits, cats; we try to do all we can in those terms. But she's never been a little girl who runs out and plays with her friends. If a friend calls she'll say, no I don't want to go out. She never goes out to anybody's house for tea.

They're both very protective towards him: they look after him at school, take him to the toilet, change him for PE. They're both little mothers before their time.

You can't go off and do things as a family; you can't take the children out for the day because you have to be so prepared. You are a handicapped family, not just a child. (Christine Martin, talking about her two daughters, aged 8 and 10. Her disabled son, Mark, is 7)

In the past, once parents had died or were getting old, the care of a disabled child would pass to the nearest available female, usually an older sister who would be expected to sacrifice everything for her disabled sibling. Today's parents, however, no longer automatically expect other children to give up their own lives in this way, although some hope that the responsibility might be taken on voluntarily.

When other children, usually daughters, take on part of the responsibility for disabled brothers or sisters, they have to grow up very quickly and have little real childhood of their own. This can lead to emotional conflicts for the child, especially as she approaches puberty and adolescence.

My daughter, she's been good; but she's drifting away – not as good as she has been. I'll hear her saying to Matthew, when she's washing him: act your age, why do I have to do this for you? She needs it (affection) as well – and she's not getting it. She's never really had a proper childhood; she's almost a woman now. This is when they go and get pregnant; they are seeking affection, because they didn't get enough at home. I do feel guilty. She wants to go out today. Normally I wouldn't let her: I've got to go to work and she's got to see to Matthew. She resents it. She didn't at first, she does now.

My oldest one, he felt I shouldn't have had Matthew in the first place; he was horrified at me having another baby – and then when he was handicapped. The younger one, he's 19, he left this year; he used to bully Matthew a lot; I didn't like that. If he got smelly because of the incontinence, they were unkind; I didn't like that. Once he pushed him down the stairs – I don't know if it was an accident – I was horrified: I said, you've got to go – after all Matthew is my son.

My six-year-old really takes the mickey. He says: use your brain, think before you speak, go and get my shoes Matthew. (Louisa Price, talking about her daughter, 13, and her three other sons, aged 25, 19, and 6. Her handicapped son Matthew is 10.)

How particular children react to a disabled brother or sister will depend on many factors and is subject to the same rivalries and tensions which develop within 'normal' families. Growing up with, and becoming familiar with, disability can give children a rare sensitivity, understanding and gentleness, just as effectively as it can bring out their brutal side. The relationships which develop between siblings and a handicapped brother or sister are often loving and protective.

Care in the community – money, services and support

Research has shown that having a disabled child often leads to long-term and chronic financial hardship, especially among families who are already on low incomes. Most families can expect to be relatively hard up during the years when the children are young and when there is only one wage-earner, but the parents can usually look forward to being more comfortably off once the children grow up. Families with disabled children do not have this option: as one researcher, writing in 1985, put it, they can become permanently held at what is normally the poorest stage of the family life-cycle.

These families suffer further losses of earning power if the fathers refuse promotion or overtime, or take less well-paid, more convenient work in order to cope with the pressures of bringing up a disabled child: one survey showed that men with disabled children earned on average £8.20 a week (1978 figures) less than other fathers.

They also have all the extra expenses which bringing up a disabled child can entail, in terms of extra clothes, bedding, special footwear, extra transport, special toys and even the extra wear on carpets and furniture. One large-scale and detailed study, first published in 1981, indicated that such families on an average income spend about £15 a week (1984 prices) on extra costs.

These additional financial costs are considerably more than the support parents receive from the state allowances and benefits that are available. One of the main problems is that there is no single allowance which specifically addresses the problems of disabled children: families have to claim the same disability allowances as everyone else – allowances where age-limits have often been fixed arbitrarily. This means, for example, that there is no statutory cash help available for any disabled child under two years old*. The qualifying age for the Mobility Allowance is five, even though for many families transport costs in the first few years of a child's life are a major problem; the Mobility Allowance also excludes many children who may be technically able to walk but who have difficulties doing so because of severe mental handicap or behavioural problems. The Attendance Allowance, introduced in 1971 for anyone in need of constant care, is only payable to disabled children aged two or over, even though costs in the first year of life tend to be very heavy, particularly because of hospital visits and men's earning losses; in addition, families whose children have to go into hospital for four weeks or more, temporarily lose this allowance, even though they may have to travel to hospital for lengthy visits and pay child-minding costs for their other children. And, since this Allowance places a premium on dependence, it penalises children who strive to be independent.

As is the case with other carers, many families either do not know about the benefits which are available or do not claim them, sometimes because they feel that doing so carries a stigma. Others do not fulfil the stringent conditions attached to benefits such as the Attendance Allowance.

There has only been one initiative taken in recent years which was specifically aimed at families with disabled children. The Family Fund, set up in 1973 after the Thalidomide scandal had drawn attention to the plight of all

* The present government has accepted that there is a case for giving more financial help to families with severely disabled children under two. But it has put off taking any action about this until the survey of people with disabilities, undertaken by the Office of Population Censuses and Surveys, is completed.

disabled children, has been a valuable source of one-off financial help: for buying expensive items such as washing machines or extra bedding, for example. But the Fund, set up by the government but administered by a charitable trust, is discretionary, and cannot fill the gaps in social security and service provision for disabled children.

In addition, it was only recently – in June 1986 – that most mothers of disabled children were granted compensation for loss of earnings through the Invalid Care Allowance. Before this date, married women were ineligible for the ICA. It has also been predicted that the system of income support which is currently being introduced to replace supplementary benefit may hit some low-income families with a disabled child.

The practical support provided to families with disabled children is not only inadequate: research shows that it is at an even lower level than that provided to elderly people and their carers. For example, families with a disabled child are unlikely to be receiving the Home Help Service, and much less likely than other carers to be visited by a district nurse; more important, the evidence indicates that health visitors – who should be playing a key role – have little contact with them.

I've got a health visitor who came along and said, you need help; she promised to help but she made it worse. She said I had the wrong kind of nappies and she'd switch them; the next thing I knew I wasn't getting any nappies. I was desperate. When I phoned up, they said they'd been cancelled. She'd cancelled them without ordering any others.

You're told what's wrong in the hospital, then you're left to get on with it. Parents like us are sent away, pushed to one side, left high and dry. (Christine Martin)

A decent education?

I don't like special schools: they're not helping children. There's a lot of time wasted: instead of teaching them how to cross roads, they spend time slapping paint on paper; they're not going to get anywhere like that. The children have got potential, but they're not being worked out, they're regressing.

The children aren't matched properly: if a child can talk a bit, he should be with children who can talk even more, but they don't group them like that. If another child starts making noises, Matthew comes home doing it; if the child's crawling, he starts crawling. Despite the hassles, I'd rather have my child at a normal school. I know he's not going to be academic, but he'd have to learn because it's so competitive. I've been the one who's had to teach him his name, address, where he lives and his phone number. (Louisa Price)

The last two decades have seen some improvements in education for disabled children: gone are the days when they had no right to schooling, when many were dismissed as ineducable, and when thousands more received no education at all. Today, thanks to legislation passed in 1971 mentally impaired children have access to specially trained teachers, facilities and new teaching methods; while the 1981 Education Act, based on the Warnock report, gave all children with special needs the right to individual assessment and an appropriate education, whatever their disability. Segregation in special schools is also beginning to disappear.

But, despite this progress, parents still face problems over their child's schooling. Many still feel that their children – especially those who are mentally impaired – are being siphoned off into segregated 'dumping grounds', and not encouraged to reach their full potential; while others worry that the moves towards integration into mainstream education mean that their children may lose out, get neglected or 'go under', unless ordinary schools are provided with the specialist facilities and resources they need.

Despite the substantial legal rights they were granted under the 1981 Act, parents are also kept in the dark by many local authorities about their children's schooling: one recent survey of education authorities found that only one-third even inform parents about their rights to be consulted over their child's education, and half fail to tell parents anything about the assessment process itself. Parents are also not told about their children's legal right to stay at school until they are 19, and their right to continuing education –

something which may be crucial for a child with learning difficulties.

Out of school

Just as they're just beginning to know what they want, they're dragged out of school and put into ATCs (Adult Training Centres); they are literally put on a production line, doing mindless industrial tasks – counting out ball bearings, putting together colostomy bags. At 19, she'll have to go to an ATC, a dump. Training for what exactly? Most stay there the rest of their lives; they don't move on anywhere. (Margaret Tass, mother of Rosa, 19).

Worries over schooling are followed by even more anxiety for most of these parents: what will their child do next? Leaving school is a crucial period, a time when a young disabled adult faces an uncertain future: in the past school leaving was the time when admissions to mental handicap hospitals peaked. It is also the time when services and support from local authorities tend to be at a minimum; although the Disabled Person's Act 1986 contains clauses which will force local authorities to assess the needs of disabled school-leavers, and should therefore help to relieve the burden which parents face.

For the moment, though, some parents have no option but to have children who have left school – especially those with severe behavioural problems – at home all day. Other mentally impaired young adults may still be shunted into the glorified production lines which are called Adult Training Centres – or, if they are lucky and able enough, into low-paid casual work. Despite the government's (widely ignored) quota scheme, whereby disabled people should form 3 per cent of the workforce of larger companies, most disabled young people will find it difficult to earn a proper living. Instead, once they have left school, they are forced to rely on social security benefits, which are usually inadequate; many remain financially dependent on their parents.

Growing up

He's been maturing over the last two years. He's become sexually aware; which is another problem – he's inclined to expose himself, want to show everybody. When I tell him, you don't touch your willy, he says, it's mine not yours! (Louisa Price)

He loves jigging about. Most weeks he's got a different girl's name – he's quite keen on the girls. He likes to think he's got girlfriends. Sometimes he asks me: Mum, why haven't I got a wife? I say (laughs) well, no one will have you. (Patsy Brown)

The transition their offspring make from childhood to adulthood is one which most parents find difficult; but it can be especially so for parents who have been single-handedly caring for a child for years, and who may have acted as their nurse as well as their parent. Nowhere is this more true than in the realm of sexuality. Sex is a powerful issue because it involves fundamental notions of individuality, independence, freedom and identity, and it raises the question of how we view disabled people: whether we transform them into objects of 'care' and pity or see them as people with the same physical and emotional needs as everyone else.

In the past, the idea that disabled people might have sexual desires was viewed with fear and distaste, or morbid curiosity. Thanks partly to the confusion between mental illness and mental impairment, mentally disabled people have always been the subject of myths about their 'animalistic' and 'uncontrollable' sexuality, attitudes which partly derive from the once widely-held theory that 'defectives' should be stopped from breeding. Today, as we have become more open about sexuality in general, ideas have changed and many now recognise that disabled people have the same emotional and physical needs as everyone else.

However, this has left many older parents in a dilemma: some deny that their disabled children have sexual feelings, while others worry about mentally handicapped daughters being exploited, or getting pregnant, a fear which has been highlighted by the recent debates over the sterilisation of mentally handicapped young women.

She has a Down's syndrome boyfriend, they enjoy a cuddle; they say I'm going to marry you darling – it's a nice caring relationship. But there are problems: I've caught her having a good play with herself; I've told her, you can't do that in public. We're a very tactile family, so Rosa is used to being stroked and tickled. That places her at risk: there could be someone out there who's going to abuse her. (Margaret Tass)

The problem of 'letting go' is not just confined to the area of sexuality: as ideas about disability change, young disabled adults are rightly being encouraged to run their own lives and live more independently. This can raise problems for parents who have looked after them.

Parents are always accused of being overprotective these days – but they're the ones who have to bear the consequences of taking risks. You're the one who bears the brunt if your son gets lost and the police bring him home. (Philippa Russell, Voluntary Council for Handicapped Children)

Adolescence is also the time when other people shy even further away from disability, especially from mental handicap, which is so often confused with mental illness; when, for instance, the Down's syndrome boy who was always thought so lovable as a child ('they're so affectionate') may now appear to be a large and powerful adolescent whom outsiders think odd or even frightening.

People are kind on the surface but I know they're afraid of him. Most of them are. Even my sister. Nobody's been nasty or anything but we feel they look at you sideways. (Margaret Mason, mother of Kevin, 26, physically and mentally disabled by brain damage)

Leaving home

For an able-bodied child, one of the biggest steps to independence is leaving home – whether that means getting married, moving into his or her own flat or moving away to college or university. Yet despite all the policies aimed at 'normalisation', setting up home is one right not extended to most disabled young people, who have no choice but to stay with their parents. A range of group homes, flats and hostels are being developed to replace hospital beds, but their numbers are still inadequate, and they are mainly designed for those coming out of hospital, not for children already living with their parents. And because many boroughs have not yet developed their own community facilities, living away from home may, for a disabled young adult, mean moving to a totally different part of the country – something which can be a traumatic experience for both parent and child.

The system of disability benefits can also make it difficult for a disabled child to leave home: many families exist on a complex – and often precarious – package of benefits and allowances which have over the years become an essential part of the family income. They may have helped to replace parental loss of earnings and opportunities, for example, or to top up supplementary benefit or a reduced pension. Once such a system has been established, it is often financially difficult for a family to survive without it, as it would be forced to do if a child left to live elsewhere.

Some parents feel so protective, that even if a place in 'the community' is offered they find it difficult to let a child go, or feel guilty about doing so. There is also concern about standards in many group homes.

They're very kind at the hostel, but when he comes back from a week there I don't feel he's as clean as he could be; he usually comes back losing somthing. (Ted Brown, Patsy's husband and father of Simon)

The first time away from home she cried all weekend. Also I had this terrific guilt: I thought it was the first step to putting her away. You go home and she's not there, you feel terribly lonely. There are six of them in the group home and a member of staff who sleeps in. Social services are looking at ways of cutting corners, and now there's this suggestion that it doesn't need 24-hour staffing; so they'd be left to their own devices. (Margaret Tass, whose daughter Rosa now lives most of the time in a hostel)

Letting go

He's settled down pretty well, but I feel terrible: I feel I've lost an arm and a leg. When someone's so dependent on you, in a way you depend on their dependency. He's a lovely boy; everything was geared to him. (Olive Wylie, whose son John has just gone to residential college. She was almost grieving the loss)

Most boys leave home at 17 or 18, to live on their own; that's what I'd like for Matthew. But then I think: it would be nice if he doesn't – when the normal ones go at least I'll have Matthew. It's selfish I know, but we're all selfish. (Louisa Price)

The intense and prolonged relationships which build up between disabled children and their parents, and the disadvantages and isolation they face in the world outside, can lead to the development of emotional bonds which have more to do with mutual dependency than disability. It could be argued that the nature of the parent/child relationship means parents are not always the best people to be supporting disabled adult children. Perhaps in the future, young disabled adults and their parents will be offered options for living which will enable them to separate emotionally.

I'd say (to someone in a similar position), give yourself until they're 18, then you've earned the rest of your life to yourself. Get them into a school or sheltered housing. OK, they may not dress as well as you dress them; they may not shave; but at least they're doing it themselves. (Meg Townsend, mother of John, 32, brain-damaged at birth)

The future

For the future I'm a very determined person. I will never accept Matthew the way he is: I'm working very hard to make him fit in; I will do as much as I can, until the day I die, to make him as independent as possible. There might come a time when he goes to college – I hope so – when he might decide he will live in the community. I'm hoping he will be able to work, to look after himself, to look after a bed-sit. I'm even hoping he'll get married and provide me with grandchildren. People think I'm crazy when I say this, but these are my aims and I've got to aim high. (Louisa Price)

The number of children with severe disabilities has increased in recent years, although whether this will continue is uncertain. As medical technology becomes more sophisticated, it is likely that growing numbers of children with certain kinds of disabilities will survive into adulthood: better surgical techniques and neo-natal care facilities, for example, will mean that more premature, low birth-weight babies, who are at more risk of disability, will survive. Other developments, however, such as improvements in pre-natal screening facilities and the availability of abortion, may mean a drop in the number of children born with severe malformations of the central nervous system.

What is certain is that disabled children born today can expect to live well beyond the lifespan previously expected of them; many will survive into old age. As to the future: the closure of the large 'subnormality' hospitals and the moves towards independence for disabled people are optimistic signs that, in the long term, society will take a more positivie view of disabled children. In the short term, and under the present government, it is debatable whether they or their families will get the resources they need, and to which, morally, they have every right.

Love and regret

I have enormous respect for Annette. She's very dignified. The only way any distress can be seen is through her eyes: have a look at her eyes – they're clear and bright. One of my mates in the post office asked: why do you bother with her? I said: well, primarily love and hope. He said: what does that mean, define it. I thought for a moment. I said: to love someone is to know the worst but only see the best; to hope is to seek a way to change the worst and bring out the best. (Edward Oliver)

I just love her, I think she's great. She's a character; she's the one that keeps you laughing, that's quickest to forgive. (Margaret Tass)

I just wish sometimes he was normal. (Christine Martin)

7

Growing older: Elderly parents caring for their adult children

With an elderly person there is an end to it: they're not going to go on much longer than 95; whereas with us, the only thing which is going to put an end to it is our own deaths. (Bill Clifford, 65, father of Peter, 39, who has cerebral palsy)

Some 50,000 parents are believed to be looking after severely disabled adult offspring; an estimated 10,000 of these parents are elderly, with children who are nearing middle age. They have already spent a lifetime looking after their children; many, like the father quoted above, know that caring is a burden from which they will never be free.

In those days

In those days there was no special provision, either in terms of education or medicine, there was nothing. There was nothing; no special treatment at all. It meant a fight for most of us: for medicine, education, for what happens after leaving school. Nowadays they would start training someone from the age of a few weeks, so they couldn't develop the wrong pattern of doing things. They know so much more. (Bella Clifford, 66, Peter's mother)

They did these IQ tests to determine if it was worthwhile tyring to educate them. If the IQ was less than fifty, it wasn't justified to try and spend the money. (George Burford, 71, whose 39-year-old son Charles was brain-injured after contracting meningitis when he was 10 months old. Charles was classed as ineducable and never went to school; instead he went to a junior training centre)

In those years, there weren't any societies, you felt alone. I didn't know there were centres they could go to, didn't know anything about it at all. You didn't meet other mothers. Other mothers walked their children to school, he was picked up in a taxi. You felt a bit alone. (Patsy Brown)

138

Vic and May Hopkins

Vic and May Hopkins' only son Gary, 25, has cerebral palsy, a disorder of movement and muscles caused by brain damage. He has no control over his balance, wears irons and uses a wheel chair – although he can get about a little inside the house with a stick and some support. He needs to be washed, shaved and bathed; and has to have his bowels evacuated. He can be left for about an hour. Gary's great hobby is music of all sorts. 'There's not much you can teach him music-wise; he's got all the records and discs, classical and anything else – he devotes his life to it,' says Vic Hopkins.

Vic is 66 and retired from his job in the electronics industry. He has an ulcerated leg, which he plays down but which makes walking difficult, and he loses his breath quickly. His wife is 50 and has had two nervous breakdowns: one when Gary was seven and another a few years ago. Every afternoon, she travels to Kingston to look after her mother, disabled by arthritis. 'My whole life's been my son and looking after my mother,' she says. 'I have had a lot of worry all my life; I looked after my mum and dad when I was young. I haven't had what you would call a happy life, not as such. I've had a hard life, it's not been easy.'

There are no other children, although Mrs Hopkins says she would have liked to have had more. 'That's one thing we couldn't have – I was told it wasn't advisable,' says her husband.

They live in Surbiton, in a council house with an upstairs lavatory: which means every time Gary wants to go his father has to lift him up the stairs. They thought about an extension but were 'put off by all the forms'. Since Vic's retirement they share Gary's care. Vic says that when he was working the entire burden fell on his wife, who, before they got the mobility allowance and a car, used to carry Gary about everywhere. 'By the time I came home at six o'clock she used to be absolutely whacked. If we didn't have the car we'd be in Queer Street completely; we'd only be able to push him up the road and back.'

Every day is the same routine: they get Gary out of bed, washed, dressed and ready for his day at the local Spastics Society work centre; at 12.30 Mrs Hopkins leaves for her mother's. 'I think she (her mother) feels she'd rather have her daughter than other people,' says Vic. 'You know what elderly people are like; they don't want strangers coming in. I can't expect her to do miracles (here); she's got enough to do going down to her mother's.' At 4.15 Gary comes home and they have dinner: 'By the time we've cleared up and washed up it's usually about 6.45 before we've sat down.' Gary goes upstairs to bed at 9 p.m.

I ask them if they've had any support from social or health services. 'Good gracious me no, love; we never had any help, we've done it all ourselves.' Financially it has been a struggle. 'His boots and irons: I used to have his boots and irons soled and heeled; it used to cost me a bomb.'

Mr Hopkins does most of the talking. His wife, he says, had a difficult labour, a breech delivery and an emergency Caesarean. 'I was asked whether I wanted a baby or wanted my wife saved. I said, a baby is all well and good but I want my wife saved every time. They said, we'll see what we can do, Mr Hopkins, we'll try and save them both.' At first, they were told Gary was 'perfectly all right'; it was about eight or nine months before they realised something was wrong. He couldn't see his parents; he didn't sit up for about two or three years, and couldn't hold his head up. The hospital, however, wouldn't give any details. 'If I knew then what I know now through my GP, I would have had them,' says Mr Hopkins. 'I think it's just fate, you can't blame anybody,' says his wife. 'I don't think you came blame anyone.' One of the worse problems, he says, is that they can never find any company for their son.

People don't realise and they don't want to realise. You start to speak about these things – they couldn't care a damn, it's a waste of my breath. The people next door, they couldn't care a damn. One old chap, he's 80-odd, he'll have a chat (with Gary). But people in general: they might see him out – it's, hello Gary, and that's about all. They don't make no conversation with him. The poor little devil makes his own conversation.

On Sundays now, my wife's down her mother's all day; I don't see much of her at all. That poor little devil is up in his bedroom with his music and tapes, all on his own. I've been trying to get someone in, someone to come and listen to it with him. You try and get someone in: it's impossible. He says he doesn't mind being on his own; I think he does. You try to get someone round . . . I hope your book brings this home to someone.

Frankly, I think the future, it's very bleak. Because I can't see: if anything happens to me, my wife would cope up to a certain point; but Gary is so much older (now), much heavier, she won't be able to

140

cope. Then, on the other hand, what's going to happen when both of us go? What will happen if anything happens to us? If they send him where I think they want to send him, I'd soon put a stop to it. I don't want him out in the desert, to that one (hostel) in Leatherhead; it's miles from anywhere. It's like in the old days when they stuck anyone disabled miles from anywhere. It's a colossal place, about eight miles away from any shops. I think he (Gary) does think about the future sometimes: he speaks to me sometimes about it; I say, I'll manage, don't you worry my boy, don't you worry.

Would they like to see him married?

We have hopes – we often talk about this. I don't know what chance there is, I wouldn't like to say. I would like to see him, very much so, being taken care of by other people, but the chances are . . . unless some good capable person comes along.

Where music is concerned: that's his life, his music. He gets a little bit of money, he gets what he wants and he's as happy as a sandboy. But that is *all* what he has in life. I'd like to see the poor little devil have more entertainment, go out more, get friends in.

I get the impression that once you're disabled, once you've got a disabled person in the family, nobody really wants to know you. You lose friends generally in your own way of life. You've either got to put yourself out and talk to them or you just get completely ignored and that's it. Say we want to go out for a night and you ask someone to come in; they'll say, oh yes, they'll do just that. But as soon as you mention they are a disabled person, they'll find an excuse immediately: I'm sorry I've got to do so-and-so tomorrow, this and that. Straight away, you're finished.

They'll come with pleasure if it's a normal child, but as soon as they know it's disabled, they don't want to know. The simple reason is they don't know how to cope: in case he has a fit, or a stomach upset or something like that. The old chap next door – he's 85; I know he would do it for a couple of hours. It's the same tomorrow: I've got to go to Woking, for a funeral, and my wife has to go down her mother's, so supposing I'm not back in time?

It's always been the same, for years and years and years. It never alters and it never will. Except years ago when if you were disabled you were put in the workhouse and that was it. Unfortunately, it's going back that way: look at the hostel in Leatherhead, who'd want to go there? What entertainment is there, where is there to go?

141

Nowhere. It's all newly built, but it's so cut-off. The attitude is: they're disabled people, that's it, get them out of the way.

Supposing, though, a suitable place was found for Gary?

The effect on us would be tremendous. It's no good saying it wouldn't because it would. Until you got used to it. If he wanted to go, I wouldn't stop him – provided the place was clean and tidy and they looked after him like we looked after him. I want him looked after properly, because he didn't come into the world of his choice like that. If he left he would feel the draught just the same; although he says he wouldn't, I say he would. I say, it's no use talking like that, my boy, you won't get everything done for you like you do at home. He speaks to me sometimes about it, but a lot of it I let go in one ear and out the other, because I know it'll never happen; because I know he'll never go into the hostel while he's got a mother and father, because they wouldn't take him – even if he wanted to.

He is keener on the local hostel but says Gary is too dependent to live there; he also says it has too few staff.

The way things are going, the way things are being cut down: they've got four staff on days and two at night – two to get everyone into bed. What I've heard, some of them won't be going to bed until twelve or one o'clock because they don't have the staff to get them undressed.

He'd like to be more independent I think, but as I've said, I doubt whether he'd like it, going away. He goes away once a year for a holiday with the Scouts; he thoroughly enjoys it because he's looked after properly. We've seen the camp site: it was very, very good, with properly trained doctors and nurses on site and fully qualified helpers.

Vic and his wife once went on holiday without Gary, when he was with the Scouts.

But Gary was there; he was in your mind, wondering what he was doing. It was in his mind as well: he said, I thought of Mum, I thought of you, Dad, at such-and-so times. It was in his mind as well.

I feel sometimes that disabled people do get more irritable: they're frustrated and they've got to let off steam sometimes. If you hear what he calls me sometimes, it's nobody's business. I say (to him): I don't care, I've had fifty years in a factory, I don't care, take it out on me; but as long as you never take it out on your mother – and he doesn't, and I'm glad about that. Gary and I might have our little arguments. Nine times out of ten he comes home and says, I'm sorry Dad. I say, there's no need to say sorry, boy, forget it.

I can cope with it all right; I say I can cope with it. Some nights I feel a little bit more tired; I do get a little bit down sometimes, but I soon pull myself out of it. I just can't afford to let it get me down: I've got to keep myself going, keep on as cheerful as I can.

Coping in retirement

Even now, when I'm retired, we're very restricted in what we can do. We can go out for the day, but we have to be back by four o'clock. A lot of interests and activities: we just can't get involved in them. A lot of National Trust activities we'd have liked to get involved in, but we can't. I remember thinking: when we retire we must join the old-time dancing – but you can't do that you see. (George Burford)

When we were younger we would pride ourselves on the fact that everything Peter could do, everywhere we went, everything it was possible to do: we did it. As you get older you can't do as much yourself. The feeling is always there: if he takes on something new, what is it going to involve you in? Peter has a passionate interest in cricket; he and I have, for the last ten years, gone to Surrey County Cricket Club. But I find it more difficult now to spend a whole day watching cricket than ten years ago; then I feel guilty, because if I stop going, he'll have to. (Bill Clifford, 65, Peter's father)

Many of these older parents have the health problems common to their age group, but these are exacerbated by the constant care they have to provide for adults who are probably heavier and stronger than they are. They often feel unable to relax and enjoy their retirement; guilty for no longer having the kind of energy to do the things for their child they did when they were young; and increasingly responsible, not only for their child's physical well-being but for his or her emotional welfare as well. The social isolation of adult disabled children is one of their biggest problems.

Sometimes he spends a lot of time in his own room – but wouldn't you or I if we only had the company of our parents? This is one of the greatest troubles: if only they could live with people of their own age. (Bill Clifford)

143

He loves going out; he just can't stand being at home all the time. I have to take him out every Saturday somewhere or other; he expects to go some-where. Every Sunday, he asks where he's going to go next Saturday.

There's no one else to take him. We never see anybody here: they don't want to be involved, they don't want to know. (George Burford)

Elderly parents feel tremendously protective towards their adult disabled children and carry a heavy burden of anxiety for their future happiness. Many hope that their child will marry; will meet an 'exceptional' person, who will look after him or her and provide the only safe alternative to the loneliness and desolation of institutional care – whether provided in hospital or in 'the community'.

What happens when we die?

Let's say within the next ten years we won't be capable of looking after him any more. Even now my wife would find it very difficult on her own. He needs help with dressing and washing and toiletting and bathing. You can't leave him to go out on his own: because of his mental condition he hasn't the road sense. He doesn't know money; he can't read or write. You see, there is nothing, and no plan for anything. If the occasion arises where it is essential for him to go into care, they'd send him anywhere in the country where they could find a vacancy – it might be miles away. He's not mentally capable of worrying about that. He is aware that he will have to go somewhere; he realises this. (George Burford, talking about his son Charles, 39, brain-damaged by meningitis)

I think what worries me is: if he had to go into a home, how would he react if he had to disperse all the things he's got, a great drawer full of records, a mass of jigsaw puzzles? I think he'd prefer it if he went in while I'm alive, so I could go and visit him and get him settled in. If anything happened to George, I just couldn't manage him: he's so much bigger than I. I couldn't take him out because I can't drive and he can't get the bus. (Martha Burford, George's wife)

There is nothing, literally nothing. If we had an accident and were killed, the borough would find out where there was a residential home with a vacancy which would take him. It might be anywhere in the country, which is appalling because he wouldn't know anyone, he would have no work centre; this is the worry for all of us. You can't just leave the house so Peter

144

could go on living in it, we've got a daughter to provide for as well. Even if he could: who's going to look after him? Who's going to make sure he gets the right care? (Bella Clifford)

The major worry for all these parents is what will happen to their children when they die. In the past, as they grew older, many mentally handicapped children would have gone into the old 'subnormality' hospitals, but most of these are now closing their doors to new admissions, and are being replaced by a range of community facilities such as hostels and group homes. The development of these new facilities, however, is patchy, delayed by lack of both resources and political will, as well as by public opposition; in any case, in the main, they are designed for mentally handicapped people coming out of hospital, rather than those living at home. Moreover, many parents of severely handicapped adults, who have spent their whole lives being looked after on a one-to-one basis, feel that community hostels and homes would not provide the kind of care their children need.

The ideal solution would be a gradual transition from parental home to community facilities, while the parents of the child are still alive, so that both sides have the opportunity to adjust: the child to a more independent life, and his or her parents to a life no longer dominated by the child's needs.

Most local authorities, already overstretched by the problems raised by 'community care' and the closure of the large hospitals, have not begun to even tackle the challenge of middle-aged, handicapped adults still living at home, and neither, at the moment, are they obliged to: unlike the health authorities which ran the large hospitals, and which operated under different legislation, local authorities are under no obligation to provide residential care for their mentally handicapped adult populations. This means that many will act only when they are forced to: in an emergency, when a parent dies or grows too old to cope, at which point the handicapped adult child is likely to be removed from the home he or she has always known to wherever there is a bed –

sometimes a residential home, or 'boarding out' facilities (often in a different part of the country), or, increasingly, a private home. The private sector that caters for disabled adults is now flourishing and is thought not to be monitored adequately, giving rise to a growing anxiety about standards.

Some innovative projects to help younger handicapped adults live independently are now being developed; but they are still few and far between, and may prove irrelevant to the needs of highly dependent middle-aged disabled adults who have never lived away from home before.

Also, these projects need plenty of preparation on the part of the parents: allowing a teenage disabled child to start spending weekends away in a hostel, for example, is one way of getting everyone used to the idea of him or her going permanently. The need for that kind of preparation means that such schemes tend to be taken over by middle-class parents, who would anyway expect and prepare a 'normal' child to leave home for university, college and an independent life. In many working class and ethnic minority families, young adults, especially daughters, are not expected to leave home until they get married. This difference in outlook – as well as privilege – means that working class parents, like the Hopkins family, will have little access to, or success with, these new projects.

Accidents and injuries

Time goes so slowly. People say: is it really five years since the accident? It seems more than that to us: it seems like a lifetime. (Eileen Monkton, 56, whose son Philip, a former policeman, was severely brain-damaged in a car crash)

Another group of older parents are looking after adult children who have unexpectedly become disabled through accident, injury or illness. Probably one of the largest groups of this kind are those whose children – usually, like Philip Monkton, men in their twenties – have suffered severe head and sometimes spinal chord injuries following motorcycle or

146

car accidents. There are also thousands of parents caring for children who develop mentally disabling illnesses, such as schizophrenia, in their teens and twenties. In rare cases, parents are looking after adult children who have become severely disabled after brain haemorrhage or some other unforeseen illness.

In many ways, the problems these parents face are no different from those facing all parents of adult disabled children, except that they have to cope, late in life, with something that was completely unexpected; and, sometimes, they have to bring back into the home a child who had already made an independent life elsewhere. Acceptable alternatives to living at home are particularly difficult to find because few specialist residential facilities exist for some of these mental and behavioural disabilities: in the case of a young adult brain-damaged by head injury or illness, the alternative to being cared for at home is usually an NHS psychiatric ward or a nursing home more suited to elderly people with dementia.

Many such parents are having to cope, not only with their own misery, but with the frustration and resentment expressed by a damaged adult who is used to leading an independent life, and who is now forced back into a state of childlike dependence. For the first time in their lives, they will also have to learn to deal with numerous professionals – in the case of brain damage, with neurologists, psychologists and psychiatrists – and with services which are often sparse, fragmented and unsatisfactory. Unlike other older carers they do not have years of experience to draw on.

Most parents of disabled children have problems in obtaining professional help, but those looking after brain-damaged adults often find it impossible to obtain the intensive and long-term rehabilitation services which they so badly need. The specialist help needed, for example, to begin the painfully slow process of helping someone learn to walk, talk, or even move and think again, may be provided in the first months following an accident or illness; but in most parts

147

of the country, it is simply not available on a long-term basis.

A minority of brain-damaged adults and their families, who have won some kind of compensation claim – for medical negligence following an operation, for instance – will have the money which is needed to buy specialist private care: not only nursing care but also physiotherapy and psychological help, which can be obtained in the private sector. But, in the UK, obtaining such compensation depends on being able to prove that someone, usually a doctor, was to blame for an accident; even for those who might qualify, this usually means fighting a lengthy and difficult battle through the courts. There is no 'no fault' compensation scheme available for those who, like Philip Monkton, are damaged by accident.

This means that, like most carers, these parents are dependent on welfare benefits. Not only that, they also have to stand in line for NHS rehabilitation services, such as physiotherapy or occupational and speech therapy; and wait months for the occasional visit to scarce specialist facilities, which might be miles away.

Many parents will devote their own time and energy – often sacrificing their jobs and the rest of their lives – to providing the physical and mental stimulation that may help their child at least gain recovery of some of his or her faculties; often at the expense of their own health, and with little support from statutory services. Unfortunately, the complex relationship between parents and children suggests that, in many cases, they may be the wrong people to be doing it.

Ray and Eileen Monkton

Eileen Monkton nursed her son Philip for a year after his car accident. Throughout that time he was in hospital, unable to speak or move; she did everything for him at first – even working to get him to swallow. Now he lives at home with his parents: he can just about shower, dress, get out of bed, move from his wheelchair to his toilet seat, and make himself understood.

Ray Monkton, Philip's father, is an agitated, nervous man, who

148

smokes constantly; he says he cries a lot. He took partial early retirement from his job as a factory inspector to spend more time with his son, and is currently fighting a compensation case on his son's behalf. He has recently had several operations for cancer of the bowel, a disease which he believes has been brought on by stress. 'As a pilot in the RAF I had two crashes. I walked away – no problem. But now: you get uptight, blow up for the slightest reason.'

Eileen Monkton:

The worst thing is obviously the lack of short-term memory. He has long-term memory: he can remember when he was seven years old, when we lived in Cheshire; he even told me how he went to the end of the road and turned right to get to school – he knew exactly how to get there. We took him (back) to the senior school; do you remember the headmaster, we asked, and the music master who everyone adored – he vaguely remembered him.

He doesn't remember much after that, though. He can remember the names of people, but can't put faces to them. He wasn't in the police long enough for it to really sink in: we took him to the police station – it just didn't register at all.

In fact, it was a long time before he remembered us. He had this blank look in his eye at first. I was there bathing him; the nurse suddenly turned and said, he knows it's his mum. He immediately looked round and there was some recognition. I thought: yes, he does know me.

He can read, but, because he has no short-term memory, by the time he's reached the bottom of the page he's forgotten the beginning. He can't enjoy a story. But he can play a game of chess; and bridge – you need a memory for bridge. This is instinct: he's always liked playing bridge. With head injury, the concentration lasts for such a short time, even with something they really enjoy. With bridge, he'll sit down and really enjoy it. What life is left though? – just sitting down and playing bridge and cards; it's not that rewarding.

We've had the piano teacher in to revise his piano playing; that all comes back – that's long-term memory. It's the short-term memory: he's got to learn everything and do it enough times so it will stick in his mind.

The problem with something like brain injury: it takes a special expertise and knowledge, you have to track people down. He got into some intensive rehabilitation at Wimbledon; we had a very long wait, but skilled staff are few and far between. It was a great ordeal for us, travelling to Wimbledon, 120 miles there and back every weekend.

More physiotherapy, this is what we need; it would take so much weight off our shoulders. There's that place in Hungary; people have sold up and gone to live there so that their children can go to this school.

No one's said, do this or that; it's what we've worked out all the time, it's what we think should be done – because we've had no advice. I'll get an article and read it to him, ask him questions, but no one's actually offered anything. When he was at Wimbledon, because he'd been in horticulture, they gave him lots of jobs pricking out the tomato plants. He gets fed up with that; it's not easy to do if you're spastic in one hand.

He hasn't any friends, he wasn't in the police force long enough to make friends. There's no on to say: right, I'll take you to the pub – this is the problem. There's nowhere he can meet people, not people of his own age – this is what he needs. Everywhere he goes, we have to take him.

The one thing which really upsets you: he can't get a girlfriend, he so desperately wants one. Any young lady who comes here, he'll look to see if they're married. I say: you might meet someone even yet. He'll say: what age was Dad when he got married. I'll say: he was 28. He'll say: I've still got a year or so to go.

It's a miracle if they (women) can fall in love with someone like that; they'd have to be an exceptional person. It has happened; look at that person (on TV) the other day, the lady with Thalidomide who married and had a baby. Obviously she was like that when he met her, and they've managed to make a life for themselves.

I'm fortunate Ray hasn't said, I'll leave you to it. We're at each other's throats more than we used to be, because of the stress of it all. Ray is definitely packing up work completely at the end of the year; he wants to spend more time with Philip. I don't know whether that's a good thing or not: at least his work takes his mind off it. I feel Ray needs to rest, but he won't take advice; there'll be arguments if I try to stop him from doing too much.

We do feel suicidal sometimes. Philip says: I sometimes wonder if I'm the lucky one out of that car crash, whether I'd be better off dead. I'm usually too choked to reply.

Ray Monkton:

The worst thing is his reactions – when he starts to hit his head against the wall and scream. He's never gone for anyone else, always himself. If you've seen or heard this, it just rips your guts out; you stand there wondering what to do. And often you don't know, you don't understand what you've done wrong, you've been trying to help.

He always flew off the handle quickly. He still does, but more so now. We're so emotionally involved, it's our only child. Everyone said he'd do well in the police, he'd found his niche. Everyone said he'd do well; it's really hit us so hard.

He'll sit and listen to any kind of music, he used to sing in the choir and play the cello; he loved music – one of the reasons why we thought he might have a go now. We've got a cello here; it cost me £150, which we paid for. We've had to work very hard for the money: will you play it? we asked. Yes, he said. But he doesn't – I've got to make him.

I used to take Philip swimming at the public baths. I used to carry him into the water, literally. He has great guts: he would be drinking the water and screaming with frustration. If you keep talking with them, excite them, aggravate them, it all helps.

Reggie and Kate Garton

Reggie and Kate Garton are in their seventies and live in a spacious, elegant flat in the centre of London. Two years ago their daughter Gill, 43, suffered a massive brain haemorrhage which virtually destroyed her memory. Once an ambitious academic and poet, with a string of degrees behind her, she is now unable to hold a conversation, to remember to go to the toilet, or to go out alone: she would never be able to find the way home.

Gill got a first-class honours degree in English at Oxford and has lectured at universities in the UK and the USA. Her life, however, has not been without its difficulties: she had had a drink problem for about ten years; had been through a brief and unsuccessful marriage to an American academic; and she suffered from Crohn's disease, a severe disorder of the bowel. At the time of her brain haemorrhage, she had just taken early retirement from a lectureship at a British university, ostensibly to concentrate on writing poetry; but 'it was partly because they wanted to get rid of her,' her mother says later.

'She was extremely disruptive in the department, always having ideas which probably rocked the boat like mad. You know what university's like: people who have ideas always make others feel uncomfortable. Partly they wanted to get rid of her.'

On Christmas Eve 1984, Gill was taken into hospital coughing up blood and suffering from a bad headache; by Christmas Day she was very withdrawn and barely able to speak; by the day after Boxing Day she had fallen into a coma and had to undergo a major operation for a subdural haematoma – massive bleeding in the head. She was in intensive care until February and then spent four months in rehabilitation at a specialist unit, during which time she managed to get back on her feet and retrieve the beginnings of speech. She was finally discharged in June 1985, and has been living with her parents ever since.

Gill spends most of her time reading – anything from French poetry to old comics, none of which she really understands – and watching television. Now a large woman, whose speech is slow and who walks heavily, she has little motivation and gets easily frustrated and bad tempered. Her parents are proud of her past academic achievements: 'At Oxford she was the youngest Senate member, that sort of thing,' says her father. 'She's an unpublished poet; she wrote some very good poetry. We're in the process of trying to get it published.'

The Gartons both come from upper-middle-class backgrounds. He was in the Navy, and they spent the first twenty years of their marriage moving around the world, until he took an Admiralty post in 1959. Small, thin, upright and impeccably polite, he has, since his retirement, been awarded an OBE for his voluntary services to the NHS and to charity. He speaks first, concentrating mainly on the treatment Gill has received at the hands of the NHS. The Gartons have spent the last two years taking her to, and getting second opinions from, a variety of neurologists, psychologists and psychiatrists. They have learnt from a clinical psychologist in Oxford that, although Gill is mentally handicapped and amnesiac, she still retains much of her intelligence and her background knowledge. The same psychologist told them, however, that little more can be done for her.

Reggie Garton is obviously dissatisfied with the health service: one consultant neurologist treating Gill refused to have anything to do with her parents. 'He was a research chap. He was interested in *the patient as a specimen. He wasn't interested in us because we couldn't contribute to his research.'* What no one told them for some time, he says, was that Gill *'has absolutely no memory, she's totally amnesiac; she can't find her way round, can't remember anything. We were never given the real prognosis – I don't believe they knew.'* The current lack of knowledge about brain injuries is, he believes, compounded by a refusal to communicate by the professionals. *'In brief there is a tremendous gap in sympathy for the people caring, trying to use their common sense, trying to use such skills as they have. Even with my knowledge of the health service I couldn't do very much. I absolutely shudder to think what most people (do): they must just give up'.*

Mrs Garton describes their daily lives in more intimate and more graphic terms. Gill, she says, *'can do everything. She can walk, but she doesn't know where she's walking. She can dress, she can eat properly; although now she eats like a pig. She's extremely greedy because everything she eats she thinks it's the first time she's eaten – if there's a biscuit on the table (she'll have it). She can bath herself, she can wash her hair.'* She's also doubly incontinent (Gill could not re-learn continence, she says, *'because she doesnt "get the ping on it" like the rest of us').* *'She could cook but I won't let her cook because it's so difficult for me. She can make her bed. The operative word there is can.'*

The main problem, says Mrs Garton, is not just loss of memory, but complete lack of motivation.

I don't suppose she'd ever go to bed unless someone told her to. She certainly wouldn't get up. Most of the time she sits and reads: anything from the cereal packet to Italian or French poetry. She can read all sorts of things; but she has no idea what she's read; no idea what she's seen on TV. She plays draughts, she plays patience with me, mahjong. She cannot write – nothing comes out of her head and this distresses her terribly.

She asks for nothing: she asks for absolutely nothing – except food occasionally. If we're drinking coffee, she'll say, I want something to eat. You'll say, but darling. She's put on four stone since she left (the hospital). She used to be so slim, so petite. I should think it's compensatory, don't you?

She doesn't come forward with anything. Occasionally, when her friends come in – she hasn't got many left – she will chip in. Her speech is terrible; she's terribly lazy. The only way I can get her out is to go shopping. She walks badly too.

What was she like before? She was fantastically good-looking, terribly slim and petite; she was an academic climber: when she was successful it was never enough. This you hear of quite often; we had another friend who was brilliant – he had a drink problem because he thought he was never achieving enough. This was Gill's problem: she never felt she was getting where she ought to be. She had a personality which went down very well, lovely manners; she was very kindly about people in distress. Her students adored her, absolutely adored her; she always had time for them. In the last year, before she retired (from university), she got five firsts among her students.

She was passionately involved: nuclear disarmament, apartheid, unemployment. She was also very knowledgeable about all the arts, well-informed. She had an absolutely vibrant personality; the Americans loved her, they loved her liveliness and ideas. At the time she was ill she was looking for a job in America. I think, once she'd retired, she felt there'd be more scope there.

She's never been happy – at least that's my summing up. I feel she's never been happy. She was a feminist – very much so – but she would have loved children; the domestic life would have suited her very well. She belonged to a generation which didn't, which couldn't, have both. Today's women can choose both if they want to, but she was just ten years too early, and she chose a career. She was bitterly lonely. By the time you're 40 you're rather scraping the bottom of the barrel, and you tend to bring in anyone who will ease your loneliness; and if there is no one you'll bring in a bottle of vodka.

We talked the same language: she would ring me up to say, I've just written another poem, can you listen to it. I terribly miss Gill's intellectual stimulation, it used to be wonderful; I was always getting intelligent ideas from her. I miss that very much. Gill and I; at times, I suppose, we used to screen Reggie out – we'd talk about poetry and literature. We were totally, totally equal – except that she was more intelligent than me. We've always used Christian names, always looked on each other as friends.

I always wanted a daughter, and, with the weakness of parents, I wanted her to do all the things I hadn't been able to do. I suspect – if one had to confess one's sins to one's Maker before one died –

probably the only thing was that I pushed Gill probably too hard; she must have felt these expectations; it probably added to her feeling of not achieving.

Kate Garton herself has never had a career, and only worked outside the home in later years, as a domestic bursar.

I was a service wife you see, one moved around. I suppose I was a doctor *manquée*; I'd loved to have been a doctor, but my parents didn't think it a good idea that a girl should be trained in anything.

Since the illness my husband has been absolutely marvellous. With all the information he's got about the health service he's invaluable. He knows exactly who to approach, when to approach them and when not to. It's made him very tired. Living with the worry: he'll be exhausted. Emotionally it hasn't changed him at all. Has it changed me? I don't know. When I'm tired, I'm more short-tempered. I think I've always had a very, very swift temper, but it was under control for many years; it's not as under control as it was.

It hasn't done anything to our relationship in any way at all – it certainly hasn't done that. We're totally different: we disagree, occasionally we get cross; when one gets tired, one gets cross – but no way has the bond been damaged. One's not just holding together because it's necessary, but because we're very fond of each other and we are both sharing this burden, this burden of sorrow, really.

We've divided the work. Reggie does all the washing – all of it, the whole of it – and the ironing and everything. He's always been absolutely wonderful, you almost have to chase him away. He does all the cleaning – I do a bit. The reason we don't have anyone in, is it's more trouble than it's worth. I do all the shopping and cooking. We share trying to take Gill out. I have to go away occasionally – he's perfectly capable of handling her.

I get up myself about twenty to eight. I am myself then, as I'm talking to you. About 9.30 I say to Reggie, I must get Gill up. I go in and I can hear my voice change completely. I become a nanny: 'Come on darling it's time we got up. All right now, if I leave you on your own? I'll get you some coffee'. That's how it's changed me.

I think probably I treat her too much like a child. She's too comfortable here, therefore she won't make the effort. There are times when she hates me, when she says: I don't care if you do die. The next minutes she says: Kate, I do love you so much.

155

One is fairly proud: I can't bear her going out looking like a slut, with her hair untidy or her face dirty. I was washing her hair (recently) when she became particularly difficult – my temper snapped and I slapped her. She quite rightly reacted very strongly, she's very big now, about 11 stone; she went for me. As she always did when she first came out of hospital, she went for me, pushed me and bent my back over. Fortunately, I've got Reggie to shout for.

At our age, one expects to live one's own life. Instead we're looking after a highly intelligent child; a woman who is much more intelligent than we are, but who can't even remember to clean her teeth, go to the loo, who can't remember how many pads to put on or when to come for meals.

I think one of the ghastly things is: nobody seems to understand the strain, mainly emotional, when you've got a middle-aged person that you're looking after. There's terribly little comprehension of the sudden mess-up of one's life when this happens in advancing years. You hear of people – one woman, her son of 19 had a driving accident and lost his memory – but this woman was the same age as Gill; she had a husband and other children; there was a nuclear family to support her. Then parents who are looking after Down's syndrome – a great deal has been done for these people. There's very little comprehension of what happens at the age of 65 or 70; you're presented with an extraordinary tragedy which causes you to alter your whole life.

If it's a husband or wife ill, you can probably call on your peer group, your friends, to support you – we can't get anybody. If I call people in they're my age, and it's the wrong age for Gill. I'm missing terriby the peer group, that's one of the hardest things, the peer group. Who at 43 wants to sit and talk to a 70-year old? I've got a lot of good friends in the parish, but they're not really Gill's sort.

Yes, it's very isolated. I more than Reggie, because Reggie's not gregarious and I am. We've got three good friends who drop in occasionally – being service people we haven't got many friends round here.

I'd just started having rather posh dinner parties. I did rather exciting cooking asking the local judge, those sort of people. I can't have dinner parties, I'm not free to. I can't go to the church at the time when all my friends are there; I can't go out on the spur of the moment. I miss being able to go to 9.30 church, where I'd be surrounded by friends, the family church. I have to go at 8.

156

The major effect? One's sadness. One lives with sorrow. Not from day to day, day to day is easy. I live with the sorrow that somebody you hoped so much for is really a dead person: a dead person who's alive.

That is the thing which has altered our lives: living with sorrow.

And the anxiety for the future. We're both 70 now: what will happen when we're dead – that anxiety is ever-present.

There is nothing for the future. I've rung up lots of people, the Cheshire Homes et cetera, made an awful lot of enquiries. The answer is always: if she was physically disabled we would help, but as she is mentally disabled we haven't got the facilities. She's not mad you see – she doesn't fit anywhere.

There is no provision in the health service: the only solution they've got is a psychiatric ward. That is not for Gill – she's very, very aware what's going on around her.

Either she's got to live with us for the rest of her life, or she goes back to her own flat, with a companion, which is becoming increasingly impossible. As one of our friends said: she'll be desperately lonely. Or else she ends up in a psychiatric hospital, which we're not prepared to do. We'd have to put her in a private nursing home, it would have to be an Alzheimer's home because no one else deals with young amnesiacs. Alzheimer's homes: everyone says don't send her there because they're all too old.

She's never going to use her head again. I'd like to see her somewhere where she could look after the chickens, do a bit of housework, have all the time in the world for reading, where people are gentle, imaginative, sensitive and intelligent.

The Gartons have another child, a son four years older than Gill, married with two children, living in Wales.

They (her son and daughter) have never been close. Michael is a practical man, he's a builder; he buys old houses and does them up. Of course he's concerned, and his wife is certainly concerned. Anne (his wife) would always have Gill; she said she would have Gill. I believe she would, but Anne's got her elderly mother (to look after), she couldn't cope, it wouldn't be quite right. And they've got nothing in common, nothing to talk about. At least Gill and I have something from the past to talk about.

She can't see beyond the present: she can't think about what will happen when we're dead. I think, deep down, she has this terrible

157

fear. She keeps asking: why aren't I back at work? I think she's frightened, frightened, frightened.

If you give birth to somebody, you've been desperately fond of them, you've watched them and hoped they will achieve their own happiness: the thought of her being in a psychiatric hospital . . . it's so ever present, it's like a great cloud.

If I've learnt anything about love, I've learnt it from Gill. I don't think I can even elaborate on that. I love her very, very deeply. I'm quite prepared to see her faults, but I love her. I would do anything for her. I know there's a bond from the other side, I know that I have always been Gill's anchor, and especially now.

We always gave her freedom: she could do exactly what she liked, and did. I remember saying to her: if you go on drinking like this you'll kill yourself. She said: I'll last longer than you. And God hasn't it been proven: she will last longer than me – but what a state to be in.

8

·

Men: Caring husbands, sons and lovers

Not any man could do it – you've got to be a caring type of person. There'd be some men who'd say, sod this I'm off round the pub, or, she'll have to go into hospital. I couldn't. (Wilf Gibson, 62, who has looked after his wife Jean, who has premature senile dementia, for the last twenty years)

It is not known how many men have the major responsibility for looking after a disabled relative, but their numbers have probably been underestimated: although most research indicates that 75–85 per cent of carers are women, one recent study suggested that men might form about 40 per cent of those looking after elderly people. Whatever the current figure, there is no doubt that, given changing employment patterns, the rise in single parenthood and an elderly population which far exceeds the numbers of available female carers, the number of male carers is likely to grow in the future.

The majority of men who are caring for someone full-time, as opposed to just 'helping out', are looking after either disabled wives or mothers. Rising divorce rates and changes in patterns of custody also mean that there is smaller group of single fathers looking after disabled children.

The male advantage

It was clear that the men were receiving more from both informal networks and from the services. Women were more likely to be undertaking caring tasks without any support, whilst men often had help from a number of different sources.

The allocation of service support . . . is mediated by a set of expectations

159

which assume that it is appropriate for women to undertake a heavier burden of care than might be expected of men.

(Equal Opportunities Commission, Carers and Services. A comparison of men and women caring for dependent elderly people, *April 1984)*

The small amount of research which has been carried out into male carers indicates that, generally, men do not fulfil the caring role in the same way as women: they do not sacrifice as much to it in terms of their work, independence, freedom and spare time, as women do; nor are they expected to by their friends, families, by statutory services – or by themselves or their dependants.

Studies comparing men and women carers, for example, have found that men face less restrictions on their lives than women; men are more likely to carry on a regular social life and less likely to give up work or take time off. They are also less likely than women to carry out intimate personal care for a relative. Also, men get more help from statutory services, which still tend to see the male as the 'breadwinner' who must be kept at work, and which are therefore more likely to provide services such as home helps and Meals on Wheels. Studies also suggest that men get more help from relatives, friends and neighbours.

Disabled relatives, especially if they are female, have different expectations of men caring for them than they do of women: mothers being looked after by their sons, for example, will often struggle on trying to dress or wash themselves for far longer than they might had they a daughter available to take over. Elderly women are also far more likely to carry on with tasks such as housework and cooking if their carer is a son, and they are often more willing to accept that a son will continue to work, have a social life and go out in the evenings.

Research also suggests that when a disabled relative becomes severely dependent, he or she is more likely to be admitted to residential care if living with a son than with a daughter. Men carers are also more likely to receive help at an earlier stage in the onset of illness – in the form, say, of a relative's admission to hospital for assessment – than are women. Female carers are given more help in the form of short-stay relief and day-care than are men – but as a means of helping them carry on a little longer, rather than as provision of substantial support. According to the EOC survey quoted above:

Where the main source of care is a man, the need to restore the elderly person's ability to cope independently might seem more urgent than where a female carer appears to be coping with day-to-day needs.

It comes as little surprise to find that some studies comparing men and women carers have found that men tend to feel less depressed about caring than women, and that they find it less stressful.

Despite these findings, few of the male carers interviewed for this book conformed to the stereotype of the 'bread-winner' male who still managed to pursue both a career and social life: most of them had given up work to care, and in most ways seemed to bear the same burdens and the same restrictions on their lives as women carers. Only one man had been sufficiently cushioned by social services to keep his job; aged 62, and caring for a wife who was partially paralysed by multiple sclerosis, he had regular daily help from both a district nurse, who got his wife up and dressed, and a home help – he only took over caring completely for his wife at the weekends. This man was clearly a forceful character who said he had fought 'tooth and nail' to obtain a specially adapted home and all the equipment his wife needed – including an electric recliner, ripple mattress, an electric lock on the door, an electric lift upstairs and an electric hoist in the bathroom. Men are perhaps more likely to resort to 'forceful' tactics than are women to get what they want: another man, looking after a wife totally paralysed by multiple sclerosis, recalled how the local wheelchair centre 'couldn't run a booze-up in a brewery' and recounted the story of how, when he rang his local wheelchair centre for a new battery, he received five visits from various personnel – but still no battery:

Finally I rang up the manager, I said: if you haven't got a battery on its way within a few minutes, I'm coming to take it out of your car. Within a few minutes the man arrived with a battery.

Yet this kind of forcefulness is not typical: most men carers are no more effective in their dealings with the welfare bureaucracy than are women. What determines the level of support is not just gender, but other factors such as personality, income, class and the availability of local resources.

As is the case with women carers, most men are middle-aged or elderly and in ill-health themselves; many are under both physical and emotional stress, socially isolated and un-supported by statutory services.

In other ways, however, a man's experience of looking after someone who is disabled differs significantly from that of a woman's. For a woman, especially if she has already brought up children, caring for a dependent or handicapped relative is an extension of what she has always been expected to do for her family; it is carried on in a domestic world, on territory with which she is already familiar. Expected for the most part to act as providers for their families, and to partici-pate in the public rather than the domestic world, most men, especially from this age group, have had little previous ex-perience of caring and are unfamiliar with the intimate physical and emotional contact which it involves. Male carers have to cope, not only with the sacrifice of their masculine public role, but also with a complete reversal of their normal domestic and emotional relationships.

This is not to caricature men as being unable either to care or to deal with the domestic work which it entails: most of the men interviewed for this book had been caring for years, were as competent – and as comfortable – with domestic life as women, and had few problems with cooking, cleaning or housework. Nor is it to assume that all men are necessarily at ease with the masculine roles they have hitherto been ex-pected to fulfil.

Nevertheless, the role-reversal involved when men become carers, means that they face particular problems.

162

James Lenagh

Bridie, she doesn't know where she is; she talks the old Irish, the Gaelic, from forty or fifty years ago. One or two of me mates – when they speak Gaelic to her, she'll switch on.

James Lenagh, 39, lives with his mother, Bridie, in a desolate, run-down block of flats on the outskirts of Glasgow, on an estate which looks more like a barracks then a place for people to live: the stairs are filthy and marked with graffiti; the shopping centre is half boarded-up; there are dogs wandering around, and a bleak-looking pub made of concrete. James says he can't sleep for the noise at night; he has a drug pusher as one of his neighbours. 'I'm either kept awake by Bridie or the night parties. Then first thing in the morning there are the caretakers with the bins. And when it is quiet, if it's too quiet I can't sleep.'

Bridie, 79 in October, is an advanced case of Alzheimer's, one of the major causes of dementia. A small, thin, wizened old lady, she sits in the kitchen, a plastic beaker with a few inches of whisky on the tray in front of her, murmuring and rubbing the arm of her chair repeatedly. He has to keep her in the kitchen, James says, because of the incontinence: the mess would get into the carpets. She has just come home from a visit to the hospital but is minus her false teeth, which, he discovers when he rings the ward, have been given to another old lady. She can still feed herself, but has to use plastic bowls and cups; in the kitchen she had strewn bits of her corned beef sandwich all over the floor.

His mother's personality has completely changed, James says: 'Even her looks have changed. Years ago when I was a kid, she was one of those Irish Catholic type of women, so strong-willed, strong-minded, domineering; our mother was always the boss of the household. Now she's just a wee wain. I'm now the parent, looking after the child.'

Born and brought up in the Gorbals district of Glasgow, James left home in his teens and went on the road, doing casual work in the building trade, moving about with his mates, and, when the money ran out, moving on to another job. He came back – from Aberdeen – seven years ago, when his mother started 'acting very queer'. She was diagnosed as suffering from dementia, and was taken into the local psychogeriatric hospital – 'pure bedlam'. He took her home because he thought she would be dead in a few weeks. 'She was getting punched by other patients; the nurses were short staffed, they hadn't been feeding her. I thought she wouldn't last more than a month; I said I'd take her to get the hell out of there.' Seven years later, he is still looking after her.

I thought I was bringing her home to die, that it would be a question of weeks; not one single doctor told me otherwise. I think they're afraid of carers learning too much too quickly.

At the beginning it was very difficult: can you imagine having to wipe your own mother's backside, clean her, change her? At the beginning it was reminding her to go, then showing her where the toilet was, then helping her to undress, then helping her to sit down – it was a gradual process. Now she's become just like a wee wain: she soils herself. You've got to take her in there, change her, wash her. She can be sitting there quite happy, and suddenly she'll change completely. She can soil herself, take her pants off, leave them lying in the middle of the floor. That's why I keep her in the kitchen; because of the carpets.

You can't leave her at all except maybe to go up to the shops for five or ten minutes. It's not so bad now she's no longer mobile; when she was mobile there would be this non-stop walking up and down the hallway. Now her balance is starting to be affected, she has dizzy attacks; she can only walk with me in front of her, holding both her hands.

James chain smokes, likes a drink when his mates come round – is by his own admission a 'hell of a boozer' – and is friendly with Johnny, another man looking after his mother over the way. Rose, another neighbour, does the cleaning: 'she comes down normally on a Monday, gives the place a complete going over, changes the bedding'. The flats are very friendly – 'it's like a village'. If James needs to go out for more than an hour he'll leave the keys with the caretaker. His clothes are cheap and slightly grubby. Poverty: 'we have corned beef sandwiches in sliced white and slightly mouldy bread, and cheap coffee with chicory added.' He draws around £130 a week in benefits for both of them, and doesn't consider himself badly off compared with most families on an estate where unemployment is rife; anyway, he has little to spend it on.

We're a lot better off than other people, pensioners, people on supplementary benefits. I'm a cunning little bugger: after six years I've found my way round the system. No one sat down and explained what I was entitled to. The supplementary benefits officer who used to pay a weekly home visit was always asking, is there anything you want, Mr Lenagh? But how can you say if you don't know what you're entitled to?

He has no visits from relatives – despite the fact that his mother was one of sixteen and 'there are millions of them in Glasgow'. None ever come near the door. 'They feel if they come up they'll put too much of a burden on me. Another reason: they're afraid – they no longer want to see Bridie the way she is now, they prefer to think of her as she was years ago.'

His parents came over from Ireland as teenagers: his mother to work as a maid in one of the big Scottish houses, his father to work as a labourer. The family lived in the Gorbals for twenty years.

She was a terrific housekeeper, the house was always spotless, there was plenty of food. Things were difficult for every family in the Gorbals: there were too many chapels, too many pubs, not enough money to go round them all.

My mother and my father never spoke to each other except in emergencies. She hated the drink, and he liked his pint on a Friday night when he'd finished work. I think he drank because she dinna speak to him, and she dinna speak to him because he drank. He was strong in his own way, but too quiet. If that had been me: if a woman doesn't get a strong enough character in a man, they do try and dominate them, and the more they dominate the worse they become. If he'd asserted himself when sober it wouldn't have been so bad.

They used to sit in this cramped room in the Gorbals, she buried in her book and he with his newspaper. But they did really love each other: when he died, she broke down.

James left home in his teens, after his father – the parent he was closer to – died of a heart attack: 'fell down the stairs and smashed his brains out. That really hurt me, that's when I left home.'

He also lost a younger sister – his favourite – when he was 26: 'she died of pneumonia, died in my arms'. His older sister, an ex-nun, was about to get married at the time their mother became ill. 'My sister more or less puts it to me: either she gets married or she gives up the chance.' Life before he came home, he says, was 'carefree. I made money, I spent money. I thoroughly enjoyed every

*second of my life; I could come and go as I pleased. I'd just work at
a job; if I got fed up with it I left it. I've been a sales rep, a lorry driver,
a bus driver – various jobs. I've travelled every single inch of Britain.'*

*He was never interested in marriage: 'So I'd nothing really to tie
me down. I had the freedom to go out whenever I wanted, to make a
few bob as required. If one of the contracts was finished, we could
go out and blow the money.' Now, though, he is 'so tied'.*

Does he regret taking it on?

No. I don't believe in locking up old people in the funny farm. People
who throw them in homes, I've got nothing but contempt for. I've
seen them in the geriatric unit, they come up to visit their mother; all
they do is look at their watch until a decent time has passed and
they can go. That's one thing the professionals are so keen on, they
keep asking: why don't you put her in a home? I said: why don't you
give me the backing I need?

He is immensely cheerful.

You've got to be. I'm lucky, I've got one of those daft personalities,
like a rubber ball. There's times I feel like banging my head against
the wall. There have been times I feel like screaming. Or going mad
altogether. I was always an extrovert, I think that's helped me. But I
do feel isolated. I have got people, but there's times I don't want to
see anyone. Especially after a bad night with Bridie.

There will come a time when she will have to go into hospital,
when she will not walk, when she'll have to be spoon-fed. Then I will
not do it, I will have to put her in. If I put her in now, it's like six years
of my life wasted. She can walk and talk a bit, and eat. I know there
will come a time.

*His biggest worry is the future, about what he'll do for work when his
mother dies, by which time he could well be in his mid-forties: the
danger is that, with high unemployment, he could end up on the
road, living in hostels and doing casual work.*

Half of me is saying I have to plan for the future, get some training or
trade – there's plenty of training available, with this unemployment.
But I can't sign on (for it) because I don't know how long she's going
to last. Part of me wants to go into the likes of some form of social
work and welfare to help others in my state. The other half says:
once she's away, to hell with it – I don't want to see sick people.

166

The moment she's dead, and everything's finished, I'm out of that door. I want a complete break, away from everything I know. I could pack a suitcase and walk out of here in the morning.

Giving up work

I didn't want to give up, I loved my work; I was always good at my job, top man. I'm a doer rather than a talker. I thoroughly enjoyed work and the good money. It was a big decision to make but I decided that she was more important than anything. (Max Harper, 61, who took voluntary redundancy twenty-two years ago to look after a wife paralysed by multiple sclerosis; he had been earning good money as a supervisor at Ford motors)

I had a very good life: I used to go abroad a lot; I was an export manager, I travelled, entertained – a great working social life. I'd worked forty-six years – I'd started at 14. I'm a corporate member of the Institute of Export, London and Manchester. I've moved around – and I've been successful. (Edward Smith, 62, who took early retirement to care full-time for a mother of 92 in the early stages of senile dementia)

For many men, giving up work or taking early retirement to look after a disabled wife or mother is one of the most difficult steps they will ever have to take. It involves not only the loss of a regular income – one usually relied on by the rest of the family – but also the loss of an important social and public role; one which still is probably more important and integral to most men's sense of identity than it is to women, despite women's increasing participation in the job market. For these men, the masculine role they are used to playing in the public world is replaced by a private and domestic role with which they are usually unfamiliar.

Mornings: I have a cup of tea, get up, tidy up, get her up, give her a blanket bath in bed, cook breakfast, shower, do some physio, housework, cooking and shopping and washing and ironing. I make her dresses – she was always very fashionable. I bake bread, cakes. I enjoy doing the work, I enjoy cooking; I can cook better than most women.

I have a bit of a temper. Recently I brought in dinner; she said, there's a lot of cauliflower here. I haven't been feeling very well lately, under the weather and headaches; I snatched it back and threw half of it in the dustbin. At one time I would have chucked the whole plate into the air. But

167

when we go to bed, I make her comfortable, cuddle her up and kiss her and it's forgotten.

When other men see me shopping in town, the attitude is: you've got it made, you've pulled a fast one. They don't realise the effort. To go to the town centre, I will have lifted her about eight times: out of the shower, into the wheelchair, into the car, out of the car, and four more times to come home. And when he's knocking it back in the pub, I'm still on duty. (Max Harper)

Jean gets up at seven; her nappy will be soaked and maybe fouled as well — if you leave her she's on the move all the time, so it gets trodden into the carpet; so the first thing is to wash her down and dress her. Then breakfast, washing up, a cup of tea. After washing I do the dinner, then the washing, and ironing. She needs changing about every half-hour. (Wilf Gibson)

Every night I see her into the bath, lay out her nightie, return her clothes; she has been a little bit incontinent — we have to watch that all the time, she gets so upset about it. I lay out her clothes in order of dressing. When I'm cooking she stands there like a shadow. I say, sit down love, it's easier. That's one of the things that rankles me. I'll send her into the lounge and say, you can set the table; I know it might hurt her but she really does get in the way. (Alfred Long, 73, caring for a wife with dementia)

I take her a cup of tea in the morning. She usually gets up on her own, slowly: it takes about one-and-a-half hours. Then we have a cup of coffee mid-morning. Then we get stuck into getting the lunch ready. Afterwards, I wash up, then she'll have a little nap; at about half four we have another cup of tea; then we start to prepare for tea at 6.30. Mother sits and watches 'Crossroads', and after that she'll be sound asleep. (Kevin Sofer, 41, caring for a mother of 73 with rheumatoid arthritis)

Some men find it especially difficult to cope with the more intimate physical care which is needed by their wives and mothers, especially when it involves incontinence. Incontinence in a dependent relative is always a problem, but where the carer is a man, and the dependent usually a woman, dealing with it raises particular social and sexual inhibitions.

It's not an easy job, a man to look after a woman. When she has an accident, I have to wash her down, even her private parts. I go and heave my heart up. (Edward Smith)

168

It's constantly on my mind if we go out: how long are we going to be here? Will she be dry? You can't go out for longer than an hour. (Wilf Gibson)

To make life bearable and more comfortable, her major concession was to have an ileostomy. Had it not been for that twelve years ago, we probably wouldn't have been together. Before the operation I would bring my wife into town, get her out of the car and the first thing to do is put her on my back and look for a toilet. It wrecks your life. Now life is very much easier. Now all we have to do is empty it out. Had it not been for that I would probably have gone. I've been involved in MS societies: if it's a woman, and it usually is, the man looking after her will get fed up and go off. (George Brook, 62, caring for a wife, 58, paralysed by multiple sclerosis. An ileostomy is a major operation which involves replacing the bladder with a stoma bag)

The physical strain

Most of these men, whether husbands or sons, are conscious of their own increasing frailty and ill-health, and worried about whether they will be able to cope as they grew older; many are also conscious of the fact that the woman they are caring for, whether a mother or wife, may well outlive them.

I've got a constitution like an ox, never flu or anything. I've got arthritis in a shoulder now, so I have started to lift her from bed to chair with one arm, which is always difficult. My own health: that's what worries me more than anything. If anything happens to me during the night, how long is she going to lay there before anyone realises something is wrong? Will the milkman continue to leave pints on the doorstep? There might come a time when I'm not able to look after her any more – I try not to look too far into the future. (Max Harper)

Energy, that really is the problem. I don't know what would happen if I suddenly couldn't . . . it's slowed me right down. I was always an agile man, but the last three years have absolutely slowed me down to a dead stop. (Alfred Long)

Men carers tend to take on a greater physical burden than they can manage, often because they, or others, feel they ought to:

We go away but you can't call it a holiday for me because I'm still doing the same thing. We go camping actually; before, we used to go to hotels. I'd tell them about the wheelchair, they'd say, that's fine; then you'd go, and find eighteen steps up to the front door and a spiral staircase. It's not a holiday for me. There's not only her: I usually get collared at these disabled places – I get more to do then you would at home, lifting and carrying. It's hard work. (Max Harper)

Social isolation

Despite the evidence that men get more help from neighbours and relatives then do women, they experience the same social isolation. They are often particularly bitter about the attitudes of female relatives and friends, from whom they expected more support.

The trouble is here, there's no woman comes. I used to ask the neighbours and that to go up and see the wife, even if it's just for a wee blether; women's talk, that's what she needs, see what I mean? I used to say, come up and see the wife sometime; they never came.

I have a younger sister, she has a car and she can drive, in the car it would be a ten-minute run; she said she'll come down when she's passing – she's never been passing. My own sister, she comes down here to the shopping centre, but she's never been passing. We get postcards, from Yugoslavia, the Costa Brava and all those places (laughs). But she can't come down the main street along here; she's never been passing. (Robbie Naylan, in his seventies, looking after his wife Letty who had a stroke three years ago)

We've a daughter, 43, she lives seven miles away and we haven't seen her for eighteen months. We have three beautiful grandchildren we never see. The daughter has never even offered to have Mary (his wife) for a weekend – she's never even combed her hair.

The neighbours have never looked in; they never have done. Lots of people – if I'm working at the front of the house, they'll stop and ask, how's your wife? I'll say, OK, why don't you go in and say hallo? They'll say, I'll do that. Then I'll look up and they'll have disappeared. When I used to work away from the house every ten hours, she didn't see anyone. (Max Harper)

My brothers' wives, they don't work, I don't speak to them. My brothers will come to see her for an hour a week. The youngest one always stresses that his wife has to do for her own mother, says: she has her own mother to look after. The other one says there's no room; his wife never visits, he comes alone. One of them has a wife, no children and two bedrooms; but they only have one bed so they never have anyone to stay. They should take Mother on a rota basis – they won't take her. (Edward Smith)

Wilf Gibson

Wilf Gibson, 61, lives in a bungalow on the outskirts of a small village in Kent; we talk in the kitchen while his wife Jean, suffering from premature dementia for the last twenty years, chatters and laughs just outside the door.

He is quiet, stoical, and uncomplaining. There was never any question of him not looking after Jean, he says: she is the girl who waited for him five years during the war when she 'could have had the pick of anybody'. He shows me photographs of them when they were younger – Jean was very pretty – and of their wedding with him in his sailor's uniform: 'That spirit, the old wartime years, has gone; people were always in and out of each other's houses.' They met in London where he was an apprentice fitter at a gasworks in the Old Kent Road and she was a machinist, making babies' coats. In the navy he used to drink and be a 'bit boisterous', but 'that all stopped once John came along'.

The house is like an institution; it lacks the homely, 'feminine' touch: there are clashing floral curtains and carpets, and odd bits of furniture stuck in corners. He says he finds housework relaxing – 'an old sailor can do anything' – and likes 'messing about' in the garage.

What he really finds difficult, though, is Jean's constant incontinence: he is painfully embarrassed that a visitor is in the house when he has to change her nappy, and finds the idea of taking her, for example, to the dentist very worrying. 'I shouldn't be embarrassed but I'm afraid I am. Will she be dry? Will we have to wait?'

He took early retirement five years ago from his job as an engineering supervisor. Their only child, John, is married and lives quite near. 'Once a week we go to the boy's and that's for the whole day for dinner and tea. We used to have a regular Sunday outing to Jean's sister, but she couldn't cope with seeing Jean like this.'

He says he hasn't really asked for much help, but that the community nurse keeps an eye on him; and he has two volunteers – 'the two girls, they're a blessing' – who visit once a week and help

171

him get her in and out of the bath. 'With Jean, there's a lot of lifting to be done; having had a rupture I'm a little bit scared of that.' The worse thing, though, is the long wait for the chiropodist. 'Jean's toenails are bloody terrible. I try to cut them, but she's got such hard skin.'

He would never consider putting Jean in hospital and looks contemptuously at me for even asking the question. For him, it is a question of morality, and of marriage being forever.

Do you think . . . for a girl who waited right through the wartime . . . and then goes and gets ill, that you can abandon her? Love her? Of course I love her. The doctor, the district nurse, the social worker – they've all mentioned it. I said no, I'm not going to part with her.

Yes of course you have your moments. But I'd rather have it this way. She's been in hospital on two occasions (when he also had to go into hospital) and they put her in a ward with a lock on it. The doctor told me she'd last eighteen months in there – it was a terrible place.

I don't worry about the future, but it's always at the back of your mind. I must admit I cried my eyes out the time she had to go into hospital. I know what would happen to Jean (if he died). I've invested the severance money and I've got a few savings. If Jean goes there's enough for a decent burial.

Does he ever think it might be better if Jean died? He pauses:

Sometimes I have thought that. But I would hate the day. I have thought: you've suffered a bloody long time Jean, why suffer any more? (He has tears in his eyes.) But I'd miss her.

Husbands

A wife looking after her husband might find it easier – the things which have to be done are second nature. It hasn't come easy to me but I've trained myself gradually. (George Brook)

Often middle-aged or elderly themselves, husbands looking after disabled wives are usually coping with mental and physical disorders such as dementia, stroke and multiple sclerosis, in women who were previously at the centre of their domestic lives; women who probably looked after them in the past. In most respects, these men face the same

172

problems as do wives caring for disabled husbands; but, unlike the women, most of whom expressed a desire for a separate life of their own outside the home, few of the men interviewed for this book expressed any wish for a life beyond the domestic routine they shared with their wives. They appeared to experience neither the intense conflict between their own desires and the demands of their partners nor the same levels of guilt and resentment as were common among women. It was almost as though, if they were given more freedom or time to themselves, they would not know where to go, or what to do with it.

Going to the pub for a drink? It would make me feel guilty; while I'm up there she's by herself. I can't be in the position where she wants something and can't get it – she can't even switch the video on. I really don't know what I would do if I was free one night. I'm not the sort of person who can sit in a pub and drink pints of beer on my own. I've got no friends. I might go to the pub or something for the first half-hour, but I'd feel lost and lonely. (Max Harper)

My wife said a couple of years ago: go out, go down the pub. But I'm uncomfortable going down the pub. I would if I'd got someone with me. (George Brook)

I only wish he would go out. He's not housebound, don't get that idea; not housebound at all. (Mrs Brook)

This difference may reflect the fact that most women take on caring at an age when their children have grown up and they are ready to spread their wings; whereas for men, this is the time when their working lives have often become less important, and when they become more attached to domestic life – and to the wife who is usually at the centre of that life, however disabled. It may also be that men carers express their feelings of conflict, guilt and resentment less then women do.

We get on very well together. For eleven years we've been together twenty-four hours a day and neither of us is showing any sign of madness. I don't particularly want to be away from her for a long period of time. She's said to me, why do you stay? I say (jokingly), I've got no one else; it's true I

haven't got anyone else, there is nobody else. (Max Harper. He has to do
everything for his wife, who is totally paralysed by multiple sclerosis – even
blow her nose; usually they share the same plate and even the same knife
and fork. 'That might shock you but it's easier')

Similarly, whereas wives tend to speak of disabled husbands
as demanding and dependent children who have to be kept
happy, husbands express more protective, more sentimental
feelings towards the women who still occupy centre-stage in
their lives. Unlike the wives caring for husbands with dementia, for example, few men with demented wives believe
that their relationship is over.

The love, it's as strong as it ever was. (Alfred Long)

The loving relationship – it's been there all the time. (George Brook)

Robbie and Letty Naylan

*Robbie and Letty Naylan are in their seventies and have lived in their
Glasgow tenement flat for the last twenty years. They live in one
room, with a double bed in a recess, two armchairs, a television,
stove, fridge and table. There is another room, the 'best room',
occupied by their son, 47 and unemployed, who came home when
his marriage broke up a few years ago.*

*Robbie Naylan is talkative, sharp, and has a shock of white hair:
Letty is quiet and looks at him contemptuously from time to time.*

*Three years ago she had a stroke, or, as he calls it, she 'took the
shock'. Despite the doctor's advice that she needed to go into
hospital, 'she didna go, I thought it was a temporary thing', he says.
It has left her incontinent and unable to walk without a frame, but
she still has the use of her arms and her speech. He cooks, cleans,
helps her get dressed and does the laundry. She can still feed
herself and manages to wash herself. He rarely goes out except to
do a bit of shopping and collect the pension; they sit in their
respective armchairs all day, watching television. They fight like cat
and dog – about money, about him going out: she is constantly and
publicly accusing him of going off with other women (he was, he
says, a bit of a lad when he was younger).*

*Next to the bed is a commode, and the floor near the bed is
covered with newspapers because she cannot always get out of*

174

bed and onto the commode on time; he has to sleep on the inside of the recess. The room is narrow, gloomy, high ceilinged. It's on the first floor, which means she hardly ever goes out as the only way she can get down the stone stairs is backwards.

They have no money to buy a retirement bungalow or a car with special seats, and have no washing machine to cope with the incontinence – he does the washing twice a week, in the bath. During the night she gets up about three times – 'sometimes I sleep through it and she manages'.

Robbie was turned down three times for the Attendance Allowance – although he receives it now – because she could feed herself and cut her own food. 'Four doctors there were altogether who came to see us. Can she cut her own food? they ask me. How do they think the plate gets to the table, the food gets to the plate from the cooker, see what I mean? It's because I'm retired, they think I've got nothing else to do; that's the impression I get.'

He is also angry because his superannuation – from his job as a council worker in public lighting – comes to over £18 a week, so he's not able to get any extra money from the DHSS; he describes how someone from the DHSS came and asked him what help he needed, and then turned around and said he didn't need help because he had his superannuation pension. 'So I didn't require assistance,' he mimics. 'If we only had the OAP I'd have got that £15. But I didn't require the supplementary.'

When he first retired he used to go on outings to the countryside for the day – but 'since this happened you can't go no place'. They sometimes go out when the younger son, married with two children, comes to take them out in the car.

The son living at home is not much use, according to Robbie. He used to have a good job as the manager of a creamery and had a big house, but when he was made redundant his marriage broke up. 'It's no very handy, him being of the male sex; if it was a daughter, she could help out.'

His wife will not have any sitters: 'she doesn't like strangers, especially when she has to hop back and forward.' A 'green nurse' (the district nurse's uniform is green) used to call to give her baths; 'but she wouldn't have it, they're strangers. They said to her: but they're women too; she says, he can do it, he's my husband.'

Letty does, however, go to a 'geriatric place' twice a week, which is good for her, he says, because she needs to talk to other women.

175

Married fifty years, they recently had their Golden Wedding anniversary: 'We went no place, no party or nothing. We got a lot of cards.'

They bicker constantly, Robbie says. 'She says to me, you've nothing to say. What have I got to talk about, when I'm sitting here quiet – see what I mean?'

She suddenly interrupts: 'He never opens his mouth. What makes me so angry, he's got nothing to say in here; but he'll talk the hind leg off a donkey – and it's usually a young lady he's talking to.' He laughs.

Much of the bickering is about money: he nags her for spending the Attendance Allowance on cigarettes, a habit she'd managed to give up before the stroke. 'It's my money', she says (technically, she is right), but he says it belongs to the house. 'He collects my allowance but he takes £10 of it,' she says bitterly. He says it goes towards electricity bills.

He repeats how he wishes he'd had a daughter. 'As I've always said, if I had a a daughter, you know what I mean – if she lived here, if she was willing. With a son: he's not that handy, he has to go out of the room when she wants to use the commode.'

Sons

It's always been a mother/son relationship. I'm still her little boy, having never left the nest. It's just a situation you've got to accept. She can't help it, I can't help it; it's the situation you find yourself in. I worry a lot; yes, I have been a worrier. I'm learning not to: you've got to, haven't you? If you don't, you just go under. I worry about my mother dying; obviously it will leave a hole in my life. (Kevin Sofer, 41, looking after a mother of 73 with arthritis and a slight heart condition; the two of them live in a pair of identical whitewashed bungalows whose front doors face each other, on the outskirts or a small Norfolk seaside resort. He suffers from colitis – a nervous stomach complaint – and has not worked for several years)

Many single sons looking after their mothers are only children who have never left home or who have failed to properly establish separate lives from their parents. They have often taken on an emotional 'caring' role from an early age. Now middle-aged or elderly, they find their lives dominated by a parent, usually a mother, who may, despite

176

disability, be stronger than they are, and who will, in many cases, outlive them. It is probably no coincidence that the single sons interviewed for this book were nervous, highly-strung men with stress-related diseases of the stomach and heart, while their mothers were women suffering from the illnesses of old age, such as rheumatoid arthritis and dementia.

Edward Smith

I don't see any future. I think I'll go first. Friends say she'll put me away, and I'm beginning to believe it now. The doctor told her: 'Edward's not fit to be looking after you.' She just says, go away. This is my home, she says.

Edward Smith, 62, tried to commit suicide only a few months before this interview, after five years of looking after his 92-year-old mother with dementia. 'There's nothing to go on for; she's the healthy one and I'm not.'

The third of four brothers, and the son of a master butcher whom he also looked after, Edward took early retirement from his job and has never left the home he now shares with his mother: a large, gloomy, Edwardian house, full of solid, dark furniture, in the well-to-do suburb of a large northern town.

He is especially bitter about the attitude of two of his brothers – both retired businessmen – who, he says, visit for an hour a week, but whom he hardly speaks to. 'They say Mother is my responsibility. You've lived on the cheap for long enough, they say.' There is also unease between the brothers over the inheritance of the house and their father's investments. 'All the books are kept, so there's no hanky-panky. I wouldn't touch it, I don't want it, I'm not interested.'

Edward is an anxious, highly-strung man, who himself became ill with heart disease three years ago, and who has a growth on his bladder; he now needs hospital treatment every six weeks, during which time his mother has to go into respite care. 'Mother takes it reluctantly, very reluctantly. She told the doctor to go away, ordered him out when he tried to talk about it. I don't want to see that man, she said. Or the social worker – it's always "that woman".'

There's favouritism in families: her favourite was the youngest and father's was the eldest. Most women in those days had big families, never wanted them really. She didn't have any affection for me at all – the others maintain they didn't get it either. I spent a lot of time with my granny. I was there all the time; she nursed me through my illnesses. That's why I'm different from the others, that influence.

Father was a businessman, his life was his work. The marriage – they got on. Father was Victorian and it was the same with his family; that's why I never got on with him. But she was spoilt, she could always get her own way. They were both selfish people. I try not to be like that; I think I've achieved it. As you sow in this life, so you reap. I believe; I'm a Christian; I still do for people when there's time – I help when I can.

They amazed me at the home she went into while I was in hospital: they said, she undressed herself; they said, what did I do it for? She's conned me; she makes me get her on and off the commode. When I became ill I said, Mother, you'll have to manage yourself; after the doctor told me not to do any lifting, I said, Mother, the commode's there, the paper's there, the frame's there – you can do it. She says, it's hard; she says, I don't love her any more. I say, Mother, I love you as much as you love me.

I'm sick of it, to tell you the truth. I could have gone out for a meal yesterday, but said I didn't want to and lay on the bed. I told the doctor, I'm becoming unstable. The tranquillisers make you into a zombie: I've not got the interest or initiative in anything. It's taken all my social life, even my other interests. I don't read books, don't play my hi-fi. I just go to bed when I've put her to bed. I'm too depressed and exhausted. The others don't help: they say Mother is my responsibility; you've lived on the cheap for long enough, they say.

I had a very good life, I used to go abroad a lot; I was an export manager, I travelled, entertained, had many lady friends – a great working social life. I was always out at night, every nightspot in London, or visiting overseas; a good life in commerce. I've moved around, and I've been successful: you should have seen the letter I had from them when I left.

I wanted to finish at 60, to travel. I'd worked forty-six years – I started at 14, I had to learn at night; I'm self-educated. My idea was to retire, to travel, to keep up my interests and my friends. I've friends all over; one in Hampshire, one down in Somerset. Lots of lady friends. I've never brought them home: my mother has always been jealous; I was the last one at home and she didn't want me to go off. So I've had lots of lady friends; I'm still in contact with them.

I would like a relationship. In the past Mother has soured the woman before I identified what was wrong. One woman said, I've always loved you; she was a businesswoman, came a few times and felt unwelcome. She's now married for the second time. A lovely person. Every woman says I would have made a good husband.

He's gone out with his widow friends, Mother says. She'll be very caustic about it to the young man who gardens; she makes it very difficult – I get word about that.

I won't make the decision (about putting his mother into care), it will be a collective decision. The family want me to do it, but they've told me it's my decision, so they can turn round afterwards and say: Edward put her in a home. The social worker says it shouldn't be my decision. The social worker is most supportive: she saved me from suicide.

None of the family back me up. It's because of this place (the house): there's a feeling that I will be the beneficiary. They tell me I'm living on the cheap; I tell them they should be contributing. They don't want to cross her, they want to stay friends with her. She thinks it's marvellous that they come and sit with her; doing nothing. They just don't want to get involved, they think they're doing the job with a visit once a week.

They don't ask us at Christmas or New Year; I just sit looking at the wall. It's only March since I had it out with them, since we finished as a family. I became so depressed in March that I went and arranged my own funeral. I want it strictly private: no one is going to my funeral.

Men who don't care

Not every man with a disabled wife or other relative will choose to stay and look after her: the evidence indicates that husbands find it far more difficult to adjust to a wife becoming disabled than do their female equivalents. One study from 1979, found that only 4 per cent of disabled men were divorced, compared to 16 per cent of disabled women – both compared to a national divorce rate of 7 per cent. Another study showed that marriages were more likely to break up where a wife rather than a husband became disabled.

It is difficult for anyone to come to terms with the problems caused by severe disability in a relative, particularly in a partner, and it is no surprise that some marriages break down under the strain. But whereas most women whose husbands become disabled will view their role as carer as an extension of their traditional nurturing function, many men find it difficult to accept the role reversal involved in becoming a carer rather than someone cared for; to come to terms with looking after a wife or mother who has previously always looked after them.

Younger men can have particular problems in coming to terms with a wife's disability. They may be simply too self-centred, too stuck in a demanding 'little boy' syndrome, and too dependent on their conventional social role, to be able to cope; the only way they can react to disability is by running away from it and denying their responsibility. One young man deserted a 'very good wife', who had been severely disabled by an accident, apparently because their relationship had relied almost completely on her being a good hostess, a good cook and a good mother to their children.

Obviously, whether a husband can cope with disability in his wife will depend on the underlying strength of their marriage: the male carers interviewed for this book – the men who had stayed – were in long-standing relationships which had survived many crises, and the raising of families, and which had gone beyond conventional social roles to a deeper comradeship.

Not all marriages, are so strong or so long-lived. The marriage of one woman, Mary, in her early forties and crippled by multiple sclerosis, had broken down completely: although their financial situation made it impossible for this couple to separate physically, the husband was never present and behaved more like a lodger than a partner, spending whatever time he could out of the house – either in the pub or at work.

As is often the case where a husband deserts a disabled wife, the care of this woman had been taken over by her daughter, Joanne, who had left school at 16 to look after her. The two women are hardly on speaking terms with the father; they lived together only because there was no alternative.

Joanne: In the beginning he was really, really good, he did housework, gardening; he helped Mum with everything. But the years have gone by; it's got less and less, and he's more unwilling to do it. I think he thinks he's been given a rough deal.

Mary: He's taken to drinking. Money burns a hole in his pocket even if it's not his.

Joanne: He's always at work, he's at work so much it's ridiculous, if there's any overtime going he takes it; he'll work rest-days just so he's not here. If he's here, he goes up to his room.

Mary: He drinks in the garage and at home. He's got a dual personality; he's so charming and witty and nice to people; as soon as they go out of the back door, that's it, his ordinary self, dead miserable. He's not happy unless he's miserable. He used to take me out Saturday nights, but he loathed anyone seeing him push a wheelchair; he'd bump into people, I'm sure on purpose.

The husbands of disabled wives are not the only men who cannot cope with caring: many fathers find it difficult to came to terms with a child's disability, especially if they are clever, ambitious men who cannot accept that the child is less than they had hoped for.

One woman was caring for a 30-year-old son who was slightly retarded at birth and who was left brain-damaged by a haemorrhage three years ago. Her husband is a retired stockbroker who, she says, has never been able to accept his son – 'he always says he will never take Michael anywhere again.'

He's a very active man, a very high powered person, he was on the stock exchange council; then there was this brain-damaged son he just couldn't accept. They didn't get on that well before; Michael wasn't that bright. My husband has a very high IQ; he's a very high-powered successful type of man, and my son has always been a dreamy type. My son also had dyslexia – my husband just couldn't accept that, he couldn't accept the idea he could read back to front. He was always calling him 'that bloody boy';

181

even now he'll say it, over some pathetic little thing Michael can't help.

I just don't say anything any more; it's just too upsetting. He can't accept him. I don't think men . . . they think of children as adults and wonder why they don't lead their own lives; but as a mother – who else will love and care for him?

My husband is now vice-chairman of the health authority; he loves it, he's totally reorganised one hospital; he's absolutely marvellous. He's done amazing things with outpatients. He was absolutely appalled at the situation – he's taken over all their finances. This is all voluntary, he doesn't get paid, he loves it; it drives me mad (laughs).

I have an awful sense in my heart of hearts that I let him down by having such a slow child. We've a rather clever daughter, that's the awful thing, and a boy who was slow – if it had been the other way round it wouldn't have mattered. He favours my daughter, she's very bright; lots of O and A-levels. My daughter has always protected him (Michael) because he's always been very slow; but unfortunately she is married to a very brilliant man, selfish to the core. Michael never goes up there, he senses his brother-in-law doesn't want to know. My daughter has taken to coming down here during the day; I don't think she tells her husband. It's dreadful; I never comment or ask because I don't want her to feel divided loyalties between her brother and her husband.

The clever ones – it's funny: for them it's like coming down a mountain; it's like coming down a mountain where they're at the top. They never mix with slow ones: they went out with bright children, bright girls, they've always avoided the dunce; and then suddenly they find they have a slow child. Take my advice: don't ever marry a brilliant man.

Men looking after men with AIDS

There is in Britain a growing number of men who are looking after other men, and whose roles as carers have so far been unacknowledged. These are gay men whose partners, lovers and friends are suffering from Acquired Immune Deficiency Syndrome (AIDS). Many such men have lost several friends and lovers over the last few years; one AIDS counsellor, who was interviewed for this book, described their experiences as comparable to those of living through a war.

One of the biggest problems of caring for someone with AIDS is coping with the stigma attached to this disease. While there are many families, professionals and volunteers who are committed to fighting this illness and to supporting those who have it, there is mounting evidence that gay men who have AIDS, or who are known to be HIV positive (carriers of the Human Immunodeficiency Virus which causes AIDS) have faced abuse from neighbours and work colleagues; hostility and suspicion from health and social services staff; discrimination from employers and housing agencies; and sometimes, rejection by their own families (although this is not always the case: as with any crisis, the issue of AIDs can provide a chance to resolve family conflicts over homo-sexuality). On the employment front at least, it looks likely that discrimination will increase: one in five companies say they would ask someone with AIDS to resign, according to a survey undertaken in 1988 by the magazine *Chief Executive*.

The panic which the subject of AIDS provokes has affected not only people with AIDS, but anyone associated with them, including their carers. Unlike other people caring for someone with a terminal illness, who can expect sympathy and support, carers of men with AIDS are, except within their own community, enormously isolated. Also, gay couples are usually not accepted as being partners in the same way as heterosexual couples. Unlike wives caring for sick husbands, gay carers are unlikely to be offered respite care, for example.

Gay carers come from a far younger age group than most other carers. As single, self-sufficient men, the majority will have never before experienced serious illness or disability. Many will find their new roles of carers hard to adapt to, especially in the context of sexual relationships.

Because of the nature of the illness, a man looking after a lover with AIDS will also have to cope with feelings other than pain at the prospect of losing someone close. These include guilt, if he thinks he is responsible for infecting a partner; anger, if he feels his partner is the one to blame; and anxiety, about his own health and his own future: indeed, some gay men caring for a sick partner are themselves ill. The onset of AIDS in a partner may also cause hidden uncertainties or feelings of guilt about sexuality to surface.

At present, most people with AIDS are admitted to hospital for treatment only during acute periods of the illness, an approach which is designed to enable them to remain at home for as long as possible.

But most people with AIDS do not live in nuclear families; like many other young, single people living in large cities, they do not have conventional networks of support on which they can draw. Many live alone; and their chief carers and supporters – their partners and friends – are usually unable to give up full-time work; so the provision of adequate community services is particularly important.

The needs of people with AIDS are similar to those of other groups with disabilities living in the community. The fatigue which AIDS causes, for example, means that many sufferers need help with housework and meals; while the diarrhoea which is a common symptom of the infections associated with AIDS, and with the drugs used in its treatment, makes the provision of laundry services essential. If still at home in the final stages of their illness, they will need intensive nursing support. Yet, although some extra money – £6 million in 1987 – has been allocated to the regions hit hardest by AIDS, community services provided by most local and health authorities are still inadequate: in an era of tight resources, people with AIDS have to take their chances like everyone else. Some of the more enlightened local authorities are beginning to develop specialist support services, but these are still in their infancy. Outside London, AIDS sufferers fare particularly badly. Also, the stigma attached to the disease has meant that some staff such as home helps have been reluctant to provide community services, although some local authorities are now beginning to educate community staff about the nature of the illness.

The system of disability benefits has taken little account of the special requirements of people with AIDS, who may face a large drop in income: many go straight from being comparatively high earners, with mortgages and other financial commitments, on to means tested state benefits. AIDS patients may find it difficult, for example, to obtain the Attendance Allowance, since the claimant has to be in need of attendance for at least six months before being eligible for this allowance, by which time someone with AIDS could be dead; and, few AIDS patients will be able to meet the stringent qualifying conditions for claiming the Severe Disablement Allowance. Housing can be another problem, especially for those who are thrown out of private rented accommodation. Few local authority housing policies include people with AIDS on their priority lists of medically vulnerable people.

Over the next decade, the AIDS crisis will continue to grow, and with it the problems faced by gay carers. In Britain, by 1987 some 1,123 people had been diagnosed as having AIDS, of whom over 600 had died; a further 40–50,000 are estimated to be infected with HIV. There is little hope of a cure in the near future, or even of a vaccine against HIV within the next five years.

The development of certain drugs and more knowledge about management of the disease, however, could mean that people with AIDS survive for longer periods than the current average, which is between nine months and two years; so, for people with AIDS and their carers, the provision of adequate community services is particularly crucial.

Kevin Brompton

Kevin Brompton lives in an inner city district of London, in the house he shared with his lover Alan, who died of AIDS four months previously. They bought the house two years ago, and spent time and money renovating it: the furnishings were all chosen by Alan, he says. He has no desire to change them.

Kevin is 35 and works as a computer operator; Alan was 32 and an accountant who was made redundant just before he became ill. They met over seven years ago: 'Seven very wonderful, wild magical years – that's the only way you can put it. I expect everyone thinks

185

their other half is the most wonderful person in the whole world, but this really was a very special relationship.'

Alan was diagnosed as having AIDS in December 1986, when an acute chest infection forced him to go for a hospital check up. He was found to be suffering from pneumocystis carinii pneumonia, a rare illness indicative of immune deficiency. He was prescribed an antibiotic by doctors, and after a few weeks in hospital, recovered sufficiently to come home; but he never returned to his normal strength. Over the next few months, he was constantly in and out of hospital: he suffered particularly from psoriasis, a skin complaint, and had bad pains in his arms and legs. Six months after his diagnosis, Alan was admitted to the specialist AIDS ward of a London hospital; by this time he was virtually unconscious. Kevin and several close friends were with him when he died.

The hospital doctors decided against investigating the specific infection which finally killed Alan; it was felt he was too weak for tests to be carried out. 'The attitude was: we want to let him be comfortable and go with dignity,' Kevin recalls. 'I can't speak too highly of the people at the hospital.'

I suppose, looking at it now, all of last year on and off he was ill: there were lots of silly little things. If you're gay it's always at the back of your mind – every time you sneeze. He had had psoriasis, it got very bad; he had had problems with his bowels, as well as shingles and gout. He'd always been quite healthy before; he was the sort of person that everyone said: it will never happen to Alan.

I suppose, at first, we both sort of hoped we'd got a couple of years. We thought we had plenty of time for them to get a cure: in that situation, you grasp at any straw.

Alan's parents, who live in a different part of the country, do not know that he is dead: there had been no contact between him and his family for years.

There was a big bust up several years ago; they weren't happy because he was gay. At a later stage they said maybe they'd been a bit hasty, but it was too late for Alan. He got rid of everything to do with them: in all his belongings there was nothing, no papers or anything, not one reference to them. He didn't want them to know that he'd got AIDS, and he said they weren't to know about his death.

186

My own family have been as supportive as they could be. My father and stepmother: we're quite close, although we never openly discussed the fact that we were gay. It was referred to obliquely though. Just before Alan died, they guessed what was wrong.

We've got lots of very good friends, mostly gay, but some straight: they've been absolutely marvellous, and they still are. I don't think I could have done it otherwise, to be quite honest. In the last few months there were not enough hours in the day; I was working, but we had a rota of friends with keys who would all pop in.

Alan was always OK to be left. I used to give him his breakfast and leave a meal out, and a friend would drop by to see if he was OK; then he would snooze until I got home. I'd see to all the lotions and potions and ointments for his skin; he needed special cream for his fingers and feet. When he was in hospital I used to bath him.

He was on numerous drugs: anti-inflammatories for his legs, sleeping pills, and Largactil (a tranquilliser normally used in the treatment of nervous disorders). The Largactil was absolutely wonderful, it had the most amazing effect. When he came out of hospital he couldn't relax at all; he was constantly walking around the house, he couldn't read, or concentrate on TV. He was never really the same after being in hospital – whether it was the AIDS or the antibiotics, I don't know. The Largactil turned him into a normal human being again.

At the time of Alan's diagnosis, they were told that the hospital where he went for treatment would have the drug AZT (an anti-viral drug used in the treatment of AIDS) within a few months; at the time the drug was due to become available, however, the local health authority said they could not afford to buy it. Kevin wrote letters of protest:

To the Prime Minister, the Health Minister, Princess Di – I got replies from them all, all non-committal. I got a letter from Edwina Currie promising that everyone who needed AZT would have it. But there are still people who need it who aren't getting it.

Within a few weeks the money had come through; but anyway, by the time the drug was available, Alan wasn't well enough to have it. It's quite a toxic drug and you need to be fairly strong.

When Alan first went into hospital, there was no proper AIDS ward. It was a fairly old ward and fairly crowded: not a very wonderful place. But later, when he went back, there was a new

187

ward: they'd obviously spent a lot of money. Most of the time he had his own room with a shower, his own TV. The attention and love they got from the staff – it was quite exceptional. Especially the nurses. The doctors were good as well; but then, doctors have to be doctors, don't they?

He went on benefits when he became ill. I can't remember what we were getting but I know it came to about £50 a week. Alan was the sort of person who didn't really like charity, but I didn't think £50 a week was enough to live on. I said to him, if you're ill you should have enough money to live on, if you didn't have me, how would you live?

We tried to claim for some things, but I was so busy I didn't have time to sort it out; every time you telephoned you couldn't get through, or it was engaged. Just before Alan died, a social worker tried to sort out the heating: we got an allowance of £1.60 a week. What's £1.60 a week? I had the central heating on all the time: he felt the cold; you can't let them be cold when they're ill. When he first got made redundant, there was an awful lot of money, but by the time he died, the money had just about gone. I used to think – thank God we haven't got to live on what they think we should live on. I was grateful we had the money.

After Alan died I felt physically and mentally exhausted. It's really only recently I started to feel stronger. I put on a very brave face to the outside world. It's a cover: I just get through day by day. Alan would want me to carry on and not be miserable. He would have wanted me to meet someone else; the chances are extremely remote, for lots of reasons, but I know that's what he would have wanted me to do. He's a hard act to follow, though: he was so special to me, I don't think anyone else could make up.

He was the sort of person – if he had a cold he would take to his bed. But all the time he was ill he wasn't like that at all, he hardly ever complained about it. I think he accepted it. We've both got quite a strong faith; I think it helped us both an awful lot. We were both Christians. I'm quite happy I know where he is. I hope I'll be there with him one day.

My only regret is that we should have been more honest with one another about our own feelings. I wouldn't tell him I was desperately worried and upset because I didn't want to upset him, and I'm sure he was doing the same for me. I think – if we had talked, maybe we could have been closer. But then again, I don't think two human beings could have been closer than we were. I had never thought before, that this person is the special one, that it would go on for ever and ever. Whereas I was quite sure it would with Alan and he was with me.

People used to say to me: what does it mean for you? I would say: well, I don't know (whether he is HIV positive) and I haven't got time to think about it. When you've got somebody very ill, you haven't got time to think about yourself. Even now I think: who knows? It doesn't worry me much. I've got friends in a similar situation who have been tested; some have been found completely clear, others are positive. I don't particularly want to know.

We never discussed where the virus might have come from. We were not completely monogamous but almost. You have to remember, the latency period with AIDS could be up to ten years – my guess is that Alan became infected a longer rather than a shorter period ago, before we knew each other.

But there was no point in talking about it really. Because there is no way of ever knowing.

I think it's affected all of us really. I can't speak for the whole of the gay community, of course; I can only speak for my circle. We all think we've got to live very much for today, but then most gay people have always felt like that.

He knew I'd look after him and I did, as best I could. That's all there is to it, really.

9

·

Black carers: Caring within ethnic communities

*Back at home, family will look after you when you are old, but here they
are too busy because they all go out to work.*

*I didn't know about 'pensioners' until I came here . . . we don't call people
old. We don't throw people on the scrap heap.*

*In England, when you reach 60 or 65 years old, you become a social
problem. No one cares about you. If you're ill, that makes it worse. In the
West Indies, you don't finish at 60 or 65 – you are respected. The older you
are, the more respected you are.* (From Anil Bhalla and Ken Blakemore,
Elders of the Minority Ethnic Groups, *All Faiths for One Race (AFFOR)*,
Birmingham 1981)

As is the case with indigenous carers, most carers within
different ethnic communities are looking after relatives who
are growing old: there are about 396,000 immigrants of
pensionable age in the UK, some 52,000 of them from the
Asian subcontinent, 16,000 from the Caribbean and 20,000
from Africa, including Asians from East Africa. A further
859,000 people from the ethnic minorities will reach
pensionable age in the next twenty years. Several ethnic
groups have made their home in Britain for generations and
there are many black British who would rightly object to
being referred to as 'immigrants'. This chapter, however,
concentrates particularly on people of Afro-Caribbean and
Asian origin who have come to this country only relatively
recently.

Many of these elderly people were already adults when
they came to Britain. Many have experienced poverty, flight
from persecution and exile, traumas which may have con-

tributed to both the high incidence of premature ageing and psychiatric problems which have been found in some ethnic communities. As a report on Britain's ethnic minority elderly, funded by the DHSS and published in 1985, points out, the loss of homeland, social status and a familiar environment which many of them have experienced can make them particularly vulnerable to confusion, depression and severe anxiety. Dementia is still relatively uncommon among the ethnic communities, since this older generation is still relatively young, but the report's author, Alison Norman, predicts that it will become a major challenge in the future.

Some black elderly people face particular health hazards: among Asian women living in Britain, for example, shortages of vitamin D have lead to a high incidence of anaemia and osteomalacia, a form of old-age rickets; while those from the Caribbean and Africa are at risk from diabetes, hypertension and stroke, according to a research report published by the Centre for Health Service Management Studies in 1984.

Not all of these dependants, though, are 'elderly' in the usual sense of the word: many who first settled in Britain twenty or thirty years ago and are now in their fifties and early sixties, are experiencing the illnesses and disabilities normally associated with old age. Migration, poor housing, diet and working conditions, racism and the stress of unemployment, have no doubt contributed to their plight.

Poverty and poor housing are two particular disadvantages faced by elderly black people; both factors are thought to affect both their physical and mental health. These 'elderly' tend to be concentrated in inner city areas, in either high rise council properties on unpopular estates, or in private property in poor condition. The AFFOR study, quoted above, which interviewed 400 Afro-Caribbean pensioners, found that over half of them were dependent on supplementary benefits, compared to one in five of Britain's retired population as a whole.

The growing numbers of older immigrants – often living in the worst housing in the country, on inadequate pensions, some of them speaking no English, separated from their families and with no idea of how to deal with the bureaucracy of state services – has finally begun to arouse concern among policymakers. As the 1985 report points out, they are a group which lives in triple jeopardy: of old age, racism and lack of access to statutory services.

Little attention has been paid, however, to ethnic carers, and little is known about their numbers or circumstances. Some are themselves relative newcomers to Britain and share all the disadvantages faced by the elderly relatives they are looking after. These carers in a second homeland constitute one of the most invisible and neglected groups in the country.

Karim Ismail

Karim Ismail is a 37-year-old Ugandan Asian who came to Britain to study accountancy in the early 1970s. He was unexpectedly followed here by both his parents, when, like thousands of others, they were expelled by Idi Amin in 1974. His parents lost everything they had – they had owned a small shop on the outskirts of Kampala – and, while they stayed in an army barracks turned refugee camp, he left his studies and supported them by working on a market stall. All three now live in a small and gloomy London council flat.

His mother, who can speak no English, was already physically disabled and needed an ambulance to fetch her from the plane which brought her to England: the trauma of expulsion has affected her greatly. Karim began to look after her full-time about two years ago when she started to develop dementia. He returned home from the US, where he had developed a promising career in accountancy, to do so. He does everything for his mother, including giving her baths and coping with her incontinence. 'I used to have a barrier against it, I could not undress her. That has all disappeared now.'

Karim also looks after his father, who suffers from chronic bronchitis. His father, he says, does not understand dementia and will often start screaming at his mother: he takes everything she says seriously. Theirs was an arranged and not very happy marriage, undertaken in the state of Gujarat when his mother was 14.

His mother no longer recognises her children and lives for the most part in the far-distant past. The children she does remember, and now weeps for as if they had died yesterday, are the three she lost in infancy, when she was a young mother and the family still lived in India. One of them, a brother who would have been eight years older than Karim, died of smallpox. Karim had no idea his mother had been so poor or had lost three children, until, in her ramblings, she began to talk about them for the first time. 'Everything just started to come out, she started talking about the poverty in India; she had had a lot of suffering, she kept it to herself. In many respects I learnt a lot through my mother's illness.'

Like many Asians, he feels that in England 'people are on their own' and that the culture here is changing the outlook of his compatriots: that they are becoming more interested in 'bettering themselves' through jobs, cars, bigger houses. 'It's not the way it used to be in Uganda. Here, people have their necessities of life, but they're trying to be more materialistic. They don't have enough time. For instance, before people used to come and visit once or twice a week, but now they are busy in their own selves. It's the circumstances they live in: people here are less open.'

In Uganda, he says, someone like himself, looking after a disabled person, would not be so isolated: there, life is lived on a more public level and the community is very important.

In Uganda the whole attitude of people was very different. Not only the Asians but also the Africans: they are very open people. You don't suddenly become alone, wherever you are you're part of it. Every day in Uganda, in the evening, people used to come and visit my mother – it was just like a very big family. And she could communicate with people, because she could speak Swahili. The kind of house we had was very open, built around a very big courtyard; a person could walk around. Now she doesn't recall Uganda but she recalls India. The only way she remembers Uganda is when I speak to her in Swahili. She was 35, 36 when she left India. They left to better themselves.

His father joined the army to serve under the British in the Second World War and was in Kenya in 1945; husband and wife went from there to Uganda in 1952, attracted by the economic incentives offered by the British. Karim was born in India but went with his parents to Uganda when he was three years old. He has returned twice to India.

He feels that the poverty his family and others like it have experienced, and the constant uprooting have produced a great insecurity in people, expressed as a need for self-advancement. 'I used to have frustrations before, basically very selfish, trying to attain a certain goal – I'm learning now. You're always aiming at the highest possible – salary, entertainment – you always want to create an image. You're trying to be competitive, to create an impression, a race where there's nothing to achieve. I saw it at its worse in the US: you're always trying to fight for your position.' Now, he lives on supplementary benefit of around £50 a fortnight and his parents get a supplementary pension.

His mother is a large woman with a long grey plait. She has been asleep on her bed for the afternoon; normally Karim does not let her sleep during the day. On the wall hangs a faded picture of her own mother, in her nineties and still living in the village in Gujarat. Karim's grandmother had many children, several of whom died in infancy. 'I've grown very strong from the inside' he says. 'I thought caring was a duty of one person to another human being. It has brought a lot of change within me to face.'

Bharti Hiram

Bharti Hiram is a 28-year-old Hindu woman with two young children. She came to Britain from her family's village in India after an arranged marriage eight years ago, and speaks little English. She now looks after both her husband's mother, an old lady of about 80 with high blood pressure, and a sister-in-law, Daksha, aged 40, who is mentally handicapped. The latter, who only speaks Gujarati, sits at home all day; she is frightened of the day centre and cannot be understood by staff there.

At the time she was married Mrs Hiram had never met the mother-in-law and sister-in-law she was to look after: the Hiram family had already settled in Britain. She and her husband live in a rented house in North London in a borough which has one of the largest Asian communities in Britain.

In many ways, Mrs Hiram's problems are the same as those of any other carer. As well as looking after two young children, she has the physical burden of washing, dressing and cooking for her husband's two relatives. Neither Daksha nor her mother-in-law can be left alone for long: Daksha because she needs help in going to

194

the toilet, her mother-in-law because she is not very mobile and is subject to fainting fits. Like other carers, Mrs Hiram is extremely isolated and virtually housebound; but her problems are exacerbated by the fact that neither of her dependants speaks English and she herself speaks only very little. There are plenty of Asian community organisations in this area, most of them based on religious centres: but they tend to be geared more towards men than women. These three women live in what is virtually a prison, with little contact with the outside world.

Mrs Hiram says she has put on weight since her marriage and looks far older than her age. She is proud of the two colour photographs of herself and her husband on the mantelpiece, taken at their wedding in India eight years ago; she looks a very beautiful young girl in her red and gold wedding finery.

The privately rented house in north London is decorated in Western style, but in each bedroom there is a small Hindu shrine to the gods, and in her mother-in-law's room, hanging on the wall, is an imprint of the feet of her dead husband. Unlike Mrs Hiram's family, who have never left India, her husband's family are widely travelled: along with thousands of others, his father left India for East Africa after the war.

Mrs Hiram smiles politely during most of the interview; towards the end, however, she starts to cry. Her own mother has been very ill recently and Mrs Hiram wants to pay a final visit to her village, to see her mother and to go to her sister's wedding.

'I want to see her; I don't know what to do. I'm just alone here. No one is here in my family, I'm the only one.' She did not particularly want to come to England, she says, but it could not be helped: she married a man whose family was living here already.

She longs to return to India, if only for a visit, but she and her husband cannot afford the fare: Mr Hiram works in a factory and earns very little; and there are other things which have to come first, such as buying a washing machine for all the extra washing, and a television to keep Daksha occupied.

Mrs Hiram also has problems with her own health: she has been on the contraceptive pill since the birth of her second daughter and would now like a son, but she hasn't had a period since coming off the pill a year ago, and is now being treated for infertility. However, she keeps missing hospital appointments because there is no one to keep an eye on Daksha and her mother-in-law when she goes

195

out. In addition, her husband has developed high blood pressure –
so she feels she has to contain everything rather than share her
problems with him.

Things have improved since the time, several months ago, when
she threatened to leave home unless her mother-in-law stopped
nagging her. 'Sometimes my husband gets annoyed with me; he
takes her part all the time. I said to my husband: either she goes or I
go; I'll stay at my auntie's house.' Since then the mother-in-law has
been more subdued. Would she have gone permanently? 'Only to
teach him a lesson.'

The loss of traditional community support

For those carers who are also first generation immigrants,
looking after a disabled dependant in this country can be an
isolated and alienating experience. Like Karim Ismail, many
come from communities where there exists a more
communal way of life, and where caring for an elderly
person, for example, will often involve a far wider support
network – of extended family, friends and neighbours – than
it does here. In addition, in Africa, Asia and the Caribbean,
old age is more often than not seen as a time of wisdom and
experience, and 'elders' are people to be respected and supported: attitudes which are completely at odds with the
disregard and impatience with which old people are generally
treated in Britain.

Not only do many ethnic carers lose their traditional networks of support, they often have no access to indigenous
welfare services, where the attitude has often been that
'these people look after their own' and need no help from
outsiders. Ethnic minority carers can thus find themselves
falling between two systems: one of which is breaking down
and the other of which ignores them.

As is the case with the indigenous population, the burden
of caring among ethnic communities falls mainly on women:
they are automatically expected to look after elderly relatives
and are probably under greater social pressure to do so than
are their indigenous sisters. This is partly because their tra-

ditional obligations are stronger but also because they have no alternative: residential care as a system is unheard of in many ethnic communities and the idea of putting an elderly relative 'away' into a home – especially one which will not cater for their diet, customs or culture – is abhorrent to most such families.

Many young Asian women are in the same position as Mrs Hiram: brought over to England by their husbands after an arranged marriage, they are expected not only to leave their own parents behind, but to take care of their husband's family, most often his mother-in-law. Back in their home country, these women would have joined their husband's parents' household, and become part of an extended family which offered social and financial support and demanded mutual obligations. In Britain, however, they will still be expected to meet the obligations even though they are not receiving the support. As a consequence, many Asian carers feel overwhelmingly isolated, powerless and depressed. The situation is worse if they speak little English themselves and, like many women from the subcontinent, are dependent on their husbands for their dealings with the outside world. Their own families and parents may still be 'back home', their brothers and sisters dispersed; there is little left of the old extended family to turn to for support.

It is small wonder that there is so much depression and mental illness among Asian women; problems, according to one survey, which are often expressed in physical terms such as constant back or stomach pains and which therefore go undiagnosed.

To make matters worse, ethnic minority women are likely to get little support from their husbands in caring for an elderly relative. This is not just because caring is still traditionally regarded as a female obligation: it is also because of the problems facing ethnic minority men themselves. Many men from the Indian subcontinent put all their energies into providing financial security for their families. They work long hours for little pay and suffer many stress-related illnesses. In addition, there is evidence that the experience of exile, unemployment and poverty has led to high rates of alcoholism, suicide and mental illness. This situation in turn leads to many cases in which Asian wives are caring for chronically ill or disabled husbands. Women who in the past may have rarely been out of the house on their own, and may speak little English, and who may have always been dependent on, and subservient to, their husbands as head of household, find themselves suddenly having to deal with a world with which they have hitherto had little contact. In this situation, the burden of managing household affairs will often fall heavily on the children, who have more contact with the indigenous culture. An eldest daughter, especially, may find herself coping with the burden of family finances and housing problems, and dealing with welfare agencies. In an Asian family, an eldest daughter is often the link to the outside world and the prop which virtually keeps a family going.

Access to services

Little information exists about the use of the welfare state by people from ethnic communities; but the evidence which is available suggests they have little access to, and receive little support from health and social services. Services for the elderly, those who often need them most, are particularly poor: as the 1985 report pointed out:

Hospitals are frightening and confusing places for elderly people from any background; much more so if the staff cannot understand what you are saying and cannot make themselves understood, if you cannot eat the food, and your body is exposed and handled in a way which you find shaming and distressing. (Alison Norman, Triple Jeopardy: Growing Old in a Second Homeland, *Centre for Policy on Ageing, 1985)*

The same problems exist within the domiciliary services, which are barely used by the ethnic minority elderly. Few Asians appear to use the Home Help Service – one of the main pillars of support for elderly people in our society –

partly because often, it is not provided in a way which is acceptable to those from other cultures. Likewise, the Meals on Wheels service – the other mainstay of dependent elderly people in the community – rarely takes account of the different dietary requirements of the ethnic minorities.

In some parts of the country, where ethnic communities are concentrated, genuine efforts are being made to meet their health and social needs. Some of the more enlightened boroughs have, for example, developed Meals on Wheels which cater for ethnic diets, appointed Asian workers, supplied day centres with interpreters and given extra training to their health and social services staff about the language, lifestyle and culture of their clients.

Yet in some areas, these kind of services are either non-existent, or provided in a way which is grudging and tokenistic. Services are sometimes provided 'for Asians', for example, without any account being taken of the differences between different Asian communities; in some hospitals, the 'ethnic minority diet' still consists of a tasteless vegetarian curry; and some health and social services staff seem determined to remain ignorant of different cultures. Small wonder that many people, especially the elderly, refuse to go near an NHS hospital or health centre; and that many remain ignorant of the services which do exist.

If the basic needs of minority elderly people are only just beginning to be recognised, then those of their carers are still being ignored. In the last few years there have been important developments in the support services directed at carers rather than their disabled dependants, initiated by both voluntary and statutory services – respite care and care attendants who can 'sit in' and replace the carer in the family home, for example. Yet so far, these new developments take little account of the needs of minority carers. Few of the new 'care attendants' are themselves drawn from the ethnic communities, for example: little of the respite care provided in NHS homes and hospitals caters for differences in diet and language. While such services are still patchy and unsatisfactory for indigenous carers, they are virtually non-existent for carers in the ethnic communities.

The needs of ethnic minority carers should not be set apart as 'special', nor their values and requirements seen as somehow 'exotic'. Most ethnic communities do not wish to be though of as 'these people', as a group with special problems which somehow have to be 'dealt with' by the relevant authorities. Like everyone else, all they want is a genuine recognition of their problems, as well as a genuine respect for their cultural traditions.

10

·

No place like home? Residential care in homes and hospitals

One year after our first interview, Christina Stanson, whose experience of looking after her mother was described at the beginning of this book, herself suffered a small brain haemorrhage; she was forced to put her mother permanently into a ward in the local geriatric hospital. She had cared for her mother – a stroke victim – for five years. Tina's children have grown up over this time: 'Harriet was only 9 when it happened and she's 14 now; Robert was 17 and he's 23.'

Now in her early forties, she visits her mother regularly and continues to assist her father, aged 80 and still living at home. She is under hospital treatment for the numbness and pains she gets in her face and hands, and still has dizzy spells. 'The consultant said: no way can you look after her again. Once she went in I knew I wouldn't bring her home.'

'I just felt with Mum and then Dad, and then this happening, I was going to end up absolutely barmy. I wouldn't recommend anybody to care; it's destroyed me, it really has.'

She's fine in there. She's on a ward for patients who've had strokes. Most of them aren't long-term like Mum; most are in for assessment and then going back home. But there's five who are in there long-term like her, and they're going to open a little ward for Mum and the others. There is nowhere else; there's nowhere else for her.

They're keeping Mum really as a favour. It's lovely: the nurses are very kind – I know them, they're very good; and Mum loves it, she loves it. It's just me who can't come to terms with it. The nurses say to me: don't come up.

It's quite a lovely ward: it overlooks the common, it's not a long corridor – all the beds are in little bays. They've got a day room, they (the staff) do their hair, they give her a bath every day. The nurses are excellent, nothing's too much trouble; they take her out, to do

201

her Christmas shopping and so on. Of course it's not like home; it can't be. When Mum first went in, I was looking for every little fault.

It was awful, when I was ill and when she first went in. I had to get the social worker to tell her; I couldn't do it, I couldn't tell her. The social worker said, Tina's unwell. They had to put her on anti-depressants, she was so low; she kept on saying, I'll be going home. She has accepted it now. She'll always say, Chrissie's a good girl. I think she understood I wasn't well. She's been very good, very good.

My brothers and sisters still don't go to see her. All the time I was ill, I didn't get one get-well card. They were the ones who wanted her to be in a home, but they've never been to see her, or Dad.

I've become very close to Dad since she went in, he's more like a friend. I've got to know him very well, he's been really supportive. Mum's illness was all too much for him. He's not like he was when she was at home. He's looking after himself; he's much better. He has Meals on Wheels, and I go down once a week and clean the house and do the laundry and take him to the hospital. He's a little bit more independent now. We have a much better relationship – we were always fighting before.

Me and my husband, we've stripped the house and decorated it, and Patrick's bought me a brand new car. I've had my hair cut short and I've lost weight. I manage to do lots of reading. I'm seeing friends more. It's taken me all this time to get back on my feet, though. The stroke did frighten me: I'm not afraid of death but the thought that I'd be left like Mum – I couldn't stand that.

She'll stay in the hospital now. She knows that. She loves the priest; she has communion every week. She would like to die: she says, I wish God would take me. She's been in so much pain, what with the abscess on her back and kidney infections. She's 76 now; she was 70 when she had the stroke.

She's accepted she'll die in hospital. She's said to me: you won't burn me, you will have me buried? She's a Catholic as well – her Catholicism, it goes way back.

We get on much better now she's in hospital: I can go and see her, I take her some flowers, I take her for a walk on the common, and – and then I hand her back. Dad and I can go and talk to her; when she can read a little bit we take her magazines.

She's much more independent: she'll help them get her into bed, she helps them to lift her, she wouldn't do anything like that before –

202

she left it all to me. Partly it was my fault, because I was a perfectionist: I wanted everything done the right way. You can't do things all the right way with someone like Mum.

She knows all the nurses by their first names; they're all very, very lovely to her.

Mum has looked so much better since she was in hospital than at home. It was so intense, so emotional; we're all better off for not having that. She doesn't have to be alone at night. I'm not wondering if she's struggling in wetness: she's got a nurse there all the time.

Of course it's not like home. I do all Mum's washing because I prefer her to wear her own clothes. She's had a few falls in hospital; I wasn't very pleased about that. But she's heavy, I suppose. They shouldn't drop them but they do.

There are a few things that worry me: sometimes all their dignity, their rights seem to be taken away. It's not perfect, but they do try. It can't be perfect with people like Mum.

The cleaning's not up to standard – but then my standards are so high that if I ran that ward I'd be dead in six weeks. Then there's the way the meals are served: you'd like (them) to have a nice glass, you'd like a napkin – what comes up on the plate is not fit for the cat. If only once a week they could have a nice meal, with candles, or something. It's when you're old; it's as though all that's taken away from them.

The nurses are inclined to talk to them as if they're babies, as if they're imbeciles. Some of the ladies in there – one's a concert violinist – they're very, very intelligent people. The nurses do care, I can't say they don't care – one of them gets on the bed and has a cuddle with Mum. They do care – all the nurses. They collected nearly £500 the other week for patients doing a sponsored run.

It's just – things like – they like to get them all together to make mobiles and paint ducks. These are ladies in their eighties, they don't want to do that. Mum hates it; she won't do it.

The consultant phoned me: he said he wanted Mum to participate more. They were going to the pub – they often take them all out for the evening; they wanted her to go along in her wheelchair. I said: Dr Nash, Mum's never been to a pub in her life; she's been a teetotaller all her life. He said: she could have a lemonade. I said: Dr Nash, she's 76-years-old, she doesn't want to go into the pub. I know how she feels; I don't like organised entertainment, singalongs, I couldn't stand it.

I think: by the time you're 80, you know what you want, whether you've had a stroke or not – you're still a person.

And the nurses and doctors – they're inclined to think all the old people are deaf: they start shouting at them. Her hearing's very good.

We have had an incident with one of the nurses – it was reported by another nurse, I will say that, they are very honest. One nurse was very cruel to Mum – she was disciplined for it – she was actually physically cruel. Mum has this protrusion on her bottom . . . she had wanted to go to the loo, this nurse said Mum had got to get on a bedpan; she made her get onto a bedpan, this squashed her protrusion – it was all bleeding and everything – she really gave Mum a good going over.

Another one, she said Mum was a big fat pig. She was reported as well. It always seems to be the night nurses – they're mostly agency nurses. The sister said it was because they have different ideas: they think Mum should be at home. I said: I've looked after Mum for four years, I've done all I can; let me talk to the nurse, let me tell her. Some nurses – they see things in a different light.

You do get this from some of the nurses. I remember when Mum used to come in for respite care; they used to say, I don't know why their families can't look after them. I say to them, I've done it for four years and I know what happens: in the end it's the carer who dies and the patient who's still alive.

A close friend of mine, she used to be a nurse, she gave me some good advice. She said: never make friends with them, if there's any trouble you'll feel you can't complain. And she's right.

But I am friends with them. The little girl who dropped Mum – on her head, actually – she came and told me, she was in tears. She said: Tina, I had an accident. I didn't know what to say. She's a lovely girl but she shouldn't have been lifting Mum by herself – she's not even a nurse, she's an aide. They are short of nurses, they're thirty-three nurses short at the hospital, and sometimes only three of them on duty – with twenty-six patients in at the moment, all like Mum, some worse than Mum. When you think it took me all my time to care for Mum. They have to serve meals as well, they do the washing, they bath them, take them to the toilet.

The trays and lockers are very tatty, the blinds at the window they all need re-doing – when the sun shines onto Mum they have to put up a blanket to stop it getting on her head. And the curtains that go around the bed – they always choose that awful orange colour – they're always falling down.

I usually go to the hospital every day. I look forward to it. I like to take Mum things. I take Dad. We have a cup of tea together. It's not very far, it only takes about seven minutes in the car. I especially like to do it for Dad because he loves to go.

I am having problems; I feel so guilty. I think I had it in my mind . . . my whole world went round the idea that Mum would die at home. I've had to come to terms with the thought that she'll have to die in a ward. I didn't want that. I just didn't want that.

It's very difficult to go into Dad's house. I feel terrible when I go into Mum's room: I feel as though I can't breathe; it all comes back to me, all the memories. I wish I could have kept looking after her. Because I do love her, and she is my mother. I know I couldn't have kept on looking after her. If maybe I'd have been a different person, a stronger person, less emotional, maybe I could have kept her at home. I do love her, I can't help that; I do love her, although sometimes I feel she didn't love me. Maybe it's the little girl in me or something; maybe that's why I wanted to show her – that I do love her.

Dad's been a great support: you mustn't feel guilty my love, you've done so much for her, he says.

The way I was actually doing it – it was as though I wanted Mum to be a different person. I was trying to make Mum, after she'd had the stroke, I was trying to make her the mother I didn't have. I wanted to make it into this perfect little thing before she died. I put flowers and plants and books in her room; I wanted her to be the Mum I wanted when I was a little girl. I think maybe because I thought I had more power; she couldn't dominate any more. I was wrong, you see.

We get on much better. She has said: I do love you Chrissie, I do love you, you were a good girl, you were a good girl. I understand, she says, it was far too much for you. She looks at me in a different sort of light – she understands me now. Before, the more I did, the more she seemed to condemn me.

I think I'll go back to college and do some sort of course, maybe in child psychology. Just for myself, to get back onto an intellectual level – not all bedpans and poo.

Unable to cope

Many women are driven to give up caring for a disabled relative because they simply cannot cope any longer; in many cases, like Tina Stanson, because of a breakdown in their own physical or mental health. They are then forced to turn to what is still the only alternative to being cared for at home: long-stay institutional care in a residential home or hospital.

Carers faced with this prospect may feel guilty at doing something which was probably unthinkable only a few years previously. They may feel grief at their own inability to continue caring; anxiety at the prospect of a vulnerable relative being cared for by strangers; as well as relief at the lifting of an intolerable burden.

Most carers also face an uphill struggle in finding alternative care which is even vaguely acceptable either to them or their dependants. At best, like Tina Stanson, they might find a home or hospital ward which is relatively homely; at worst – and because this decision is so often taken in a crisis – they may be forced to 'dump' a relative in an understaffed, underfunded NHS ward or local authority home, and to watch someone they have looked after for years gradually lose all sense of dignity and independence.

The standards of care in many institutions – whether geriatric ward, residential home or mental handicap hospital – have improved considerably over the last twenty years. In many homes and hospitals, ideas are changing rapidly and great efforts are being made – often with few resources – to make conditions more homely and to encourage residents' and patients' privacy, dignity and independence. And moving into residential care is not necessarily a disastrous step: not everyone hates institutions. Many disabled and elderly people will start to enjoy the social life and the friendships which they can provide and may find a new lease of life, especially after the isolation and loneliness of being looked after at home by an exhausted and resentful carer. As is the case with Tina Stanson and her mother, such a move may even improve the relationship.

But whatever improvements are made in long-stay care, and however friendly and caring the staff, most carers and their relatives still feel there is a vast and unbridgeable gulf between being cared for by someone close, in the comfort of a family home – whatever the problems – and being looked after by strangers in an institution. Like Tina Stanson, many women are forced to accept the fact that the care received by their dependants can never be of the same standard as that provided at home. For some, it can be heartbreaking to see an elderly or disabled relative admitted to residential care, only to suddenly go downhill – or worse: the tale of the elderly person who has thrived for years while being cared for at home and who dies within a week of being admitted to a longstay geriatric ward, is still a familiar one.

Most carers feel a genuine moral dilemma when it comes to putting a relative into institutional care, especially if that relative is herself anxious and frightened about being 'put away'. This dilemma reflects the wider moral question of the options for living we offer disabled and elderly people. We live in a society where most people live in families and look after their own relatives in their own homes. For many of our elderly people institutional care is something they dread, something which still smacks of the Poor Laws and the workhouse. Many carers are forced into making an invidious choice between putting their dependant in an institution – and thereby ensuring their own survival – and continuing to provide that elderly or disabled relative with a home in which to live in relative privacy and dignity, looked after by his or her own family.

In a better world, the need for such decisions would not exist, since elderly and disabled people and their families would have a range of options for ways of living; with a network of community services and support which would render obsolete the choice between long-stay residential care and being looked after at home. In some parts of the country, these new patterns of support are already being developed, and many younger disabled people are opting for what to them are more acceptable ways of living: for instance, in sheltered flats with support services supplied, or in new residential homes where there is a far greater degree of privacy than has been provided in the past. These new models of independent living – which mean disabled people are not totally dependent on either their families or institutions – may eventually make redundant the concepts of 'care' and 'dependency'; but they are still few and far between. Thousands of carers and their relatives still face the 'home or institution' decision.

In a sense, carers are being forced to take on a moral burden which belongs to society as a whole. We have failed to provide adequately for our disabled and elderly population, or to honour their right to independence and dignity; we have failed to face up to an important collective responsibility.

What the public sector provides

There were months of wrangling about whether she was a case for the local geriatric hospital or a residential home. She was constantly shuttled around. You get the situation where the health authority, the consultant, tries to hand over to social services, saying this is a case for Part III [a local authority residential home]; and social services are saying she needs medical care so it's the health authority's responsibility. You get trapped in the middle while they argue.

We were eventually faced with the choice: the geriatric hospital, over-crowded and understaffed, or Part III where she would have had to share a room, maybe with people who would not be mentally alert and maybe even doubly incontinent. In the end I gave up work completely and took her back home. Nobody told me if I'd put her somewhere private I'd have got help with the fees from the DHSS. They kept that very quiet. This is what happens all the way along the line – an awful lot you just don't get told. (Janet Bambry, who cared for her mother, a semi-invalid after a stroke, for twelve years)

In the public sector, the two main residential alternatives for elderly people, who make up the vast majority of our disabled population, are NHS beds in long-stay geriatric or

208

psychogeriatric wards – often housed in large, isolated mental hospitals – or local authority 'Part III' residential homes; for the latter, local authorities make a minimum charge of £31.60 a week (1987 figures).

Over the last few years, many geriatric wards – the traditional 'dumping grounds' for elderly people – have been closed, the aim being to keep as many old people as possible in their own homes supported by domiciliary services such as district nurses, home helps and Meals on Wheels. The theory was that those who still needed residential care were to be housed in small local community hospitals and NHS nursing homes rather than long-stay wards.

In reality, the development of community hospitals and nursing homes has been slow while the domiciliary services intended to form the backbone of the new community care policies are grossly inadequate. The result has been that, at a time when the number of elderly people in need of support is growing, many traditional long-stay public sector institutions have been closed while no acceptable alternative has been developed to replace them.

This failure has led to lengthy delays for elderly people in need of a long-stay bed, and frequent wrangles over responsibility between hard pressed local social services departments and health authorities squeezed of both funding and places for long-stay care. The result is that many carers have to wait years before being offered a residential place.

The pressure on hospital beds has also made a nonsense of the original distinction between local authority homes and geriatric wards: local authority residential homes, known as 'Part III' (because they are provided under Part III of the National Assistance Act 1948), were originally designed and built for fit elderly peole who needed some support, but who did not need nursing care; now they are being used for very disabled elderly people. As a result residential homes' staff, many of whom are untrained, are being forced to cope with growing numbers of highly dependent and demented elderly people – simply because there is nowhere else for them to go.

Jill Fordham has cared for a husband with multiple sclerosis for the last thirty-four years. Now 60, he is almost totally paralysed and virtually helpless, and has been promised a place in a voluntary home for incurables in the near future.

We've only come to this decision with the utmost regret – we didn't want it. It was very difficult and the actual decision was made by my husband. I think he felt it was just too much to expect of me and I was getting old. He said, obviously there's no place like home; but felt in fairness to me it's what he should do. I feel he's going to get a better quality of life and a longer life there: he needs medical care and they have immediate medical back-up. There's quite a lot going on for them there: they've got all kinds of activities; they take them to the races eight times a year, to drama groups, chess clubs – they get quite a lot of visitors.

The only problem, she says, is that the home – run by a charity, but where places are paid for by the local authority – is some distance from their own home, which will make visiting difficult for her. The only alternative closer to where they live was a residential ward for severely disabled people at the local hospital.

The majority of residents on that ward – you get the feeling they're there because nobody wanted to look after them. They just sit there: there's no motivation, nothing going on. If you go into that ward you'll find six people asleep in the middle of the day. You feel such people are existing rather than living.

I feel it's the end of an era; very much the end of an era. It is very sad. I've been going through all kinds of mementoes and photographs, memories of the early days when one had so much optimism and hope. It never occurred to me, thirty years on, that they would be nowhere near a cure; it never occurred to either of us. I don't think we could have possibly carried on – we always thought, any day there'll be a cure.

Everyone I've spoken to, they've said: you've got absolutely no reason to feel guilty, you've done your best for 34 years, lots of people would have given up years ago. So I don't feel guilty – only regret; I wish I could have done it for longer. I prayed to get strength to do it, but it just didn't come. Now I feel he's likely to be in much better shape for going than if I'd hung on and on. Now I feel it's what we're meant to do.

Younger physically disabled people who are looking for a residential alternative have even less of a choice than do elderly people. This is because, in the forty years since the 1948 National Assistance Act – which provided for residential care – local authorities have mainly concentrated on providing for the growing numbers of elderly people. Even today, the only long-stay places younger disabled adults are likely to be offered are in geriatric wards or 'young disabled' units attached to NHS hospitals.

Some carers of younger or middle-aged dependants turn for help to the voluntary organisations which have over the last forty years stepped in to fill the gap. The problem with the voluntary homes is that they are unevenly distributed around the country, which means that dependants find themselves at some distance from their families. Many voluntary homes also impose restrictions on who they will admit: in a bid to attract younger clientele, for example, some impose an age limit of 50 or 55; exactly the time of life when carers themselves are finding progressive disabilities such as multiple sclerosis – the major disabling illness amongst non-elderly adults – most difficult to cope with. Or again, many homes refuse to take people with behavioural problems brought on by conditions such as head injury or Huntington's Chorea. These are cases for which there is very little suitable provision either in the voluntary or statutory sector, and those who suffer them are likely to end up in psychiatric wards once their families can no longer cope.

When hospital is home

Robert Jameson's mentally handicapped son David, now aged 36, has lived in hospital since he was 11, when his parents felt they could no longer cope with keeping him at home. 'We kept him at home in the first few years; there was never any question of sending him away,' says his father.

But David was a 24-hour-job and we had three girls. He was very hectic, he was also epileptic – he had two or three severe fits a week. There was nobody

211

to help in those days. It was a terrible decision: you can't describe the heartbreak, it's heartbreaking – you feel you're letting the boy down. But, at the end of the day, five lives were being torn asunder because of one. And David had to lose out.

The hospital where David lives, however, is now gradually reducing its number of beds as part of the move towards 'community care', replacing them with ordinary houses and hostels in the community. It is a move with which the Jamesons fear their son will not be able to cope.

'David would like to stay; a lot of them want to stay,' says his father.

Moving people out of long-stay hospitals doesn't guarantee a better way of life. You put them in a small house in any street – what happens? You find the doors have to be locked, because the staff are frightened of them getting knocked down. In hospital, David can wander round the grounds. All this will be lost to them. People have got to realise: these are people's homes we are talking about.

David is mentally handicapped: he can walk and hold a stunted conversation, but he's very childish in his ways. He can't cross the road on his own; you can't send him to the shops, he can't handle money; and he's very gullible, as most of them are. He'll need gentle monitoring for the rest of his life. They don't like change.

I think it's got to be accepted that mentally handicapped people are different. That is a fact. Quite a lot of my son's habits are unacceptable. Some of them (the residents) are quite docile and lovable, but they're not all Down's: others are mentally ill and physically handicapped as well. At the end of the day, one has got to accept that basically, mentally they are quite often children. They do need monitoring, they need 24-hour care. This business about the hospitals being isolated is a load of rubbish. Look at the thousands of elderly people in our communities: they're fare more isolated than those in hospital. A lot of these hospitals are set in beautiful areas. They get taken on holidays, my son went on holiday only the other week.

We're not saying all the hospitals are great. But let's face it, parents send their children to residential schools – look at Eton and Harrow. I was in the army for five years. There's nothing wrong in people being grouped together. What worries us is what worries most other parents: what happens when I die?

One can't praise the nursing staff too highly. But over the last two years there have been ward closures, staff shortages, low staff morale. It's very unsettling for David and a lot of the residents. It's unsettled the staff – we're very much concerned. We're saying we need an independent reappraisal of community care. We're saying this madness has got to be stopped.

These days, few parents would consider putting a young disabled child into care; attitudes have changed and today the majority of children with severe handicaps live with their families (although some handicapped children do get sent to residential and boarding schools – often to be taught social skills). There are, however, a substantial number of parents whose children do live in institutions. These are the middle-aged and elderly parents of adult, usually mentally handicapped, offspring who were born at a time when it was accepted that such children should live in institutions; when there were few support services for keeping them at home; and when parents often felt they had no choice but to have their child admitted to one of the large mental handicap hospitals, usually around the time they reached puberty or adolescence.

The era of large institutions may be coming to an end, but it is not yet over, and the major worry of parents such as Robert Jameson is the uncertain future their children face in the move to 'community care'; the transition from a hospital they regard as home to facilities which may be neither funded nor staffed adequately, and the reliance on support from a 'community' which appears non-existent.

Private homes: the new dumping ground?

We tried several different private homes over the years; I was never satisfied but we were desperate. In the first one the matron was an older lady, a stickler for manners: you couldn't put your elbows on the table when you were eating – this was at a time when I was glad my mum was getting down any food at all.

The next one was recommended by the doctor. The owner seemed a very pleasant woman; it was a nice little house, it seemed hunky-dory, but my mother started to have problems. She got terrible pains – I'm sure they were caused by sitting around in a chair all day. They said they walked the old people around, but every time I used to visit, I never saw the old people moved once: they were just left sitting all day in the chair for long periods. When I cared for her I used to walk Mother twice a day – even when she was at her worst. I suppose you could say that I'm a bit fussy, but when you look after someone yourself, you have got certain standards; you expect a certain amount.

The third one was larger, a proper nursing home. The people who ran it seemed very charming, the staff seemed very good with those who were mentally gone. I didn't know it was financially insolvent at the time, but then it was taken over by a new owner. She was a bit hard, a different type of person altogether – intent on running the home for profit.

That's when it started: there were little things, trouble with the food, the staff started to get unhappy. There was no support from the top; staff would stay for a week or two and then leave. The atmosphere got bad – it was a chaotic situation. In the end there was a tremendous turnover of staff: every time you went there was someone different. They never seemed to be supervised properly; there were kids who had never seen the old people before working on their own, washing the old people and doing all sorts of things. The owner, the matron, was busy moving house from up north, so she wasn't there very often, so everything fell on the sisters; the nurses were overloaded with paperwork and trying to do everything. There were silly, small things, things which no one took any responsibility for. Some of the old people couldn't eat, so someone was supposed to take the stones out of the fruit – but no one did, the nurses said it was the cook's job. I used to go along at mealtimes so I could help feed her. Mum suffered from glaucoma (an eye disease which causes blindness), but one girl always positioned her facing the light. I'd come in and she'd be crying: turn the light off.

About a week after Mum died I went there – to get her clothes. Mum's teeth were still in a glass; they were still in her room, no one had bothered to remove them. They'd been put in that glass when she got ill, about a week before she died, and no one had bothered to remove them.

It was difficult to complain. At one point, the owner said: if you're not happy, you're welcome to take her away, we've got a waiting list a mile long. You hear that a lot. But I couldn't take her away; I didn't feel strong enough to look for another place and she was too frail to move. We had to live with the situation. I didn't want to complain because I thought it would come back on her. When you put your mother in a home, you think: I'm an amateur, with no training, here she'll be looked after by professionals. But it isn't the case. Most of the assistants had very little training and they hadn't time to learn from their mistakes.

She hated it there. She was always saying, take me away. Caring for her at home was tough, but there's nothing tougher than visiting them in a home and hearing them say that. (Jan Watling, who cared for her mother, a confused and frail old lady in her eighties, for several years before trying out three different private homes)

For many carers and their disabled relatives, the squeeze on public sector long-stay care and the lack of any alternative support in the community means that private residential or nursing homes are rapidly becoming the only options. Private and voluntary homes have always provided a proportion of residential care places; but in recent years, the number of commercially run homes for both disabled and elderly people has multiplied, encouraged by the government and subsidised to the tune of £500 million annually by the DHSS through supplementary benefit payments. Well over a quarter of a million people are in residential care in Britain; nearly half of them are in homes provided by the voluntary and private sectors which, it has been predicted, could outstrip public provision by the end of the decade.

These private homes range from the large hotel-style chains now being set up along professional lines and run by large companies – some of which, based on US-style 'Life Care' schemes, include restaurants and bowling greens among their amenities – to the smaller, more traditional homes, usually run by married couples, which make up the 'cottage industry' end of the market – the converted Edwardian and Victorian houses which now line much of the English coast.

Despite the introduction of legislation to strengthen inspection procedures in private homes, and a new, government-approved code of practice, concern about standards in some of these establishments is growing, and there are understandable fears that they are rapidly replacing the long-stay wards as the new 'dumping grounds', especially for elderly, mentally handicapped and mentally ill people. A report published in 1986 by Harriet Harman, the Labour Party's spokeswoman on social services, for example, revealed that the tribunals which hear appeals from home proprietors refused registration by local authorities, had heard allegations that elderly relatives had been forcibly fed; tied to chairs; left for hours in soiled beds; and abused with obscene language. Some proprietors who have appeared in front of these tribunals have had criminal convictions and, once disqualified from one borough, have moved on to open a home somewhere else. An ITV programme, 'The Granny Business', which was broadcast in 1987, provided similar evidence of cruelty, squalor and financial exploitation, this time in private homes in Kent: old people, it was claimed on the programme by former care assistants, had been left tied to commodes; fined for incontinence; banned from having visitors; kept in cold and dangerous conditions; left in their own urine for hours at a time; even sexually assaulted.

The registration of a private home with a local authority is, sadly, no guarantee of standards: few local authorities, it seems, have either the resources to carry out the inspection procedures introduced by the 1984 Registered Homes Act, or to enforce the code of practice on residential care, called *Home Life*, drawn up by a DHSS-sponsored working party, which was published the same year. Neither do local authorities always have the will to shut down homes on which, in the absence of the community services needed to keep people at home, they have come to depend; this is especially so at a time when large long-stay hospitals are being closed and thousands of patients returned to the community. Some local authorities have also realised that by closing their own homes and approving private establishments, they can save money and shift the financial burden of caring on to the social security budget.

Whatever one's view about the running of residential homes on a commercial basis, it would be wrong to condemn standards in all private establishments. As in the public sector, there are huge variations in the quality of care, and some private homes have become acknowledged models of good practice. And the unacceptable conditions and degradation which have been found in private homes have, in the past, also been found in public institutions. Abuse has its roots in our attitudes to old age, and in the common view of elderly people as passive, docile creatures to be serviced as efficiently as possible rather than as adults with individual needs and with the right to dignity, independence and privacy.

As Jan Watling's story illustrates, the erosion of that dignity is often revealed in the small details of living in a residential care home rather than by dramatic evidence of brutality. Too many old people are made to eat their meals at hours which suit the staff, but which are more appropriate for children than grown adults, or are banned from locking the doors to their own rooms; too many homes are concerned with rules and regulations rather than individual needs and rights; and as in geriatric wards and local authority homes, too many are run by staff who are for the most part overworked, underpaid, unqualified and undervalued. Some take little note of official guidelines on standards.

One 1986 survey of nursing homes in the south of England found that half the elderly patients had to share a bedroom, while 10 per cent shared a room with four others, sometimes in bedrooms below the square footage required by the National Association of Health Authorities guidelines. Over one fifth of these homes did not even have a lounge or sitting area for their patients.

Are the residents sitting in chairs ringed round the room, with everybody watching 'Playschool'? Does it smell, do people cringe when 'Matron' comes into the room? Is there a strong smell of air freshener – this usually indicates that incontinence is not being managed successfully. Do staff go straight into people's rooms without knocking? Don't be afraid of domestic clutter, it's better than everything being all spit and polish. I'm very suspicious if there's a strong smell of Brasso and carefully arranged flowers everywhere. (Deirdre Wynne Harley, Centre for Policy on Ageing)

Sometimes, of course, it is the carers themselves who can make a mistake in choosing a home: feeling guilty at putting someone 'away', anxious and overprotective, or frightened by press reports of cruelty and squalor, they may want to ensure their elderly relative is 'given' care rather than allowed some control over her own life. Many families, for instance, feel happier with a 'matron' in uniform who runs a home on medical lines, believing that 'she'll be all right if she's with a nurse' and with everything being done to a timetable, than they would be with a place where elderly people might be allowed to take risks or make choices – about whether, for instance, to make a snack, or fill a kettle or a hot water bottle on their own.

One of the major problems faced by carers trying to find a suitable private home is the lack of information and advice available from statutory services – from either GPs, social workers or other professionals. Although one or two charities and commercial agencies provide 'matchmaking' services, most carers have to rely on their own judgement when choosing a home. Another problem is that whereas old people who request a local authority place have the right to have their needs assessed by professional staff and alternatives such as more support at home, considered, no such assessment procedure is needed to enter a private establishment.

The major factor for carers and elderly relatives considering private residential care is, of course, the fees, which normally range from £90 to £350 weekly (1987 figures).

In the past, most private residents paid for care either out of their own purse or sometimes with the help of local authority sponsorship; but over the last few years, a new system of funding has evolved whereby increasing numbers of less well off disabled and elderly people have been able to use new supplementary benefit regulations to help pay for care, via DHSS board and lodging payments (someone with assets of £3,000 or more – including the value of a house – has to pay his or her own fees until that money runs out, which can mean a carer living in her parents' house may have to sell the only home she has to pay for a parent to go into private care). It is this use of social security to pay for private care which has been responsible for the huge growth in the private sector in recent years.

In April 1985, the government itself took fright at the rising costs in social security payments to private homes, which for elderly people jumped from £6 million in 1978 to an estimated £280 million in 1985. It put a national ceiling on the state benefits which would be made available to those in residential care, with different limits set for different categories of dependency.

Since then, many private homes have tried to peg their fees to the limits set by the DHSS in an effort to keep clients and stay open, with the result that standards have fallen. Some voluntary homes are running into financial problems and are finding it difficult to remain viable. And, although the benefit rates of current residents are protected, the ceiling means that people in homes which put up their fees as from 1985 now have to worry about how long their own 'topping up' funds will last, or whether they will get further local authority help: they may even face eviction. In the future, many elderly people may be unable to consider private residential care at all.

Critics of the government's policy argue that the money spent on supporting those in private homes has encouraged both elderly and disabled people to go into residential care unnecessarily, and that it would be better used in providing domiciliary backup services: £280 million, is, after all, the equivalent of 10 per cent of current spending on personal social services such as home helps, social workers and Meals on Wheels.

A government committee set up to consider the public financing of private care (presumably to find a way of cutting the social security budget), suggested, in July 1987, that the whole system of paying private residential costs via supplementary benefit be scrapped, and that local authorities take responsibility for financing all residential care costs; although whether this will happen is undecided.

A major report on all types of residential care, commissioned by the government from the National Institute for Social Work and published in early 1988, made a number of suggestions for improving standards in private, voluntary and local authority homes. It also suggested that disabled people be given a community care allowance which could be spent either on residential care or help at home. It remains to be seen whether these recommendations will be implemented.

11

·

Care in what community? State support for carers and their dependants

What most carers want from the state is a system which genuinely encourages disabled and elderly people to lead independent lives within the community. This could be achieved by providing them with the health and social services they and their carers require; by devising a system of cash benefits which guarantee financial independence; and by policies which take account of the needs of disabled people through the whole range of public and social life, including transport, education and employment. In short, the growing number of carers and their dependent relatives need better support and more of it. Instead, the already inadequate system of services and benefits is if anything being eroded by cash cutbacks, by the family-oriented approach of present government policy and by new legislation which sets out to alter fundamentally the current benefits system. The danger is that, as support to disabled and elderly people is reduced, their potential for an independent life will be eroded, and the burden of looking after them will fall even more heavily on their families.

Services: the failure to provide

If, right from the beginning, someone had sat down with us and, instead of shoving her home and saying there were no problems – when in fact she was virtually dependent – if they'd said: she's going to need care and here are the ways we can help. If we'd been told about the financial help, the short-stay accommodation, given a wheelchair we could actually use. If someone had said: if it gets too much, here are the options.

What I feel bitter about is that it's a big slice out of your life. I look back

221

and think, my God – it's been ten years, ten years of my life. That's when I get angry. The services are so appalling and you get treated so badly, even the way you get spoken to. I was either not advised at all, misinformed or patronised. And sometimes when I made a complaint I was downright intimidated. You have to fight all the way along the line for everything. You don't start battling until the end, when you realise; and you wish you had started earlier.

It all happens at a time when you're emotionally distressed. You want to be kind and gentle; you don't want to have to start to get angry. The caring is one thing – it's another having to do battle with all the people who are meant to support you. (Janet Bambry, who for twelve years looked after her mother, a semi-invalid after a stroke, until her death in hospital six months before this interview)

Only the DHSS has the resources with which to make a general assessment of the degree of support given to carers and their disabled relatives by statutory services. Since most services are provided by individual local social services departments and health authorities, the levels of support carers receive varies throughout the country; depending on the local resources available and on the degree of awareness and effectiveness of individual staff, be they managers, professionals or administrators.

That said, however, the evidence which is available supports the overwhelming impression given by the interviews in this book: that conventional statutory services are failing to provide even the basic support which carers desperately need. One nationwide survey of over 500 carers, carried out in 1986, found that over 80 per cent got no help whatsoever. Other research shows that the presence of a carer – especially if a woman – actually prejudices the chances of getting help, which is still geared to the disabled and elderly living alone. The conventional statutory services, in other words, are being used as a last-ditch substitute for family care, rather than as an effective system of support for the carers.

I could have done with more nursing help at the beginning. The doctor said: you've no family at home, you'll be fine. But in hospital my husband had two nurses to lift him – he was 13 stone. They assured me – they still do – that I could do it. They say: we're very short of nurses, can't you manage? The community nursing officer suggested a nursing course. If we'd wanted to be nurses we'd have trained to do it. I said: for God's sake, we're nursing all day long, what on earth do we want a nursing course for? This is the attitude – that we need re-educating. (Pam Purdy)

Kept in the dark

One of the biggest complaints among carers is that no one ever sits a carer down and tells her what she needs, or what she is entitled to. Many are left completely in the dark about the services and benefits available, and it will sometimes take years for a carer to find out about the local incontinence service or the day centre, for example. There are carers in desperate situations who never catch sight of their GP – never mind hear of the allowances or the equipment they could apply for.

This health board is absolutely pathetic; you've got to find everything out for yourself – about the aids, the wheelchair, even the incontinence pads. No one told me about the incontinence, she was given the pants which are OK if you're slightly incontinent, but she gets so many infections, now it's a complete flood.

I only found out about disposable pads through the girl who does my washing. She said, you can get these off your nurses; but the nurse had never heard of them. I phoned up the hospital; they said every single health centre had them, you can get them off your doctor or district nurses, but mine had never heard of them. Eventually, I started buying them from the chemist. (James Lenagh)

Similarly, few carers are told what caring entails. Few are given a full explanation of what is wrong with their relative and what they can do about it. Few are given advice about how to keep an elderly relative as independent as possible. Few are told the right way to help someone with dementia keep in contact with reality, or how to lift a heavy, semi-paralysed adult out of a wheelchair.

Few carers have access to the kind of knowledge about old age and disability which would actually make their job easier;

about the fact, for instance, that it is better to allow an old lady, semi-paralysed by a stroke, to wash and dress herself than to do it for her; that is is better not to 'care too much', not to undermine independence and take control, even if it is often easier to do something for someone than sit and wait for them to do it themselves.

Even more important in many ways, few carers are given the kind of counselling which would enable them to assert their own needs, and put a limit on their caring.

This lack of advice and information is partly due to the fact that our welfare system is so fragmented that no one member of staff is formally responsible for giving a carer all the information she needs. Those carers who do have contact with statutory services find themselves dealing with a formidable array of different professionals, employed by different departments, and all dealing with different aspects of community care. What information a carer receives will often depend on how helpful an individual professional wishes to be; and especially on the attitude of the general practitioner, who acts as the 'gatekeeper' to so many other services. Many carers interviewed for this book described their GPs as 'useless' – people they never saw from one end of the year to the other.

The professionals

The district nurses are supposed to do the bladder washouts and catheter changes, but they don't. For instance, last Tuesday, the nurse came out for the bladder washout and the catheter was blocked. You couldn't get water into the bladder because it was blocked, but she kept tyring to force water in. She didn't bother to change the catheter or offer to. She went away and I changed it myself. (Max Harper)

The social worker would come in and see nicely hoovered carpets; you could see them thinking, oh there's no problem here. If you look decent and the house is reasonable you don't get any help until you collapse. I remember getting one piece of advice from a matron. She said: don't just have her come when it's all clean and tidy, let them see it as it is, let them see her not cleaned up. But none of us will do that. (Janet Bambry)

The GP is hopeless. When they hear it's senile dementia, that it's incurable, they just shrug their shoulders and write out a prescription. (James Lenagh)

The home help is no good. I'd like her to do the lampshades and dust the cobwebs, but she's not supposed to climb; they won't clean high up or low down. What do they do? All they do is vacuum. If I ask her to clean the window, she asks should she do the sill. If I clean the windows I always do the paintwork. (Betty Hampton)

She finally died in hospital. The nurses were absolutely marvellous at the end: they couldn't have done more for her or for us. If they can be that considerate at the end, why can't they do it earlier on? Instead, it was this hostile aggressive attitude. The hospital didn't want to know about her. (Janet Bambry)

Many carers are angered by the patronising, and sometimes hostile or deliberately unhelpful attitudes of 'caring' professionals; by the ineptitude of the GP who tells a daughter her father's dementia is just 'his age'; by the arrogance of the hospital consultant who tells a busy woman with three children that she has no alternative but to take her mother-in-law, immobilised after a stroke, home from hospital; by the high-handedness of the district nurse who tells a single daughter she should do less 'outside the house'.

Carers feel they get treated, not as equal and important partners in care who should be consulted and kept informed, but as relatives who are 'in the way'.

Constant delays

We were given a wheelchair but it wouldn't go in the car boot. No one suggested anything could be done. Finally we did get a wheelchair which fitted in, but if we'd had it at the beginning I could have taken her out much more. They don't tell you about the better quality wheelchair, even if it means you might actually use it instead of leaving it standing in the corner all the time. (Janet Bambry)

Many carers face seemingly interminable delays in obtaining equipment and services: a new battery for the wheelchair, a bath aid, a respite bed in the local hospital or a long overdue

Attendance Allowance. The equipment they are given is often out of date, awkward and unimaginative: hoists too heavy or too undignified to use, wheelchairs too wide to manoeuvre through narrow doors, and cheap incontinence pads which, backed with plastic, failed to 'breathe' or to do the job they were designed for. One elderly woman, caring for both herself and her husband, had a disease which was crippling her hands. Her social services department had given her a primitive wooden contraption which was meant to help her pour the tea, but, when she used it, it caused her to scald herself twice.

You have to wait for everything: for prescriptions, aids, nurses, chiropodists. I was offered a lavatory handle but it took two years for them to fit it; by the time I would have had it fitted, I'd had one put in privately. I rang social services; I said I wanted an overbed table. She said I couldn't have one, I'd got one already. I said I'd bought that one so I'm entitled to one. They said, oh no, you've got one already. I bought my own wheelchair, my own bath seat; I couldn't sit about and wait for them. Chiropody – you only have a home visit every three months. Every way you turn as a carer you're told no, you can't have it. (Pam Purdy)

Of course, there is another side to the story. Despite the increasing emphasis on 'community care', both funding and domiciliary staff are at a minimum. GPs are still trained on a medical model which teaches them how to give an injection and to write a prescription, but not to offer emotional support. Community staff distance themselves from pain, disability and old age by adopting a strictly 'professional' attitude. Home helps – poorly paid part-timers who are often carers themselves – cannot be expected to do more than they are paid for. Ambulance staff, who never turn up on time to collect a disabled person for the day centre, have probably thirty others to collect at the same time.

And, of course, there are exceptions: the 'gem' of a district nurse, the 'wonderful' GP, professionals whose personalities manage to overcome the limitations of the system.

Britain's welfare state is a disjointed and uncoordinated muddle of services and benefits, and it is not the fault of its staff if they do not have all the answers. Nevertheless, by their attitudes, the professionals and the welfare bureaucracy have alienated many carers.

Caring for the carers?

She went into a home for the first time earlier this year. It had to be done; arranging it broke me up, but I had to relax and see my husband had a good holiday. We ended up bed and breakfasting in our old honeymoon hotel – it was lovely. (Julie Beale, 53, who has cared for her mother for the last forty years. This was the first holiday she and her husband had taken alone.)

In the last few years, many statutory and voluntary agencies have developed services which are directed specifically at carers rather than their disabled relatives, the idea being that unless carers are given relief, their dependants will end up in institutional care, a form of support which is far more expensive than keeping them at home.

One of the most important initiatives in this field has been the development of short-term respite care, a system whereby a disabled or elderly relative is given a bed in a residential home or hospital for anything ranging from a few days to a few weeks, in order that their carer can have a break. Short-term residential care has been welcomed by many carers as a valuable form of support. That said, the respite system still raises many problems.

First, since both resources – and beds – are scarce compared to the numbers of those in need, this form of assistance is neither easily available nor very flexible: in most parts of the country, carers are only offered respite care once or twice a year. In addition, a respite bed usually has to be formally requested weeks, and sometimes months, in advance, when often what a carer urgently needs is a weekend away from caring, not a six-month wait for her next annual holiday. Even more important, most respite care is still provided in residential homes and hospitals – the very same institutions which many carers and their relatives have rejected as alternatives to being cared for at home. Understandably, many

227

disabled relatives, especially elderly people, worry that respite care is the first step to being 'put away'; and their carers consequently feel reluctant to make use of it and feel guilty if they do so. This applies not only to elderly people but, for example, to children: few parents would want to put a disabled child into hospital even if it was only for a short period.

She has been to hospital for respite care, but she came back with bruises, scratches, scabs under her nose, fork marks in her lower lip, a needle mark in her elbow. It took her an hour to recognise I was there – she was drugged. We'd got her off all the drugs. The following night I had to go in to her every hour, just so she could be sure I was there. (Edward Oliver, talking about daughter Annette)

The low standards and unsuitable nature of respite care makes it more worry and trouble than it is worth to many carers. In the case of elderly people with senile dementia, for example, a couple of weeks among strangers can leave them feeling even more confused, distressed and disoriented than they were before. Often, such relatives emerge from respite care more dependent and in worse physical shape than they had been previously. Relief care would be more acceptable to carers if it was more easily available, more flexible and more frequently provided by friendly, familiar staff in a more homely environment.

She went into this specialist unit to give me a break for a week. Even I could see how bad it was: a lot of the patients more advanced than her couldn't talk; a lot had lost their minds completely. She kept on at me and my sister so much, we went and got her out. Another time she went into a small hospital for the elderly up the road. My sister went and got her out: she was only in there one day – she didn't like the food.

I know Mum doesn't like the idea of going into hospital much, no one does, but if I can have a break now, I can carry on. I feel rotten because I look forward to it, but I know she's dreading going into hospital; so there's this conflict of emotions in me – I look forward to it and I feel guilty for looking forward to it. (Joanne Naylor, 18, caring for a mother with multiple sclerosis)

Other valuable innovations in community care include fostering and boarding-out schemes, whereby elderly people and disabled children are placed for short-stay (and sometimes long-stay) care with a family who are paid to look after them (although some carers have criticised these schemes: Judith Oliver, founder of the Association of Carers, has asked why a 'strange family' gets £80 to £100 a week to do exactly what many families are doing for nothing); day and night sitting services, which can provide a valuable few hours' break for the carer; schemes providing disabled and elderly people with intensive domiciliary support; and individual 'packages' of care, negotiated and budgeted for by an individual professional, as in the Kent community care project, for example.

One of the best and most popular initiatives in relief care is the Crossroads care attendant scheme. This provides a trained care attendant who will come to someone's home and carry out exactly the same tasks as the carer herself would normally undertake. The Crossroads scheme, which was first set up by volunteers, is becoming increasingly popular and is now being copied by many statutory agencies.

Unfortunately, such innovations are few and far between, and they do not reach the majority of carers. Even the Crossroads scheme, for example, only helped a total of 8,000 families – a tiny proportion of the 1.3 million full-time carers – in 1986/7. Even where relief care is available, it tends to be used as a last resort, as a way of keeping carers on their feet, rather than as a genuine move towards sharing the burden of care in partnership with them.

The Disabled Person's Act

The Chronically Sick and Disabled Person's Act, introduced in 1970 and the first piece of legislation to make local authorities responsible for the provision of many specialist services, was in many ways a watershed for disabled people; yet its wording was vague enough to leave many decisions, for example about assessment of need, discretionary, and it was hardly surprising that, as the 1970s wore on and budgets became tighter, local authorities chose to conform to the Act only as far as their resources would allow. A new Act promises to rectify this situation. The Disabled Person's Act 1986, piloted through Parliament by MP Tom Clarke, does not make provision for new services; but it will, once fully implemented, lay an obligation on local authorities to assess the needs of disabled people if requested to do so. It also gives disabled people the right to appoint an advocate when negotiating with social services, and disabled children the right to have their future needs assessed before they leave school. The new Act also give carers the right to have their needs, as well as those of the disabled dependant, taken into account when such an assessment is made (although the government threw out a stronger clause which would have given carers the right to have a completely separate assessment of their own). The new Act, once fully implemented, could radically improve services for disabled people living at home, at an estimated extra cost of between £100–£150 million a year.

There are other initiatives that central government could take to improve local services for carers and disabled relatives. Carers could, for instance, be given more formal recognition, with statutory rights to services such as respite and day-relief care. Central guidelines, or norms, could be laid down on, say, the number of care attendants available for a given population, in the same way that guidelines are laid down on the numbers of home helps and district nurses (even if these guidelines are often ignored). Local and health authorities could be directed to investigate the numbers and needs of carers in their districts. Carers' link-workers or liaison officers could be appointed jointly by local governments and health authorities, with responsibility for devising and co-ordinating support, counselling and advice for carers, and for liaising with other departments such as social security and housing. Local carers' groups could be given the right to membership of local government committees and health authorities, with formal consultation and negotiating rights.

Such moves, however, would require political will as well as a substantial injection of resources. Unfortunately, the current government, for all its tributes to 'informal carers', has neither that will nor the willingness to commit those funds. Indeed, it has been dragging its feet even over the implementation of the 1986 Act.

Benefits: the failure to support

He gets assessed for benefits every three years, and every time you have a new assessment you get involved with different departments of the DHSS; you get passed from one to the other; you see one lot of doctors over the Mobility Allowance, another over the Attendance Allowance – all in different offices. Dealing with officialdom is a very big part of being a carer because it's money. You are subject to the most inordinate delays, rudeness, every sort of upset you can possibly think of in dealing with all the various departments. We can speak up for ourselves: we're vocal. But if someone's not particularly well-educated, if you're not able to speak up for yourself and make a fuss, then you go to the wall. (Bill Clifford, father of Peter, 39, born with cerebral palsy)

The cost of caring for someone with a disability, both in terms of loss of earning power and extra expense, can be substantial, and money is one of the biggest worries in the lives of both carers and their relatives. Yet the state benefits available barey begin to offset these financial disadvantages.

The Invalid Care Allowance

At the moment, the only cash benefit which can be claimed specifically by carers is the Invalid Care Allowance: a non-means tested, non-contributory benefit to compensate those who cannot work because they have to stay at home to care for a severely disabled person. Eligibility for this allowance was until recently restricted to single women and male carers; married and co-habiting women, divorced women and widows whose maintenances or allowances from their husbands were of equal value to the ICA, were not eligible.

The present government was forced to surrender on this

issue and make the ICA available to all carers, in June 1986, just as the European Court of Justice was about to rule that the exclusion of married women from eligibility for the ICA breached a European Community equal treatment directive. This turnaround, achieved after a long and determined fight by Jackie Drake – a married carer who had given up work to look after a mother with senile dementia – was a major victory for married and co-habiting women carers, many of whom have been able to claim up to £2,000 in payments backdated to December 1984, when the European directive on equal treatment came into force. The government's concession has also put a small dent in a social security system which discriminates against women, and which has customarily seen them as financial dependents of their husbands.

Yet, in celebrating this victory, there has been a tendency to overlook the limitations of this benefit. The reality is that the ICA is far from being an allowance which is granted to carers as of right, and which genuinely recognises the financial and other burdens which they face. On the contrary, it is both inadequate and hedged around with restrictions.

First, eligibility for the ICA is still limited to those carers looking after a dependant claiming the Attendance Allowance, a benefit for which it is notoriously difficult to qualify, which is not widely known and which limits the notion of caring to the most narrow of definitions (for a fuller explanation of this allowance, see later in this chapter). Secondly, since the ICA is aimed at replacing lost earnings, eligibility is restricted to carers under retirement age, thus excluding thousands of elderly people caring for parents and partners. Thirdly – and most important – the ICA is an 'overlapping' income maintenance benefit. This means that it cannot be paid to those already in receipt of similar amounts from other social security benefits, such as unemployment, invalidity, sickness and widows' benefit; and that it is included in any assessment for supplementary benefit, or income support, as it is now called. This last point means that for the poorest carers – those on income support – claiming ICA will make no difference to their income: their benefit will be reduced by the exact amount that they receive from ICA. For these people, the only advantage to claiming ICA is the fact that it credits them with a Class 1 insurance stamp and, therefore, protects their pension rights. (Claiming ICA does have a number of hidden advantages other than giving carers Class 1 contribution credits; they include a £10 Christmas bonus, as well as other more complicated financial advantages. For more details see the Disability Rights Handbook 1988–89.)

The fact that the ICA is an 'overlapping' benefit is especially hard on married couples, whose income is treated as one unit for the purposes of social security assessment. It means, for instance, that if wives looking after disabled husbands claim the ICA, the money they receive is deducted from any claim their husbands can make for them as dependants, in their Invalidity Benefit or income support. Carers of relatives other than their husbands, whose spouses are unemployed, will find that once they are in receipt of ICA, the same amount will be deducted from their husband's social security benefits.

Finally, the ICA, at £23.75 a week (1987 levels) without family additions (£14.20 can be claimed for a wife/housekeeper, and £8.05 for each child) and taxable, is a petty and inadequate sum, which bears no relation to the earnings for which it is meant to compensate, which is only worth about 60 per cent of the basic retirement pension and which, in 1987, was £6.65 less than the short term rate of supplementary benefit. It is hardly surprising that, before the long-term rate of supplementary benefit disappeared last April, nearly one-third of all carers receiving ICA relied on it to 'top up' their weekly income.

The allowance also has restrictions attached which do not apply to other similar benefits. Those who claim it, for example, have to spend at least 35 hours a week caring, and may not earn more than £12 a week. These requirements

233

penalise carers who want to work part-time; they are not made of others in caring roles – such as the recipients of child benefit, for example. These limitations discourage carers from pursuing job opportunities or from sharing care, and generally reinforce the full-time caring role.

Given the restrictions with which this allowance is hedged about, and given the fact that, like the Attendance Allowance, it is still not widely known, it is hardly surprising that it is only received by a tiny minority of this country's 1.3 million full-time carers. Even including the 70,000 married women who have recently become eligible, the proportion of carers receiving ICA is only 6 per cent of the total.

Caring – a decent income

Several proposals have been put forward recently about the kind of income which carers should receive. The Carers' National Association, for instance, has argued that carers, as partners to the professionals and essential providers of 'community care', should be seen as employees rather than clients of the DHSS; entitled to a proper income which does not overlap with other social security benefits. It has also been proposed, by groups such as the Disability Alliance and the Invalid Care Allowance Campaign, that an income scheme for carers should be made up of two components: the first would be an allowance which would be available as of right to all carers to compensate for the extra costs which caring can entail; the second, a pension, would be paid to all carers who were unable to work full-time as a result of looking after a disabled dependant. Unlike the ICA this pension would not be restricted and would be an adequate income on which to live.

There are, however, problems with the argument that society should pay carers a benefit as of right, or even a wage. Like the concept of paying wages for housework, doing so could reinforce the assumption that women should stay at home to care full-time for disabled relatives, when what we should be trying to do is to develop an alternative. In the long term, it might be more positive to talk not in terms of a wage for carers, but of a decent income for all those who, for one reason and another, are not part of the formal employment market. It might also be more useful to think about a budget or an allowance which disabled people and their carers could use as they wanted: to buy in services, for example, or to share between several different carers.

The issue of carers' incomes is part and parcel of the wider problem that our society is divided into the public world of paid work and the private world of care, and the fact that women who do not work outside the home, because of family commitments, are not seen to have the right to an independent income – they are still often financially dependent on men. In the long term, the problem will only be solved once there is recognition that everyone deserves an income which fulfils his or her needs.

Benefits for disabled people

The main income maintenance benefits on which disabled people rely include retirement pensions – since the majority of disabled people are elderly; Invalidity Benefit – a contributory benefit for those unable to work; Severe Disablement Allowance – a non-contributory allowance, also payable for those unable to work; and the Attendance and Mobility Allowances, non-contributory benefits payable on the basis of the need for attention and mobility difficulties respectively.

The maze of benefits available to disabled people is too complex to be examined in detail here; but in general the existing benefits are inadequate in several ways. First, and most important, they are set too low in relation to average earnings, forcing large numbers of disabled people to rely on supplementary benefit, or income support. Secondly, they are unfair: these benefits are based not on the financial disadvantages that disability entails, but how and when that disability was acquired; they discriminate against disabled people who have never been able to work, and who are therefore unable to claim contributory Invalidity Benefit or pension, and in favour of those disabled by war or industrial injury, who can claim special, higher benefits. Thirdly, the system of benefits is so confusing and contradictory that many disabled people do not understand it, and do not even claim the benefits to which they are legally entitled: in 1981, for example, £70 million in supplementary benefits went unclaimed by disabled people under pension age.

Because they are so dependent on state benefits, disabled people are one of the groups hardest hit by the cutbacks in the social security budget which have been made in recent years (estimated to have been reduced in real terms by £11 billion from 1979 to 1986). Nearly two-thirds of disabled people are estimated to be living on the margins of poverty; on incomes around supplementary benefit level.

In recent years, several non-contributory allowances have been introduced which are based on the financial disadvantages of living with disability, rather than on how that disability was acquired or whether the person in question has ever paid insurance or been in work. But even these allowances have done little to solve the problem of poverty among disabled people. For one thing, the complex rules which govern them mean that they can be difficult to obtain. Those claiming the Severe Disablement Allowance, for example have to prove that they are 'at least 75/80 per cent disabled' (if they are 20 or over) and/or incapable of work. The Mobility Allowance is often only awarded to those who are virtually unable to walk – and frequently withheld, for instance, from those who have difficulties walking because of behavioural problems. Both allowances discriminate against the elderly, who form the vast majority of disabled people, since they are not available to people who become disabled after they reach retirement age. Most important, perhaps, the Severe Disablement Allowance – like the ICA – is an 'overlapping' benefit which is taken into account when assessing

236

eligibility for supplementary benefit/income support, making it pointless for disabled people on income support to claim it.

As most disability organisations have argued, what disabled people need is a simple and comprehensive income scheme which recognises the extra costs and the loss of independence which disability can entail; which provides an adequate pension for those who cannot work; which guarantees disabled and elderly people financial independence; and which, by doing all this, frees their carers from additional financial hardship.

The Attendance Allowance

By the time I got through the form you have to fill out I thought I was going barmy. How often is he up in the night? For how long? Can you go out? For how long? – an hour? What relevance does this have when the man is sitting there, in front of the doctor, unable to answer a single reasonable question; when he can hardly tell you his name and address? (Rosa Petro)

One woman I knew didn't like to admit her husband took her to the toilet, so she told the doctor she crawled on her hands and knees. Because she said she could crawl to the loo, she was judged as being fit, and able to carry out bodily functions. (Eliza Ray)

One allowance for disabled people which is particularly relevant to their carers is the Attendance Allowance, since a carer can only claim Invalid Care Allowance if her dependant has first qualified for the Attendance Allowance. The Attendance Allowance is a non-contributory non-means tested benefit, introduced in 1971, and payable to all severely disabled people over the age of two. It is payable at two rates (the higher rate, £31.60, for those who need attendance or supervision day and night, and the lower, £21.10 – 1987/88 figures – for those who need it only in the day). Despite its name, the Attendance Allowance bears little relation to the cost of caring full-time for a disabled person. Nevertheless, it has proved a useful addition to the 500,000 disabled people who now claim it.

Unfortunately, many people have difficulty in satisfying

the stringent conditions for eligibility attached to this allowance. Disabled claimants, for instance, have to be in need of 'frequent attention or continual supervision throughout the day' in connection with bodily functions, or with 'prolonged or repeated attention' during the night – criteria which are not always applied consistently and which depend on the judgement of the doctor who makes the necessary medical assessment. There have been allegations that, in some parts of the country, the majority of those who qualify for the Attendance Allowance are automatically rejected on their first application – and that some claimants have died before the money came through.

A number of other conditions attached to the allowance appear to be devices for the DHSS to reduce payments, rather than genuine criteria of need. For example, the allowance cannot be claimed for the the first six months the claimant is in need of care, and neither, normally, can it be back-dated. The allowance can be cut off – and with it the carer's Invalid Care Allowance – if the claimant goes into a hospital or residential home for more than a month. This last regulation may sound logical in theory; in practice, it can mean that if an elderly or disabled person has a relapse – another stroke, for example – and has to be admitted to hospital, dependant and carer together can suddenly lose an income of over £50 a week.

The Social Security Act 1986

Large numbers of disabled people currently rely on means-tested benefits to boost their incomes. This means that they are among the groups hardest hit by the changes in benefits introduced under the Social Security Act 1986.

Implemented in April 1988, the new system, called income support, abolished the long-term, higher rate of supplementary benefit and all the associated weekly allowances which were payable to disabled and elderly people for heating, special diets, laundry and so on. These additional

238

weekly payments have been replaced by a number of specific flat rate 'premiums' for certain client groups, including two for disabled people: a basic Disability Premium (£13.05 a week for a single person 1988/89 figures) and a Severe Disability Premium (£24.75 a week). The latter was introduced as a last-minute concession by the government, partly to help get this unpopular Bill through Parliament. Other premiums are available for elderly people, and additional help, in the form of an extra premium, is available for families with disabled children.

It is difficult to predict in detail what this new system will mean for disabled people and their carers. The government has pointed out that existing claimants will be partially protected by having their current levels of benefits frozen; it has claimed that the scheme will result in a simplified and more dignified system of financial support for the disabled, and that 270,000 people will gain financially from the new scheme, against 80,000 losers. Unfortunately, the latter figure does not include disabled pensioners, who form the vast majority of disabled people. Pensioners are, by the government's own figures the biggest single group of losers in the country: 2.1 million of them face losses ranging from £1 to more than £5 a week under the new scheme. The government has promised further action, including a review of financial provision for sick and disabled people, once it has the results of the major survey of disability currently being carried out and which is due to be published in 1988.

Disability organisations, however, have already disputed the government's figures, and say that a large number of disabled people – one million, including pensioners – will lose considerable amounts of money under the new system, which, they argue, is a disastrous attempt to average out the needs of all people with disabilities. They say that the new Disability Premium cannot hope to compensate for the disappearance of the long-term rate of supplementary benefit, nor for the additional payments made to severely disabled people for such things as extra heating, special diets

239

and domestic assistance; some claimants received about £40 or £50 a week (1987) in these weekly additions. It has also been predicted that many disabled people may not even qualify for the Disability Premium at all, since the criteria laid down are stricter than those which currently apply to additional requirements.

The Carers' National Association has quoted the example of one man, a former racing driver, in his thirties and paralysed from the neck down after an accident, who eventually stands to lose £109 a week: more than half his current income, which at the moment provides him with enough paid help for him to live independently.

The Severe Disability Premium which the government estimates is payable to 7,000 people, has also come under fire for the conditions which have to be fulfilled before a disabled person can receive it, conditions which could affect carers as well as the disabled. According to the government, the premium will not, in most cases, be paid to a severely disabled person if he or she lives with a 'non-dependant' – presumably a carer – and if the carer is in receipt of the Invalid Care Allowance.

These conditions are presumably meant to ensure that the new premium only goes to help disabled people living independently – that is, alone – in the community; yet the fact that severely disabled people are disqualified from this allowance if their carer is receiving ICA is bound to be divisive. It places some carers in an invidious position, since if they claim ICA their dependant will be excluded from the Severe Disability Premium.

Two other changes in the Act have also affected disabled people and their carers. Those who are now on income support, and who would in the past have qualified for housing benefit in the form of rent and rate rebates, now have to find 20 per cent of their rates bills out of their own pockets (although some receive a notional sum within the new income support scheme as compensation); they also have to pay their water rates, which were previously covered by supplementary benefit. In addition, the legal right which those on supplementary benefit had to single payments for items such as beds, furniture, repairs and fuel bills, has been replaced by a Social Fund, operated on a discretionary basis by local DHSS officers.

The government has said that payments from the new, discretionary Social Fund will be used to enable disabled people to live in the community and to avoid the need for residential care; but it is hard to see how lump-sum grants and loans, given only at the discretion of local Social Fund officers and subjected to cash limits, can replace the current regular weekly payment made to disabled people for domestic and other help.

A further source of help for very disabled people, a Trust Fund of up to £5 million, was announced by the government in February 1988. But the move has been criticised by most disability organisations as one which replaces benefit rights with charitable handouts.

The Act and carers

The changes in social security provisions directly affect carers themselves, 11,000 of whom were previously estimated to be living on supplementary benefit. In the past, anyone caring for a disabled person, where there were no alternative means by which that person could be cared for, was entitled to the long-term rate of supplementary benefit, abolished last April. Of all the groups previously eligible for the long term rate, carers are the only ones who are not entitled to 'premium' as compensation for its disappearance. A carer's premium was unnecessary, it was argued by the Social Security Advisory Committee, because 'the basic needs of such people are not, in fact, any greater than the basic needs of other fit people of similar age.'

According to the Carers' National Association, this change, along with the new obligation on claimants to find one-fifth of the rates bill, and the loss of additional payments and single payments for one-off items, will be catastrophic for carers on means-tested benefits, some of whom may eventually lose a large proportion of their incomes; the Family Policy Studies centre predicted that many will lose nearly £12 a week. A single woman caring for her elderly mother for instance, who previously could have claimed the long term rate of supplementary benefit – £38.65 at 1987/88 figures – plus, say about £7 or £8 in additions for heating and hospital fares, is now only eligible for the basic income support of £33.40, with no premium to compensate for the disappearance of her extra weekly payments. Of course, she will not lose out immediately, since existing benefits are being frozen until the new rules catch up; new claimants, however, receive lower benefits from the start.

It is thought that the group of carers to be hardest hit by the new legislation are people under 25 looking after their parents. They, like all carers, would previously have been eligible for the long-term rate of supplementary benefit: under the new legislation, all single childless people under 25 are being treated for benefit purposes as though they were still dependent on their parents – even if it is a parent for whom they are caring. Young carers now receive a basic rate of £19.40 weekly, a figure which represents a 50 per cent cut in income.

The DHSS also appears to have used the introduction of income support to tighten up on carers' rights to claim state benefits without having to sign on for work. In the past, according to the Carers' National Association, it was relatively easy for carers of disabled people to claim supplementary benefit without signing on. But under the new scheme, the only carers eligible for income support without signing on are those with dependants who are either temporarily ill, or who are in receipt of the Attendance Allowance.

SERPS

In the longer term, carers will also be affected by changes which the new social security legislation will eventually bring about in another important area: pensions, or more specifically, the State Earnings Related Pension Scheme (SERPS). Introduced in 1978 as an addition to the basic state pension, SERPS was intended to benefit those groups of workers – many of them women whose working lives were interrupted by domestic responsibilities – who had never been eligible for private pension schemes, by providing for an additional pension based on an individual's best twenty years of earnings.

The present government has been forced to abandon its original proposal to phase out SERPS completely, but it is planning big cuts in SERPS in a bid to reduce pension costs and, at the same time, encourage an expansion in private and occupational pension schemes. For example, those who retire in the next century will find that their SERPS pensions will not be based on their best twenty years but on revalued average earnings over the whole of their working lives. This change will hit women carers, who, because of broken career patterns and part-time work, are still often excluded from personal pension schemes.

The government has made one important concession in this area: it has promised to protect the additional pension rights of those who stay at home to take on caring responsibilities, by ensuring that the years spent at home will not be counted for the purposes of working out average lifetime earnings. This concession leaves one important loophole, however: it takes no account of the women who take on part-time work during the years spent caring for children and old people. Such part-time earnings will still count towards the 'lifetime' average and will reduce that average, and any additional pension, substantially. In other words, a woman who gives up a full-time job and goes into part-time work so that she can look after an elderly relative or handicapped child, will later find herself penalised when she comes to draw on her additional pension.

12

·

The future we would like – the future which is likely

The crisis of 'informal care', as it is now called in official circles, is not going to disappear. The number of very elderly people will continue to grow over the rest of this century and beyond, and with it the numbers of those with disabilities; while AIDS can only add to the numbers of these who will need long-term care and nursing in the community. Government policies of 'community care', and the exodus from the long-stay hospitals which is now taking place, will eventually mean that there are more disabled and dependent people living outside hospital than ever before. At the same time, the role and the expectations of women – the traditional carers – are changing, with more women working than before; while new lifestyles and social trends – especially the rising divorce rate – raise crucial question marks over who will do the caring in the future.

The Thatcher years

We know the immense sacrifices which people will make for the care of their own near and dear – for elderly relatives, disabled children and so on and the immense part which voluntary effort even outside the confines of the family has played in these fields.

   Once you give people the idea that all this can be done by the state, and that it is somehow second-best or even degrading to leave it to private people . . . then you will begin to deprive human beings of one of the essential ingredients of humanity – personal moral responsibility. (Margaret Thatcher, 1978)

A senior civil servant at the DHSS, interviewed for this book, maintained that this government has taken several initiatives in support of carers. In recent years it has initiated a series of seminars on the subject at the DHSS, and published the results; it is funding important research on informal care now being undertaken at York University; it has asked for crucial information about carers from two important surveys currently being produced – the latest General Household Survey and a special disability survey whose results are expected this year (and which may reveal that the numbers of people with disabilities and their carers are far greater than previously estimated); it has helped to fund carers' support organisations – the Carers' National Association and the Alzheimer's Disease Society, for example – as well as a special support unit for carers, set up at the King's Fund Centre in London; and, most important, it has provided over £10 million for a 'Helping the Community to Care' programme – a series of pilot projects aimed at supporting families, friends and volunteers who care for disabled people.

Yet these initiatives, however valuable, are but a drop in the ocean of unmet need among both carers and disabled and elderly people. What is more, none of them address the crucial question of resources or levels of services, which the government maintains can only be determined by local agencies. For all the encouraging noises it has made about 'informal care', the government has failed to take the kind of major initiative which is needed to bring about genuine improvements in the lives of carers. For all the ministerial tributes to them, it does not have the political will, nor is it willing to provide the funds to improve the carers' lot.

The government has, in fact, a record of opposing any initiative in this area which would have cost it money. It fought a lengthy battle against giving married women the right to the Invalid Care Allowance; it threw out a clause in the Disabled Person's Bill which would have obliged local authorities to make a separate assessment of carers' needs; and, at the time of writing, it was about to axe the long-term level of supplementary benefit to which they are entitled.

The government's approach however, demonstrates more

than the usual reluctance by governments to spend money. What makes this government different is the fact that it no longer even pretends to provide adequate levels of service in the community. To do so, it argues, would promote the 'dependency culture' which it is so keen to eliminate. In the words of the senior DHSS civil servant interviewed for this book, statutory services are now seen to be what are euphemistically called 'enablers' rather than 'providers' – i.e. they no longer exist to provide care for dependent and disabled people, but only to enable others – relatives, neighbours, friends and volunteers – to do so.

Community care

This new 'self-help' approach comes at a crucial time in the development of 'community care' policies. Thousands of long-stay patients – the elderly, mentally handicapped and the mentally ill – are currently being discharged from the old institutions, and reponsibility for many of them is being handed over to local authorities, whose record so far in accommodating their needs has proved woefully inadequate. It should be pointed out that criticisms of 'community care' policies are not confined to opponents of the government: the Audit Commission, a statutory body which examines the impact of central government action on local authorities, pointed out in a major report published in December 1986, that the build-up of community-based services is slow, chaotic and disorganised; that in some places it has not kept pace with the run-down of long-stay NHS institutions; that the services provided by local authorities to replace NHS services are uneven; and that the care disabled and chronically sick people and their families receive is as much dependent on where they live as what they need.

Policies of 'community care', whereby disabled people are encouraged to live in their own homes rather than enter long-stay institutions, have been accepted for several decades. But, as the title of its 'Helping the Community to

Care' programme makes clear, under the present government, the phrase 'community care' has gradually taken on a new meaning: originally envisaged as a policy which would replace hospital services with the same level of provision and degree of support for disabled people living in the community, it has increasingly come to mean care *by* the community – by friends, neighbours, volunteers, and, above all, by female carers.

An era of cutbacks

The policies of community care are being carried out against a background of major cuts in public spending. This means that, at best, there is a failure to keep pace with the growing need for services, and, at worst, real cutbacks.

Local authorities, for example, are being expected to take over responsibility for community services which used to be provided by NHS hospitals, at a time when many of them are being financially squeezed by cuts in central funding through the rate support grant – reduced by £18 billion since this government took office. Those which increase their spending in a bid to provide the new community services are often penalised for doing so by further cuts in central government grants and by ratecapping. As the Audit Commission put it: 'local authorities are being penalised through the grant system for building the very community services which government policy favours'.

Meanwhile, the funds specifically allocated to personal social services, which include domiciliary support for the disabled and the elderly, are also feeling the pinch. In the four years from 1980–1 to 1984–5, for example, the real growth in net spending on these services, was, according to the House of Commons all-party social services committee, only 6 per cent – 2 per cent less than the government's own official target, based on the growth needed simply to keep pace with population and other changes. Many local authorities have actually been forced to cut their personal social services budgets. Data supplied by the DHSS shows that in the five years to 1985–6, three out of every five authorities – sixty-four in all – fell short of increasing spending by the 12 per cent needed simply to maintain services. In those areas, as the social services committee points out, 'there is reason for concern about the adequacy of the growth of provision'.

It is difficult to know which client groups or services have suffered the most, but it is likely that, in an era when resources are scarce, they will be concentrated on 'priority' areas such as child abuse rather than on providing the elderly with more home helps or their carers with more respite breaks. Most of the evidence indicates that traditional domiciliary services such as Meals on Wheels are at the very least failing to keep pace with increasing demand. One 1980 study, by the Personal Social Services Council, found, for example, that 80 per cent of local authorities were reducing domiciliary services – many of which already fell short of recommended levels – or increasing the charges made for them.

At the same time as local authorities are failing to provide the levels of services needed, they are increasingly relying on the private residential sector – now being funded by the government through supplementary benefit to the tune of £500 million annually – to provide for their disabled and elderly populations. As the Audit Commission points out, this growth in the private sector makes a mockery of the whole concept of 'community care', since it threatens to replace the traditional public institutions which this and other governments have been so anxious to close down with private ones.

In the health service, the evidence also indicates that spending is failing to keep up with demand. Between 1980–81 and 1985–6, for example, real spending on hospital and community health services – which account for some two-thirds of the total of NHS spending – increased by only 2.2 per cent or 0.4 per cent annually – again, less than half the official growth target of 2 per cent annually. The total shortfall in health service resources under the current government has been calculated as totalling nearly £1.9 billion.

According to a survey published in 1987 by the National Association of Health Authorities, underfunding means that most authorities are facing severe financial difficulties, delays in planned developments and freezes on recruitment. In addition, they are having to find money to deal with AIDS programmes. It is hardly surprising that in the same year, health authorities in England alone were forced to close well over 3,000 beds.

In the middle of this financial squeeze, there is little evidence that resources are being shifted from the NHS acute sector to community services. Like the long-stay institutions they are replacing, community health services look set to become the Cinderella sector of the NHS.

Other trends

The cuts in public expenditure and services have been accompanied by a huge expansion in the role of both voluntary and private commercial organisations. Voluntary organisations and staff are increasingly expected to substitute for, rather than supplement, statutory care agencies, especially in the field of 'informal care'. This raises crucial questions about the accountability of what one researcher has called 'semi-professional' staff, and the protection of vulnerable clients; as well as about the nature of funding and of voluntary work itself.

As to the private sector, it is not only private residential homes which are flourishing, but also agencies providing the commercial equivalents of domiciliary services such as home helps, day centres and Meals on Wheels; especially noticeable is the growth of agencies specialising in the domestic care of old people. Whatever one's views on the desirability or otherwise of private care, there is a real danger that the problems of abuse and neglect which have already been seen in the private residential sector could re-emerge in this new form of care enterprise.

It is not just the private sector itself which is growing, but also the notion of privatisation, competition and an 'internal market' within the traditional agencies of the welfare state. The government, for example, is now talking about hospitals and health districts competing against one another for both central funds and patients, and there are similar suggestions that the community services provided by local authorities to disabled and elderly people should be privatised.

It is hard to tell what effects these ideas will eventually have on the welfare state, but it seems increasingly likely that as more services are privatised, the character of the health service and the infrastructure of social services overall will undergo a permanent and radical change. The failure to fund the NHS and local authorities adequately may mean that the public sector is used as a 'safety net' for the poorest and most vulnerable sections of society; while the emphasis on competition, market principles and 'local' decision-making could mean that the quality and quantity of services will vary enormously throughout the country.

It is also possible that, as community services fail to develop, a new and more brutalised form of institutional care based on the private sector will evolve, and that thousands of elderly and disabled people living in private boarding houses and homes will be more isolated and neglected than ever before. It is probable that, as the number of very elderly continues to outpace the number of relatives available to care for them, a new system of care will evolve, carried out by a new army of female carers: semi-trained volunteers, and low-paid care staff.

The cuts in welfare services, together with policies of community care and the exodus of disabled and elderly people from long-stay hospitals, will mean that an increasing burden can be expected to fall on the traditional carers: daughters, wives and mothers. As public provision is eroded it also seems likely that class and income will play an increasing role in how well people cope with disability and old age, and that the differences in people's circumstances will dictate what services they receive and what choice they have – even more so than it does at present. This means that while the poorest women may have to rely on the 'bottom line' – the welfare state – others will be able to buy in the services they require. It may well be, for instance, that relatively prosperous, middle-class women will have their elderly relatives cared for by others who are less well off: part-time, low-paid ancillary staff and assistants employed by private agencies. All of this suggests that society as a whole will become even more sharply divided between the haves and the have-nots.

In the long-term however, the roles, relationships and lifestyles of women are being affected by other economic and social forces which are probably beyond the power of any government to alter, and which may well determine whether they continue to be the traditional carers. The nuclear family is on the wane; more women than ever before go out to work, a trend which seems unlikely to be reversed; while at the same time, more men are facing both unemployment and early retirement, a trend which could mean that men become more involved in the domestic world; the divorce rate is rising and the number of one-parent families is on the increase, which raises the question of whether women will any longer be able or willing to look after anyone but their own children. The expectations of women, as carers, have also risen: a woman looking after a mother with senile dementia for instance, will rightly expect more support than she might have done fifty years ago.

The government says that the growth of welfare provision has undermined the individual's sense of responsibility, and the ability of families to care for their own vulnerable members. But the experiences of the carers interviewed for this book bear little relation to the government's vision of the world: either as it is or how it should be. Their lives reveal

251

that people have as much sense of moral responsibility as they have ever had; and that they are looking after the people close to them as they always have done. The important question is whether they can – or should – go on doing so unsupported.

A new deal for carers

Women must have the right not to care, and dependent people must have the right not to rely on their relatives. (Janet Finch, 'Whose Responsibility? Women and the Future of Family Care', Informal Care Tomorrow, *Policy Studies Institute, 1987)*

In the short term, carers and their dependants need far more support, not only from existing domiciliary services such as home helps, Meals on Wheels and day centres, but also from the new kinds of more flexible and more imaginative schemes which are being developed in some areas. These services need to be expanded on a massive scale.

In the long-term, the solution to the dilemma faced by carers involves more than just increased resources.

What carers need is a new deal which will give them a genuine choice about whether or not they wish to care, and, if so, to what degree. That means providing them, and their elderly and disabled relatives, with an alternative to care within the home which they find morally acceptable – not one which is based on the existing long-stay institutions.

A bridge needs to be built between the invisible world of family care and the public one of long-stay, institutional care. A middle way needs to be found which neither confines each carer to her private hell nor condemns our elderly and disabled population to being looked after exclusively by the state and its institutions. We need genuine, collective ways of sharing care – between family, professionals, volunteers and friends. And the money has to be made available to make such developments effective.

We also need a new approach to old age and disability, to throw out our stale ideas about care and dependency, and to understand that for elderly and disabled people, as for most of us, the choice is neither dependence nor independence – but interdependence. Such a new approach could involve the long-term co-ordination of social policy across wider areas such as income, housing, transport, employment, education, and attitudes to women.

Given the current social and political climate, proposing such a fundamental review of attitudes and policy could be seen as mere wishful thinking. But the beginnings of a solution depend on recognition of the problem, and the first step towards achieving that solution is to give the carers a public voice and to listen to what they have to say.

Useful Addresses

The organisations listed below can provide useful advice, information, and literature to carers and their disabled relatives. Many keep lists of local self-help groups which can often give practical help and moral support. This list is not comprehensive. It includes separate head offices and organisations for Scotland, Wales and Northern Ireland where these exist. If an English address is listed only, this should be contacted for information about branches and local groups in the rest of Britain.

Age Concern England
Bernard Sunley House
60 Pitcairn Road
Mitcham
Surrey CR4 3LL
Telephone 01 640 5431

Age Concern Northern Ireland
6 Lower Crescent
Belfast BTZ 1NR
Telephone 0232 245729

Age Concern Scotland
33 Castle Street
Edinburgh EH2 3DN
Telephone 031 225 5000

Age Concern Wales
4th Floor
Cathedral Road
Cardiff CF1 9SD
Telephone 0222 371566

AIDS helplines

National AIDS Helpline
Department of Health
Telephone 0800 567123 for advice and counselling, or 0800 555777 for free literature and leaflets. Covers Scotland

Belfast AIDS Helpline
PO Box 44
Belfast BT1 1SH
Telephone 0232 326117

Cardiff AIDS Helpline
Telephone 0222 398258/223443

Terrence Higgins Trust
Telephone 01 242 1010

Alzheimer's Disease Society
England: 158–160 Balham High Road
London SW12 9BN
Telephone 01 675 6557

Scotland: 40 Shandwick Place
Edinburgh EH2 4RT
Telephone 031 225 1453

Amnesia Association
25 Prebend Gardens
London W4 1TN
Telephone 01 747 0039

Arthritis Care
6 Grosvenor Crescent
London SW1X 7ER
Telephone 01 235 0902

Association of Carers, *see*
CARERS

**Association of Crossroads
Care Attendant Schemes,** *see*
Crossroads

**Association for All Speech
Impaired Children** (AFASIC)
347 Central Markets
Smithfield
London EC1A 9NH
Telephone 01 236 3632

**Association for Spina Bifida
and Hydrocephalus** (ASBAH)
22 Upper Woburn Place
London WC1H OEP
Telephone 01 388 1382

**British Association of Cancer
United Patients** (BACUP)
121/123 Charterhouse Street
London EC1M 6AA
Telephone 01 608 1785

**British Limbless
Ex-Servicemen's Association**
(BLESMA)

185/187 High Road
Chadwell Heath
Essex RM6 6NA
Telephone 01 590 1124

British Red Cross Society
9 Grosvenor Crescent
London SW1X 7EJ
Telephone 01 235 5454
*Publishes manuals on caring for the
sick*

**Campaign for People with
Mental Handicaps**
12a Maddox Street
London W1R 9PL
Telephone 01 491 0727
*Works for the rights of mentally
handicapped people*

CARERS
The Carers' National Association
29 Chilworth Mews
London W2 3RG
Telephone 01 724 7776

The Carers' National Association
First Floor, 21–23 New Road
Chatham
Kent ME4 4QL
Telephone 0634 813981
*Organisation formed from a merger
in 1988 of the Association of Carers
and the National Council for Carers
and their Elderly Dependants. Free
information and guidance service
with a list of self-help groups
throughout Britain*

Care Search
1 Thorpe Close
Portobello Green
London W10 5XL
Telephone 01 960 5666/7
Lists details of every type of residential care in the country for both mentally handicapped people and the elderly, with vacancies stored on computer

Caring Costs
c/o Spastics Society
Campaigns Department
12 Park Crescent
London W1N 4EQ
Telephone 01 636 5020
Campaigns for an income for all carers

Chest, Heart and Stroke Association
England: Tavistock House North
Tavistock Square
London WC1H 9JE
Telephone 01 387 3012

Northern Ireland: 21 Dublin Road
Belfast BT2 7FJ
Telephone 0232 320 184

Scotland: 65 North Castle Street
Edinburgh EH2 3LT
Telephone 031 225 6963

Citizens' Advice Bureau
Provides free, confidential advice on any subject, including social security benefits and health matters. Local addresses found in the telephone directory

Combat
Association to Combat
Huntington's Chorea

34a Station Road
Hinckley
Leicester LE10 1AP
Telephone 0455 615558

Contact-a-Family
16 Strutton Ground
London SW1P 2HP
Telephone 01 222 2211
Link service for families with handicapped children

Counsel and Care for the Elderly
131 Middlesex Street
London E1 7JF
Telephone 01 247 9844
Free advice service to elderly people. Gives grants to help with nursing care and inspects all private and voluntary residential homes in Greater London

Association of Crossroads Care Attendant Schemes
10 Regents Place
Rugby
Warwickshire CV21 2PN
Telephone 0788 73653
Provides trained care attendants to look after disabled people at home and give their carers a break

Crossroads Scotland Care Attendant Schemes
24 George Square
Glasgow G2 1EG

Cruse
National Association for the Widowed and their Children

Cruse House
!26 Sheen Road
Richmond
Surrey TW9 1UR
Telephone 01 940 4818/9047

Dial-a-Ride
London Dial-a-Ride Users'
Association
(Public Minibus service for
people with disabilities)
St Margaret's
25 Leighton Road
London NW5 2QD
Telephone 01 482 2325

Dial UK
Disablement Information Advice
Line
DIAL House
117 High Street
Clay Cross
Nr Chesterfield
Derbyshire S45 9DZ
Telephone 0246 250055
*Free, confidential advice service run
by and for people with disabilities*

Disability Alliance
25 Denmark Street
London WC2H 8NJ
Telephone 01 240 0806
*Campaign to improve benefits for
disabled people. Runs advice service
and publishes an annual Disability
Rights Handbook, a detailed guide to
benefits*

Disabled Living Foundation
380–384 Harrow Road
London W9 2HU
Telephone 01 289 6111
*Provides advice on incontinence, aids
and equipment*

Disablement Income Group
Attlee House
28 Commercial Street
London E1 6LR
Telephone 01 247 2128/6877
*Registered charity promoting welfare
of disabled people. Provides advice
service on benefits and services*

Down's Syndrome Association
12–13 Clapham Common
Southside
London SW4 7AA
Telephone 01 720 0008

Equal Opportunities Commission
England: Overseas House
Quay Street
Manchester M3 3HN
Telephone 061 833 9244

Northern Ireland: Lindsay House
Callender Street
Belfast BT71 5DT
Telephone 0232 242752

Scotland: St Andrew House
141 West Nile Street
Glasgow G1 2RN
Telephone 041 332 8018

Wales: Caerwys House
Windsor Place
Cardiff CF1 1LB
Telephone 0222 43552

Equipment for the Disabled
Mary Marlborough Lodge
Nuffield Orthopaedic Centre
Headington
Oxford OX3 7LD
Telephone 0865 750103
*Publishes illustrated booklets on
huge range of aids*

Family Fund
PO Box 50
York YO1 1UY
Telephone 0904 621115
*Helps families of severely
handicapped children under 16.
Provides funding for items such as
washing machines, clothing, etc.*

Gateway Clubs, *see* National
Federation of Gateway Clubs

GLAD
Greater London Association for
Disabled People
336 Brixton Road
London SW9 7AA
Telephone 01 274 0107

Headway
National Head Injuries
Association
200 Mansfield Road
Nottingham
NG1 3HX
Telephone 0602 622382

Help the Aged
16/18 St James' Walk
London EC1R 0BE
Telephone 01 253 0253

Holiday Care Service
2 Old Bank Chambers
Station Road
Horley
Surrey RH6 9HW
Telephone 02937 774535
*Free advice service about holidays for
people with special needs*

**Invalid Children's Aid
Nationwide** (I CAN)
Allen Graham House

198 City Road
London EC1V 2PH
Telephone 01 608 2462
*Provides help and advice for children
with disabilities and their families*

**John Grooms Association for
the Disabled**
10 Gloucester Drive
Finsbury Park
London N4 2LP
Telephone 01 802 7272
*Provides residential care and
independent housing for disabled people*

KIDS Centre
13 Pond Street
London NW3 2NP
Telephone 01 431 0596
*Information and advice for parents,
and training programmes and play
sessions for handicapped children*

**King's Fund Informal Caring
Support Programme**
King's Fund Centre
126 Albert Street
London NW1 7NF
Telephone 01 267 6111
*A caring support programme
working to improve information and
training for carers and professionals.
(Carers with individual queries
should contact the Carers' National
Association)*

**Lady Hoare Trust for
Physically Disabled Children**
7 North Street
Midhurst
West Sussex
Telephone 073081 3696
*Welfare service for families with
disabled children and those with
chronic arthritis*

Leonard Cheshire Foundation

Leonard Cheshire House
26–29 Maunsel Street
London SW1P 2QN
Telephone 01 828 1822
Runs homes catering for physically disabled people

Marie Curie Memorial Foundation

Advice service for cancer patients and their relatives which provides day and night nursing services and welfare grants

England: 28 Belgrave Square
London SW1X 8QG
Telephone 01 235 3325

Scotland: 21 Rutland Street
Edinburgh EH1 2AH
Telephone 031 229 8332

MENCAP

Royal Society for Mentally
Handicapped Children and
Adults
123 Golden Lane
London EC1Y 0RT
Telephone 01 253 9433
Provides numerous services for mentally impaired people and their families, including welfare, legal, counselling and holidays

For Scotland, *see* Scottish Society
for Mentally Handicapped
Children and Adults

MIND

National Association for Mental
Health
22 Harley Street
London W1N 2ED
Telephone 01 637 0741

Provides help and support for mentally ill people and their families

For Northern Ireland, *see*
Northern Ireland Association for
Mental Health

For Scotland, *see* Scottish
Association for Mental Health

Multiple Sclerosis Society of Great Britain and Northern Ireland

25 Effie Road
Fulham
London SW6 1EE
Telephone 01 736 6267

Muscular Dystrophy Group of Great Britain and Northern Ireland

Nattrass House
35 Macaulay Road
London SW3 0QP
Telephone 01 720 8055

National Autistic Society

276 Willesden Lane
London NW2 5RB
Telephone 01 451 3844

National Council for Carers and their Elderly Dependants, *see* CARERS

National Deaf-Blind and Rubella Association (SENSE)

311 Gray's Inn Road
London WC1X 8PT
Telephone 01 278 1005

National Federation of Gateway Clubs

117 Golden Lane
London EC1Y 0RT
Telephone 01 253 9433

Social/leisure clubs for mentally handicapped people of all ages

National Schizophrenia Fellowship

England: 78/79 Victoria Road
Surbiton
Surrey KT6 4NS
Telephone 01 390 3651/2/3

Northern Ireland:
47 Rosemary Street
Belfast BT1 1QB
Telephone 0232 248 006

Scotland: 40 Shandwick Place
Edinburgh EH2 4RT
Telephone 031 226 2025

Northern Ireland Association for Mental Health

Beacon House
84 University Street
Belfast BT7 1HE
Telephone 0232 228 474

Northern Ireland Council for Orthopaedic Development

Room 107
2nd Floor
Scottish Provident Buildings
7 Donegal Square West
Belfast BT1 6JD
Telephone 0232 228378
Services for people with cerebral palsy and their families

Parkinson's Disease Society of the UK Ltd

36 Portland Place
London W1N 3DG
Telephone 01 323 1174

RADAR, *see* Royal Association for Disability and Rehabilitation

Royal National Institute for the Blind (RNIB)

224 Great Portland Street
London W1N 6AA
Telephone 01 388 1266

Royal National Institute for the Deaf (RNID)

105 Gower Street
London WC1E 6AH
Telephone 01 387 8033

Royal Society for Mentally Handicapped Children and Adults, *see* MENCAP

Scottish Association for Mental Health

40 Shandwick Place
Edinburgh EH2 4RT
Telephone 031 225 4446

Scottish Council for Spastics

Rhuemore
22 Corstorphine Road
Edinburgh 12
Telephone 031 337 9876

Scottish Society for Mentally Handicapped Children and Adults

13 Elm Bank Street
Glasgow G2 4QA
Telephone 041 226 4544

Scottish Spinal Cord Injury Association

Suite 3
Princes House
5 Shandwick Place
Edinburgh EH2 4RG
Telephone 031 2283 827

St Andrew's Ambulance Association
Milton Street
Glasgow G4 0HR
Telephone 041 332 4031
Provides services for sick and disabled people

St John Ambulance Association
1 Grosvenor Crescent
London SW1X 7EF
Telephone 01 235 5231
Provides services for sick and disabled people

For Scotland, *see* St Andrew's Ambulance Association

Spastics Society
12 Park Crescent
London W1N 4EQ
Telephone 01 636 5020
Welfare and advice service for those with cerebral palsy and their families. Services includes residential hostels and schools

For Scotland, *see* Scottish Council for Spastics

For Northern Ireland, *see* Northern Ireland Council for Orthopaedic Development

Spinal Injuries Association
Newpoint House
76 St James's Lane
London N10 3DF
Telephone 01 444 2121

For Scotland, *see* Scottish Spinal Cord Injury Association

SPOD
Association to Aid the Sexual and Personal Relationships of People with a Disability
286 Camden Road
London N7 0BJ
Telephone 01 607 8851/2
Provides information and advice on disability and sexuality

Sue Ryder Foundation
Cavendish
Sudbury
Suffolk CO10 8AY
Telephone 0787 280252
Runs homes for people with disabilities and provides home nursing services

Terrence Higgins Trust
BM AIDS
London WC1N 3XX
Telephone 01 831 0330;
AIDS Helpline 01 242 1010
AIDS advice and information service. Runs support groups for people with HIV and AIDS, and their carers

Voluntary Council for Handicapped Children
National Children's Bureau
8 Wakley Street
London EC1V 7QE
Telephone 01 278 9441
Runs information service on all aspects of childhood disability

Women's Royal Voluntary Service (WRVS)
England: 233-234 Stockwell Road
London SW9 9SP
Telephone 01 733 3388

Scotland: 19 Grosvenor Crescent
Edinburgh EH12 5EL
Telephone 031 337 2261/2/3

Wales: 26 Cathedral Road
Cardiff CF1 9LJ
Telephone 0222 28386/7/8

Selected Bibliography

Abrams, Mark (1978, 1980) 'Beyond three-score and ten, Two reports on a survey of the elderly', Age Concern, Mitcham

Allen, Isobel, Wicks, Malcolm, Finch, Janet and Leat, Diana (1987) 'Informal care tomorrow', Policy Studies Institute, London, Occasional Paper.

Audit Commission for Local Authorities in England and Wales (1986) 'Making a reality of community care. A report by the Audit Commission', HMSO, London

Baldwin, S. M. (1985) *The Costs of Caring*, Routledge & Kegan Paul, London

Baldwin, S. M. and Glendinning, C. (1983) 'Employment, women and their disabled children', in Groves, D. and Finch, J. (eds) *A Labour of Love: Women, work and caring*, Routledge & Kegan Paul, London

Barker, J. (1984) 'Black and Asian old people in Britain. First report of a research study'. Research perspectives on ageing, Age Concern Research Unit, Mitcham

Bartlett, H. and Challis, L. (1986) 'Time to act on what we now know', *Health and Social Service Journal*, Macmillan, London

Bonny, Sharon (1984) 'Who cares in Southwark?' The Carers' National Association, London

Briggs, A. (1983) 'Who Cares? The report of a door-to-door survey into the numbers and needs of people caring for dependent relatives', The Carers' National Association, Rochester

Briggs, Anna and Oliver, Judith (1985) *Caring, Experiences of looking after disabled relatives*, Routledge & Kegan Paul, London

Bristow, K. (1986) 'Cause for concern – a study of people who have the ultimate responsibility of caring for a severely disabled and/or elderly person living at home', Association of Crossroads Care Attendant Schemes Ltd, Warwickshire

Brody, Elaine M. (1981) '"Women in the middle" and family help to older people', *The Gerontologist*, 21, 5:471–480

Centre for Policy on Ageing (1984, reprinted 1985) 'Home Life: a code of practice for residential care', Centre for Policy on Ageing, London

Charlesworth, A., Wilkin, D. and Durie, A. (1984) 'Carers and services: a comparison of men and women caring for dependent elderly people,' EOC, Manchester

DHSS (1981) *Growing older*, HMSO, London

DHSS (1981) 'Care in Action. A handbook of policies and priorities for the health and personal social services in England', HMSO, London

DHSS (1984) 'Supporting the informal carers, "Fifty styles of caring"'. A Social Work Service Development Group Project

DHSS (1985) 'Reform of Social Security. Programme for action', HMSO, London

Disability Alliance (1987) 'Poverty and disability, Breaking the link, The case for a comprehensive disability income scheme', Disability Alliance, London

Equal Opportunities Commission (1980) 'The experience of caring for elderly and handicapped dependants: survey report', EOC, Manchester

Equal Opportunities Commission (1982) 'Who cares for the carers? Opportunities for those caring for the elderly and handicapped', EOC, Manchester

Equal Opportunities Commission (1982) 'Caring for the elderly and handicapped: community care policies and women's lives', EOC, Manchester

Equal Opportunities Commission (1985) 'Reform of Social Security. Response of the Equal Opportunities Commission', EOC, Manchester

Family Policy Studies Centre (1986) 'Caring Costs: the social security implications'. Briefing.

Gilhooly, L. M. (1984) 'The impact of care-giving on caregivers: factors associated with the psychological well-being of people supporting a dementing relative in the community', *British Journal of Medical Psychology*, 57, 33–44

Groves, D. and Finch, J. (eds) (1983) *A Labour of Love: Women, Work and Caring*, Routledge & Kegan Paul, London

Groves, D. and Finch, J. (1983) 'Natural selection: perspectives on entitlement to the invalid care allowance', in Groves, D. and Finch, J. (eds) *A Labour of Love: Women, Work and Caring*, Routledge & Kegan Paul, London

Glendinning, Caroline (1983) *Unshared Care*, Routledge & Kegan Paul, London

Harman, Harriet and Lowe, Marion (1986) 'No Place Like Home, a report of the first year's work of the Registered Homes Tribunal', the Public Services Trade Group of the Transport and General Workers Union

Harris, A. (1971) 'Handicapped and Impaired in Great Britain', HMSO, London

Henry, John (1987) 'Caring for people with AIDS' from *Carelink*, Winter 1987, Kings Fund, London

Henwood, Melanie and Wicks, Malcolm (1984) 'The Forgotten Army: family care and elderly people', Family Policy Studies Centre, London, Briefing Paper

Hunt, A. (1968) 'A survey of women's employment', HMSO, London

Hunt, A. (1978) 'The Elderly at Home', OPCS Social Survey Division, HMSO, London

Invalid Care Allowance Campaign (1985) 'Green Paper on the reform of social security: response from the Invalid Care Allowance Campaign', ICAC, London

Levin, E., Sinclair, I. and Gorbach P. (1983) 'The supporters of confused elderly people at home', extract from the main report, National Institute for Social Work Research Unit, London

McNaught, Allan (1984) 'Race and Health Care in the United Kingdom'. Centre for Health Service Management Studies, Polytechnic of the South Bank, London, Occasional paper

Martin, J. and Roberts, C. (1984) 'Women and employment: a lifetime perspective', Department of Employment/OPCS, London

National Association of Health Authorities (1987) The Autumn Survey 1987. Financial Position of District Health Authorities. NAHA, Birmingham

Nissel M. and Bonnerjea L. (1982) 'Family Care of the Handicapped Elderly: Who pays?' Policy Studies Institute, London

Norman, Alison (1985) 'Triple Jeopardy: growing old in a second homeland', Centre for Policy on Ageing, London. Policy Studies in Ageing number 3

Oliver, Judith (1983) 'The caring wife' from Finch, J and Groves, D.

A Labour of Love: Women, Work and Caring, Routledge & Kegan Paul, London

Parker, Gillian (1985) 'With due care and attention. A review of research on informal care', Family Policy Studies Centre, London, Occasional Paper number 2

Peaker, C. (1986) 'The Crisis in Residential Care', National Council for Voluntary Organisations, London

Rossiter, C. and Wicks, M. (1982) 'Crisis or challenge? Family care, elderly people and social policy', Study Commission on the Family, London, Occasional paper number 8

Social Services Committee, House of Commons, Fourth report (1985–6) 'Public expenditure on the social services', Volume 1, HMSO, London

Social Services Committee, House of Commons, (1988) 'First report of the Commons Social Services Committee on resourcing the National Health Service', HMSO, London

Tinker, Anthea (1981; reprinted 1984) 'The elderly in modern society', *Social Policy in Modern Britain*, general editor Jo Campling, Longman, London and New York

Topliss, E. (1982). 'Social responses to handicap', *Social Policy in Modern Britain*, general editor Jo Campling, Longman, London and New York

Walker, A. and Townsend, P. (eds) (1981) 'Disability in Britain, A manifesto of rights', Martin Robertson, Oxford

Weeks, Jeffrey (1987) 'Love in a Cold Climate', *Marxism Today*, Jan 1987

Wilkin, D. (1979) *Caring for the Mentally Handicapped Child*, Croom Helm, London

Wright, Fay (1986) *Left to Care Alone* Gower, London

Wright, Fay (1983) 'Single carers: employment, housework and caring', Finch, J. and Groves, D. (eds) *A Labour of Love: Women, Work and Caring*, Routledge & Kegan Paul, London

266

Useful reading for carers

Carers' National Association (1984) 'Help at Hand'. A useful guide to benefits and services. *Available from the Carers' National Association*

Darby, C. (1984) *Keeping Fit While Caring*, Family Welfare Association, London. A fully illustrated guide to lifting and handling a disabled person. *Available from the Carers' National Association.*

Gee, M. (1987) 'Taking a Break. A guide for people caring at home'. King's Fund Informal Caring Programme, London. *Available free from Taking a Break, Newcastle-upon-Tyne X, NE85 2AQ*

Kohner, Nancy (1988) *Caring at Home. A handbook for looking after someone at home – someone young or old, handicapped or disabled, ill or frail.* Commissioned by the King's Fund Informal Caring Programme, National Extension College, Cambridge

Mace, N. L. and Rabins, P. V. (1981, USA, published UK 1985) *The 36-Hour Day. Caring at home for confused elderly people*, Hodder & Stoughton, London, co-published by Age Concern, Mitcham. *A guide for carers of people with dementia*

Muir Gray, J. A. and Mackenzie, Heather (1986) *Caring for older people. A practical guide for everyone.* Penguin Books, Harmondsworth

Thompson, Liz (1986) *Bringing up a mentally handicapped child. It's not all tears!* A Life Crisis Book, Thorsons, Wellingborough

Wilson, Monica (1984) 'The College of Health Guide to Homes for Elderly People', College of Health, London

Index

independence, 134–6, 224
Indians, 194–8
injuries, disabled children, 146–8
institutional care, 201–20
Invalid Care Allowance (ICA), 36–7,
    48–9, 67, 68, 101–2, 130, 231–4,
    237, 238, 240, 245
Invalid Care Allowance Campaign,
    234
Invalidity Benefit, 101–2, 233, 235–6
Ismail, Karim, 192–4, 196
isolation, 92–4, 170
ITV, 216

Jameson, Robert, 211–13
Jarratt, Harold, 52–4
Jarratt, Joan, 19, 20, 21, 28, 31, 43,
    46, 52–4

Kent, 229
King's Fund Centre, London, 245

Labour Party, 215–16
laundry services, 26, 184
Layton, Stella, 19, 23, 57, 58, 61–2,
    66, 68
Lenagh, James, 163–6, 223, 225
'Life Care' schemes, 215
Long, Alfred, 168, 169, 174

Manpower Services, 9
marriage: disabled husbands,
    77–107; divorce, 106, 114,
    179–80, 244, 251; married women
    as carers, 40–9
Martin, Christine, 114, 123, 126–7
Mason, Margaret, 134
mattresses, ripple, 99
Meals on Wheels, 21–2, 160, 199,
    209, 219, 248, 249, 252
men: as carers, 159–89; caring for
    brothers, 69; and disabled
    children, 113–15, 181–2; disabled
    husbands, 77–107; with disabled
    wives, 179–80; gay couples, 182–9;
    reactions to carers, 42–3; sons as
    carers, 176–9
Mills, Alexandra, 42, 44
Mobility Allowance, 129, 231, 235,
    236

money problems *see* financial
    problems
Monkton, Eileen, 146, 148–51
Monkton, Philip, 146, 147, 148–51
Monkton, Ray, 148–51
Moore, John, 250
Morton, Christine, 112, 130, 137
Morton, Jane, 28, 29, 32, 63–6
multiple sclerosis, 77, 172, 210, 211

National Assistance Act (1948), 209,
    211
National Association of Health
    Authorities, 217, 249
National Health Service, 248–9, 250
National Institute for Social Work,
    220
Naylan, Letty, 174–6
Naylan, Robbie, 170, 174–6
Naylor, Joanne, 34, 57, 62, 228
neighbours, support from, 21
Norman, Alison, 191, 198
nursing homes, 209, 213–20

Office of Population Censuses and
    Surveys, 129n.
Oliver, Edward, 111, 112, 113, 125,
    137, 228
Oliver, Judith, 68, 79, 80, 99, 102,
    105–6, 229
osteomalacia, 191

parent/child bond, 30–4
Parkinson's disease, 77
pensions, 37, 233, 234, 235, 242–3
Personal Social Services Council, 248
personality change, 96–8
Peto Institute, 125
Petro, Rosa, 81–7, 237
poverty, 15, 191, 236
Prentice, Beth, 44, 46, 96, 107
Preston, Dorothy, 19, 21, 26, 28, 29,
    30, 31, 32, 38–9, 56, 57
Price, Louisa, 108, 110, 112, 113,
    123, 124, 126, 127, 130–1, 132,
    136
privacy, lack of, 45–6
private homes, 213–20, 249